The Enig  Hugh Holm

Bristol's Nineteenth Century Christian Socialist Solicitor

Mike Richardson

ISBN 978-1-911522-01-0

Bristol Radical History Group. 2016.
www.brh.org.uk
brh@brh.org.uk

Contents

Illustrations

Acknowledgements

It was never my intention to write more than a short piece on the life and times of Hugh Holmes Gore. To write his biography seemed inconceivable. However, as my research progressed I uncovered an increasing amount of interesting and intriguing material highly relevant to historians of the labour movement, the Gay community, Christian socialists and the solicitors' profession that I felt should be fully documented. I could not have done this without the support of my partner Sheila Rowbotham, who read several drafts as I attempted to write a clear and informative biography. Her editing skills, constructive criticism and words of reassurance kept me going especially during those times when diffidence in my own ability seemed insuperable. Thanks also to Paul Mangan (Breviary Stuff Publications) for applying his copy-editing skills on the penultimate draft of this book and Richard Grove (Bristol Radical History Group) who contributed his wisdom in the preparation of the cover design, images and final text for the printer. Any errors that remain, however, are my sole responsibility.

I am grateful to the librarians at Bristol Central Reference Library, particularly Dawn Dyer, and the archivists at the Bristol Record Office for their help in my research. I am obliged to the University of the West of England for the use of their facilities, as a Visiting Research Fellow. For permission to quote I'm grateful to the following: Nicolas Deakin, (Havelock Ellis material in the British Library); Sheffield City Council, Libraries, Archives and Information (Edward Carpenter letters); King's College, Cambridge, UK, Archive Centre (Charles Ashbee Papers); British Library, London, UK (Havelock Ellis Papers, correspondence and papers of Edith and Havelock Ellis, and Edward Carpenter); Images/Text reproduced with the kind permission of The British Newspaper Archive (www.britishnewspaperarchive.co.uk), and Local World Limited. Similarly thank you to the Kate Sharpley Library for the image of David Nicoll.

For quotes and references to nineteenth century British newspapers; Text © THE BRITISH LIBRARY BOARD. ALL RIGHTS RESERVED, and, in respect to the *Western Daily Press* and *Bristol Times and Mirror*, the Bristol Central Reference Library. And in regard to the *San Francisco Call,* California Digital Newspaper Collection, Center for Bibliographic Studies and Research, University of California, Riverside. I am also beholden to the following for access to their archives: International Institute of Social History, Amsterdam, The Netherlands (Nettlau Papers and Socialist League (UK) archive); Sidney Jones Library, University of Liverpool, UK (Glasier Papers); Bristol Central Reference Library (Bristol Socialist Society Minutes, 1895); Bristol Record

Office (Diary of W. H. (Harry) Bow, 1892, Parish Reports and Accounts of Holy Trinity Church, Clifton (Hotwells), and *Rules of the Bristol Conciliation and Arbitration Board, for the Adjustment of Disputes between Capital and Labour*); and the Working Class Movement Library, Salford, UK (Angela Tuckett, Papers). Thanks are also due to Joey Cain, David Sachs and to Maggie Cohen for her hospitality when Sheila Rowbotham and myself came to Salford to visit the Working Class Movement Library.

Finally I must mention the influence of the Bristol Radical History Group. They have been at the forefront of advancing and encouraging the writing of history from below in Bristol. It was in writing a Bristol Radical History Group pamphlet that I first became intensely interested in Hugh Holmes Gore.

Introduction

'What on earth is this tale about Gore? Where is the poor devil?'

A worried Edith Ellis, the new woman writer married to sexologist Havelock Ellis, put these questions in a letter to the socialist writer Edward Carpenter in November 1898.[1] Edith Ellis was sexually attracted to women rather than men and the subject of one of the few lesbian case studies in Havelock Ellis and John Addington Symonds' book *Sexual Inversion* (1897). She was able to be open with Carpenter who was himself a homosexual and had written a pamphlet *Homogenic Love* (1894).[2]

In the Victorian era same-sex attraction was exceedingly dangerous being a criminal offence for men and surrounded by moral opprobrium. Havelock Ellis and other writers on the psychology of sex created a space for the topic to be discussed behind a scientific language. On the other hand their external classifications labelled and rigidified human desires. Edith Ellis' letter hints at the personal friendship networks based on trust which those defined as 'inverts' fostered among themselves.

Who was Hugh Holmes Gore? And why was Edith Ellis so concerned about her long-standing friend in the autumn of 1898? This book explores the complexities, difficulties and significance of Gore's political, professional and personal life before his disappearance and follows what happened to him subsequently.

Hugh Holmes Gore has survived as a marginal figure, mentioned only in passing by historians of the socialist and labour movements.[3] Despite eluding biographers, Gore nevertheless featured prominently in Bristol's local socialist politics and philanthropic projects and was nationally known during the 1890s for his legal work. A focus on his life provides a means of charting the role played by an exceedingly radical solicitor active in a wide range of causes, campaigns,

---

1 Edith Ellis to Edward Carpenter, 15 November 1898, Havelock Ellis Papers, correspondence and papers of Edith and Havelock Ellis, and Edward Carpenter, (70536-70538) British Library.
2 See Jo-Ann Wallace, 'The Case of Edith Ellis' in H. Stevens and C. Howlett (eds.) *Modernist Sexualities* (Manchester: Manchester University, 2000), p. 14; S. Rowbotham, *Edward Carpenter: A life of Liberty and Love.* (London: Verso, 2008); L. Bland and L. Doan (eds.) *Sexology Uncensored: The Documents of Sexual Science* (Chicago: The University of Chicago Press, 1998), pp. 45, 48-57; H. Ellis and J. A. Symonds, *Sexual Inversion* (London: Wilson and Macmillan, 1897), in later editions of this work Symonds' name was removed on the directive of his widow.
3 Gore's participation as a candidate in the 1895 parliamentary by-election in Bristol East is the only significant event that has attracted attention of historians. See W. John Lyes, 'The 1895 By-Election in Bristol East', *Transactions*, Volume 130 (The Bristol & Gloucestershire Archaeological Society: 2012), pp. 279-293; D. Howell, *British Workers and the Independent Labour Party 1888-1906* (Manchester: Manchester University Press, 1983), pp. 386-7.

and organisations during the late nineteenth century. It also gives a perspective on his hidden homosexuality.[4]

Affectionately known as 'the people's solicitor', and an active Christian Socialist, before his mysterious disappearance Gore made important contributions both to the labour movement and to the broader push for social change. Moreover, his life of intense philanthropic and political commitment was interspersed with several dramatic personal and public episodes. Culturally and politically Gore was profoundly contrary; a rugby playing Republican, a defender of free speech, who revealed anti-Semitic prejudices, and a socialist, who came to oppose Irish Home Rule. Psychologically too Gore presented conflicting aspects, cautious and rational but prone to bouts of temper, a disciplinarian and a rebel rolled into one.

Gore's radical political views were rooted in both his High Church Anglicanism and his physical attraction to men. David Hilliard has observed that the sacerdotalism and ritualism of high Anglo-Catholicism conveyed a sense of being

> both elitist and nonconformist, combining a sense of superiority with a rebellion against existing authority. As such it provided an environment in which homosexual men could express ... their dissent from heterosexual orthodoxy and from the Protestant values of those who wielded power in church and state.[5]

This insight is most pertinent in attempting to comprehend the contradictions Gore manifested.

Drawing on material from contemporary newspaper reports and minutes of labour and socialist organisations to personal letters, this book examines the key turning points in Gore's life, placing these in the context of the society at the time. It traces his engagement in social, religious, and political movements locally and nationally, and uncovers the personal danger and psychological depression he experienced. Moreover, though it does not resolve, it throws light on the puzzle that troubled Edith Ellis.

4 Nineteenth century writers used terms such as 'Inversion', 'Urnings', Uranians', "Homogenic' and 'The Unknown People' as well as 'Homosexuality' which became accepted in the twentieth century. When movements of resistance emerged, dissatisfied by these terms, activists reinvented the word 'gay'. Both 'gay', and even more so 'queer', carry pejorative meanings but have been adopted as signalling defiance — forms of self-identification against prejudice as opposed to 'scientific' sexological type-casting. 'Queer' is sometimes used to indicate fluidity and complexity in sexual orientation and desires. I settled for 'homosexuality' because it was in use during the nineteenth century and is known today.

5 D. Hilliard, 'Unenglish and Unmanly: Anglo-Catholicism and Homosexuality', *Victorian Studies*, Vol. 25, No. 2 (Winter, 1982), p. 24.

Chapter 1

School Days

Born at Margate, Kent on 17 May 1864, Hugh Holmes Gore, the son of Thomas Holmes Gore and Ellen Martyr Gore (*née* Wild), entered a world in which Britain, with an empire that covered around one-fifth of the earth's surface, had become 'the workshop of the world'. Yet Britain was also a class-bound society, in which extreme poverty was still rife, and although there were signs of a gradual shift towards a more open and democratic society, they were slow in coming. Gore's father belonged to the strata of the aspiring middle class, which stood to be the main beneficiaries of this shift. He was a clerk to the Margate justices, having been trained as a solicitor in Birmingham and London. In 1865 Thomas and his family moved to Leyton, east London, where he took up the position of assistant clerk to the Lord Mayor of London in the Justice's room at the Mansion House, a post he was to hold for ten years.[6]

In 1873 Hugh Holmes Gore became one out of hundreds of entrants selected to attend Christ's Hospital, as a non-fee paying scholar, starting first at its preparatory school, in Hertford, before going on at the age of eleven to its upper school at Newgate Street, London.[7] The School was a charity institution; so the wealthy were excluded. It attracted, in the main, boys who came from lower middle-class families whose fathers were engaged in vocations such as 'the less affluent ranks of the Army and Navy, the Medical and Legal Professions, and the poorer Clergy' usually with an annual income of less than £200.[8] The boys who attended this school were (and are) known famously as 'bluecoats'. In Gore's time their striking uniforms comprised blue ankle-length coats, a leather waist belt, a white cloth neckband, knee high yellow socks, knee breeches, buckled shoes and a woollen flat black hat.[9]

This dress code, along with the school's other traditions, such as public suppings – 'We felt like lions at the Zoo, with a vast audience watching us eat' – and the annual loyal address to the Sovereign,[10] masked a culture of well-entrenched bullying on the part of some of the senior boys. The initial loneliness

6 Sean MacConville, *English Local Prisons, 1860-1900: Next Only to Death* (London: Routledge, 1994), p. 503, ftn. 68; 'Thomas Holmes Gore, Obituary', *Western Daily Press*, 29 September 1919.
7 K. Mansell, *Christ's Hospital in the Victorian Era* (Whitton, London: Ashwater Press, 2011), p. 389; Hugh Holmes Gore in his capacity as one of the governors of Colston School, Bristol, recalled his time 'as an old blue coat boy at Christ's Hospital, London', in an address to old Colstonians, see *Bristol Mercury,* 13 November 1895.
8 C. M. E. Seaman, *Christ's Hospital: The Last Years in London.* (London: Ian Allen, 1977), pp. 16 & 48.
9 Seaman, *Christ's Hospital: The Last Years in London*, pp. 16, 47 & 48.
10 Reminisces of A. L. Francis, *Christ's Hospital Sixty Years* Ago (Christ's Hospital publication: 1918) quoted in Seaman, *Christ's Hospital: The Last Years in London*, p. 140.

of new boys, separated from their families, in an institution which fostered a hierarchal order, based on seniority and allegiance to school rituals, created a climate of vulnerability and cruelty where brutality and beatings were assumed as essential parts of the production of ruling-class masculinity.[11] Moreover, the all-male institutions were marked by 'certain homoerotic customs, such as the formation of intimate adolescent relationships' while 'fagging and flogging were the norm'. The English Public School system in the nineteenth century was regarded as character forming. It could however be severely testing.[12]

The vulnerability of public school boys to adult homoerotic advances rarely reached public attention, unless outsiders were involved in an alleged offence. One such case, in November 1874, resulted in the conviction of Edward Ransford for sending three letters to fourteen-year-old William D'arcy Gardiner O'Halloran, a pupil at Christ's Hospital, 'seeking to debauch, vitiate, and corrupt' his mind 'with lewd, immoral, and wicked inclinations and desires, and to induce him to commit fornication and divers other immoral acts and practices.'[13]

In 1877 the reality of Gore and his peers' educational and living environment

ETON.   CHRIST'S HOSPITAL.

PUBLIC SCHOOL BIRCHES.
ETON AND CHRIST'S HOSPITAL
PHOTOGRAPHED FROM ORIGINALS

Public School, Birches, Eton and Christ's Hospital.

at Christ's Hospital was vividly and shockingly brought to the public's attention after the suicide of one of its pupils. The child concerned, twelve year-old William Gibbs, had complained about the beatings he had received from a school monitor 'to whom he was in subjection'. He had then run away,

11 See S. Poynting and M. Donaldson, 'Snakes and Leaders: Hegemonic Masculinity in Ruling-Class Boys' Boarding Schools', *Men and Masculinities*, 2005, 7(4), p. 325.

12 V. Bullough and B. Bullough, 'Homosexuality in Nineteenth Century English Public Schools', *International Review of Modern Sociology*, 1979, Vol. 9 (July-Dec.), p. 261.

13 R. v. Ransford, Court of Criminal Appeal, 14 November 1874, cited in C. White (ed.) *Nineteenth-Century Writings on Homosexuality: A Sourcebook* (London: Routledge, 1999), pp. 46-49.

only to be returned to school and birched on his bare buttocks several times for absconding. Within a week, he would have cause to leave school again, without permission, after Herbert Copeland, one of two school monitors on his Ward, struck him several times on the face, making his nose bleed. His parents took him back to school late on a Tuesday evening, knowing that he would be birched again. The following morning, in utter despair, and before his punishment could be administered, he put an end to his suffering by hanging himself on a ventilator cord.[14]

The jury's verdict that he committed suicide 'while in a state of temporary insanity' did not end the matter.[15] In fact it attracted horror stories from former pupils concerning the physical pain and mental torture they had suffered as borders at the school. For instance, one ex-Monitor reported that as an eight-year old at the school, in the 1850s, he was 'stripped in the lavatory and made to walk up and down while six of the biggest boys beat [him] on the back with twisted towels.'[16] Another, a Dr A. J. Butler, fellow of Brasenose, Oxford and master of Winchester College, and ex-Grecian (a boy who had been selected to remain at the School beyond the age of sixteen) at Christ's Hospital, wrote to *The Times* of his experience:

Sir, - As it is not eight years since I left Christ's Hospital…I can vouch absolutely for the fact, in my time, the punishments were often very cruel and revolting. Blood-blisters from caning were nothing unusual, so that the sufferer did not receive any special pity…
It is also true that the monitors were often excessively tyrannical. There was very little to control or temper their power, as the matrons who lived in the dormitories were naturally glad of a stern discipline and might easily be ignorant of excesses; while the Grecians, as in Charles Lamb's time,[17] lived above in the clouds of indifference and mystery at too sublime a distance to regard the sins and sorrows of the world below: they were too great to govern.[18]

The negative publicity that followed Gibbs' suicide compelled the government to appoint a Royal Commission of Inquiry into the circumstances surrounding the case, including the conditions at Christ's Hospital. The Commission, however, absolved the monitors at the school in general and

14 Seaman, *Christ's Hospital: The Last Years in London*, pp. 26-27.
15 *Western Daily Press*, 9 July 1877.
16 *Western Daily Press*, 18 July 1877.
17 Born in 1775, Lamb became one of the great English essayists. He attended Christ's Hospital in the late eighteenth century where he experienced violence and brutality.
18 *The Times*, 14 July 1877, p. 12.

Copeland, Gibbs' alleged tormentor, in particular, from all blame in the matter. It concluded that the school's failings, which were brought to light in the inquiry, were 'due to the system and not to individuals.'[19]

The Royal Commission's Report, as well as absolving any individual of blame, concluded 'that the school has much improved of late years',[20] suggesting that little damage had been done to the school in terms of its pupil's educational achievement. Seaman's history of the School, published one hundred years after this event in 1977, devoted a whole chapter to Gibbs' suicide, endorsing the findings of the Commission. He was sympathetic to the view of contemporaries that Gibbs was a difficult boy and 'should have adapted himself to the circumstances'.[21] However, opinion in 1877 had been divided, *The Spectator*, then a radical-liberal magazine, criticised the Commission's report and the record of bullying and cruelty prevalent at Christ's Hospital:

No other method of punishment appears to be known in Christ's Hospital, expulsion is never resorted to — from the excessive loss involved by it to the parents, the right of remaining in the school being regarded as a sort of property — and no softer kind of correction appears ever to have been heard of. The Head Master birches; and the Warden birches and canes; and the Masters cane on the hand when the offence is serious, and on the back whenever they choose; and the beadles cane; and the monitors slap the boys' faces as often as they think that required, — that is, as often as they please. The school, in fact, is ultimately governed through the fear of physical pain, and through that punitive means alone; and this the Commissioners, so long as the school remains in London, declare themselves unable to condemn.[22]

As well as bullying, pupils at Christ's Hospital endured a strict regime. They rose at six o'clock, washed, dressed and made their beds. Then they had an hour's schooling at eight o'clock, before taking breakfast consisting of a hunk of bread, and lukewarm milk. In the 1870s, cocoa, and porridge with treacle were introduced to supplement this meagre ration. Lunch comprised beef, mutton or pork – puddings were rare. Bread, butter and cheese were all that was on offer at supper time. The boys retired to bed at eight thirty in dormitories which could hold as many as fifty boys.[23]

19 *Dundee Evening Telegraph*, 11 August 1877.
20 Seaman, *Christ's Hospital: The Last Years in London*, p. 41.
21 Seaman, *Christ's Hospital: The Last Years in London*, p. 28.
22 *The Spectator*, 18 August 1877, p. 10.
23 Mansell, *Christ's Hospital in the Victorian Era*, pp. 160-1

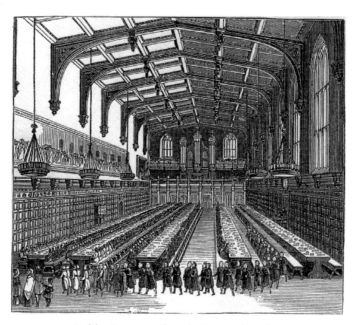

Public Supper, Christ's Hospital, 1843.

The lack of sports facilities on site, due to limited space, meant that the boys could not play the usual public schoolboy games, such as cricket. Rugby, Gore's favourite game, and football had to be played on asphalt. However, the School had a gymnasium and, from 1869, a swimming pool. Occasional cross-country paper chases took place but the growing urbanisation of London made these increasingly difficult to organise.[24]

Strict religious observance at the school was determined by the desire 'to foster and extend the blessings of a sound moral and religious education to the poorer classes'.[25] Morning prayers in the wards set the tone of the day. In the large dining hall, passages of scripture were read and graces said before meals. In the afternoons the boys, back in their wards, were divided into classes and made to repeat the Catechism and other religious material. Evening prayers were conducted on the Wards. Before 1869 the boys had to attend three services on Sundays. This number was reduced to one after the appointment of a new headmaster, George Charles Bell, in July 1868.[26]

Not all was dutiful and devout however; a Debating Society and a Literary Society enabled older boys to hone their skills, share their pleasure in literature,

24 Seaman, *Christ's Hospital: The Last Years in London*, pp. 120-3 & 127.
25 Seaman, *Christ's Hospital: The Last Years in London*, p. 18.
26 Seaman, *Christ's Hospital: The Last Years in London*, pp.73-74, & 144.

and discuss the significance of important literary works. The ethos was one of social concern and progressive modernity. Papers were given on the art critic John Ruskin, a donor governor of the School; the German composer, Wilhelm Richard Wagner whose work was just beginning to be acclaimed in Britain; the sceptical novelist, George Eliot; and the play *Brand* written in 1865 by the 'advanced' Norwegian playwright, Henrik Ibsen.[27] In Ibsen's play the main character, Brand, is an idealistic young clergyman who in seeking 'a radical new vision of humanity' sacrifices the lives of his family 'and ultimately himself'.[28]

In April 1875, just before Gore transferred from his preparatory school in Hertford to the upper school at Newgate Street, London, his father moved from Vicarage Road, Leyton to Bristol to take up his appointment as clerk to the Bristol justices at a salary of £700 per annum,[29] a position he went on to hold for more than forty years. Consequently, from the age of eleven, Gore was not within easy reach of his parents, leaving him more reliant on his school in effecting a transition from adolescence to adulthood. According to the school's biographer, Charles Seaman, 'there was, outside the classroom, no strong or meaningful relationship' between the Masters and the boys, so it appears that Gore would have had to turn to his friends and peers for companionship, guidance and support.[30]

Nevertheless, in public Gore recalled his life at Christ's Hospital with some fondness. 'He spoke of the closeness and endurance of schoolday friendship.'[31] In his last two years at the school he befriended George Jenner Rosenberg, who was six years his junior. Rosenberg, the posthumous son of the Bath artist George Frederic Rosenberg, went on to become a Grecian. He left Christ's Hospital in 1888 to study at an institution with a tradition of liberal social concern, St. John's College, Cambridge. In 1893 Rosenberg obtained a B.A. and in 1895 an M.A. In 1900, he settled into a position for life as an assistant Master at King's School, Canterbury.[32] Little is known of the young man with a wispy military style moustache and a soft face but his connection with Gore was evidently close. They kept in contact and in the early 1890s he stayed with him at his residence in Franklyn Street, Bristol.[33]

27 Seaman, *Christ's Hospital: The Last Years in London*, p. 108; Mansell, *Christ's Hospital in the Victorian Era*, p. 174.

28 A. S. Byatt, Review of Toril Moi's *Henrik Ibsen and the Birth of Modernism*, *The Guardian*, 16 September 2006.

29 *Western Daily Press*, 19 April 1875.

30 Seaman, *Christ's Hospital: The Last Years in London*, p. 150.

31 *Bristol Mercury*, 13 November 1895.

32 Cambridge University Alumni, 1261-1900, Ancestry.com, courtesy of the National Archives of the UK, accessed 23 September 2013.

33 Census Returns of England and Wales, 1891, Ancestry.com, courtesy of the National Archives of the UK, accessed 7 July 2012.

Chapter 2

Political, Philosophical and Religious Influences

By the time of his arrival in Bristol in the mid 1870s, Gore's father, Thomas Holmes Gore, had acquired great respect among his peers in the legal profession. His reputation of excellence and expertise went before him. Thus, it is likely that when the well-connected Lieutenant Colonel James Roger Bramble, who was head of the Bristol solicitors' firm of Bramble and Watts, came to sell his house, 31 Cornwallis Crescent, Clifton, in April 1875, Gore Snr. was given preference. He took full advantage of the opportunity to buy this large fashionable house which had many desirable attributes for an upwardly mobile family. It featured drawing, dining and breakfast rooms, eight bedrooms, a housekeeper's room, kitchen, cellars, and offices.[34] On completing the sale of his house to Gore Snr., Bramble and his pregnant wife moved to Woodside, Leigh Woods, overlooking Clifton Suspension Bridge; as this was just outside the Bristol boundary, it would have enabled him to escape the payment of city rates.[35] Borough rates in the city had increased sharply in the mid 1870s, mainly due to the rise in the cost of maintaining law and order, and to a lesser extent education.[36] Bramble was among those more wealthy social conservative citizens who opposed the setting of higher rates to provide civic improvements and basic public services.

Bramble was a Freemason, and a well-known Unionist.[37] Initiated into the Masonic Beaufort Lodge, 103, Province of Bristol in 1863, he quickly garnered enough support by 1865 to establish himself as Master of the Lodge.[38] By custom the Master of a Lodge on entering was identified by wearing a cocked hat that singled him out as a man of importance, one to be revered. Ostensibly a non-religious, non-political, fraternal and charitable organisation, by the Victorian era Freemasonry had assumed characteristics of a patriarchal secret organisation. Apart from the rituals, male companionship, support for the British Empire, and staunch loyalty to the Crown, the attraction of Masonic

34 Description of 31 Cornwallis Crescent (the Gores' house) found in the *Western Daily Press*, 31 March 1894.

35 *Matthew's Bristol and Clifton Street Directory* (Bristol: John Wright, 1876, compiled December 1875).

36 D. Large, *The Municipal Government of Bristol 1851-1901* (Bristol: Bristol Record Society, 1999), p. 42.

37 *Western Gazette*, 7 February 1908, Local World Limited, Courtesy of The British Library Board.

38 Obituary of Colonel J. R. Bramble, *Western Daily Press*, 4 February 1908, Local World Limited, courtesy of the British Library Board. On his death he left £70,002 to his widow, England and Wales National Probate Calendar (Index of Wills and Administration), 1858-1966.

Lieu.-Colonel James Roger Bramble.

membership was the desire to enhance business and work-related opportunities, through personal contact or connection, and the furtherance of members' professional and private interests over non-masons.[39] For Gore Snr. association with the influential and like-minded Bramble turned out to be advantageous. Gore Snr. became involved in Masonic life in Bristol and lent support to many local charities.[40]

Many Bristol charities functioned as a benign front for organisations such as the Freemasons, as well as the three Colston Societies (Grateful, Dolphin, and Anchor) founded in memory of Edward Colston (1636-1721) whose wealth was derived from the slave trade.[41] Behind the philanthropy their exclusively male members could pursue their personal agendas and interests and provide support for fellow members with a free conscience. The vast majority of the populace in Bristol, as elsewhere, were barred from joining these elitist organisations leading some charitable Clifton and Bristol citizens to eschew association with them.

The sisters Susanna and Catherine Winkworth, who had occupied 31 Cornwallis Crescent prior to Bramble, exemplify a quite different strand of philanthropy. Along with their step-mother, Eliza Winkworth, they were known for their voluntary work and for their involvement in the Bristol and Clifton Society for Women's Suffrage.[42] Susanna Winkworth was well regarded for her commitment to provide decent homes for the 'respectable' poor, and her sister, Catherine, for her work promoting the higher education for women.[43] Even though they were acutely aware that their location in Clifton was one of the most attractive and affluent areas of the city, standing high above and in stark contrast to the grimy and squalid hovels of Hotwells, St. Jude's, St. Jacob's, St. Philip's and the Dings, the homes of the working poor, it was becoming evident that charitable projects, though welcome, were 'no real solution to the nation's poverty.'[44]

In 1880 the sixteen-year-old Hugh Holmes Gore had just completed his education at Christ's Hospital and had arrived in Bristol to live at his parent's comfortable Clifton family home. As elsewhere, the philanthropic response of

39 R. Burt, 'Freemasonry and Business Working during the Victorian Period', *Economic History Review*, LVI, 4 (2003), pp. 657-688.
40 Gore Snr. is recorded as attending a grand banquet of the Bristol Freemasonry held in the Victoria Rooms, Clifton, Bristol on 27 March 1889, *Western Daily Press*, 28 March 1889.
41 These Societies deceptively focused on Colston's generosity and liberality, conveniently omitting that his wealth was slave-derived. See Madge Dresser, *Slavery Obscured: The Social History of the Slave Trade in an English Provincial Port* (London: Continuum, 2001), pp. 2-3.
42 Bramble was active in the East Somerset Conservative Association in the 1860/70s, *Bristol Times and Mirror*, 1 August 1868.
43 In 2000, the Clifton and Hotwells Improvement Society put up a blue plaque commemorating their lives on the outside wall of 31 Cornwallis Crescent.
44 J. Walvin, *Victorian Values* (London: Cardinal, 1988), p. 104.

Cliftonians to the social question was beginning to be called into question. Released from the confines of his London school, Gore became progressively more socially aware. A combination of the critiques of philanthropy, the plight of the poor and the social problems of the city were to lead him to question the present state of society. Drawing on Anglo-Catholic values, gradually Gore acquired a sense of mission and a deep concern for the working class that fired his thoughts and actions.

The Gore family home in Cornwallis Crescent was situated on the extreme edge of the Parish of Holy Trinity, Clifton (Hotwells). Coming from a High Church background, Thomas Holmes Gore, his wife, and his daughter Caroline had become active members of Holy Trinity Church.[45] It is likely therefore that their son, Hugh, also attended this church, although there is no concrete evidence to substantiate this.

After leaving Christ's Hospital in 1880 Gore was sent to Bristol Grammar, an independent school founded in 1532, to finish his education, doing particularly well in mathematics.[46] Bristol Grammar's educational standard was high. One of his contemporaries at school was a follower of John Ruskin, Bristol born Hubert Llewellyn Smith, who later became involved in the religious 'New Oxford Movement', critical of working class living and working conditions. Like Gore, Llewellyn Smith was influenced by Ruskin's social approach to economics, and was to become part of the group arguing for social reform within Liberalism. Associated with the university settlement, Toynbee Hall,[47] Llewellyn Smith's career proved illustrious: after the First World War he went on to become chief economic adviser to the Government.[48]

In June 1882 Gore sat his London University matriculation exam, a qualification for white-collar professions such as the law. When the results were announced in July he learned that he was one of the successful candidates.[49] Soon afterwards, partly no doubt thanks to his father's contacts, Gore secured a position as an articled clerk with none other than Colonel James Roger

45 Parish Reports and Accounts of Holy Trinity Church, Clifton (Hotwells) year ended 31 December 1885, p. 6; Also see *Western Daily Press*, 12 August 1942.
46 Bristol Grammar School prize lists, *Western Daily Press* 31 July 1880 and 29 July 1881.
47 Founded in 1884 Toynbee Hall was the first of the university settlement houses where, during holidays, university students could volunteer their time to work among the poor, offering education and vocational training.
48 Roger Davidson, 'Smith, Sir Hubert Llewellyn (1864–1945)', *Oxford Dictionary of National Biography*, Oxford University Press, 2004; online edn., Jan 2008 [http://www.oxforddnb.com/view/article/36147, accessed 30 Aug 2014]
49 University of London General Register, part 1, (London: Senate House Library, Special Collections online); *Bristol Mercury*, 21 July 1882.

Bristol Grammar School First XV Rugby Team, 1881-2. Gore is the first from the left in the middle row.

Bramble, in his Bristol solicitors' firm, Bramble and Watts.[50] The young Gore joined the Bristol Law Students' Society[51] and, as well as continuing his studies, he became active in local sports, particularly rugby, playing for both Clifton Rugby Football Club second fifteen, and University College in the 1883-4 and 1884-5 seasons.[52]

During this period, provoked by the painful economic depression of the 1870s and early 1880s, Gore began in earnest to explore questions about social justice, along with economic, political and religious issues, wondering if philanthropy was enough. Having encountered Ruskin's works at Christ's Hospital, Gore, like Llewellyn Smith and many others, was drawn to Ruskin's critique of *laissez faire* capitalism and the devastation it caused both to the natural environment, and to human beings and communities. By 1883 he was a committed and dedicated follower of Ruskin and had enrolled as a companion of the Guild of St. George, founded by Ruskin in 1871. In theory, at least, this involved a high level of commitment. The objects and code of the Guild of St. George were both demanding and extensive (see appendices I and 2).

50 In a case brought before the Bristol Police Court Hugh Holmes Gore is cited as being an articled Clerk, *Western Daily Press*, 10 November 1882; Gore to the Socialist League, 27 February 1885, sent on Bramble and Watts headed note paper, letter held at the International Institute of Social History, Amsterdam.
51 *Western Daily Press*, 18 May 1883.
52 Clifton Rugby Football Club History, www.cliftonrfchistory.co.uk accessed 12/01/2013; *Western Daily Press*, 4 December 1884.

The 57 members of the Guild in 1883 included the Reverend Hardwicke Rawnsley, Vicar of Crossthwaite, Kenswick, who, between 1875-78, had worked as a Mission Curate for Clifton College, in the St. Barnabas Parish, Ashley Road, Bristol. Gore became a permanent resident in Bristol a couple of years after Rawnsley had moved away from the City, but he would have been aware of the sterling work that Rawnsley had done in establishing the first Mission Church and Workmen's Club in Newfoundland Road, a deprived area of the city.[53]

An unconventional Ruskin adherent, Katherine Bradley also had strong connections with Bristol. Bradley, who wrote poetry and plays with her niece, and lover, Edith Cooper, under the joint pseudonym Michael Field, had been friendly with Ruskin in the 1870s and subscribed a tenth of her income to the Guild of the St. George; but their friendship became acrimonious, after Bradley declared that she had become an atheist, and by the early 1880s it had broken.[54] Meanwhile, Bradley and Cooper had moved to Stoke Bishop, near Clifton Down, Bristol, in 1878. Whether they knew the Gores is unclear, but they were in touch with a radical intellectual network that Gore Jnr. later entered.

In the mid-1880s Bradley attended meetings of a group called the Fellowship of the New Life at Merstham, near Reigate in Surrey. The Fellowship constituted an ethical socialist network stressing internal as well as external social change. Other members included Havelock Ellis; Edith Lees, (later to marry Ellis); Edward Carpenter; the teacher, Cecil Reddie, who was to establish Abbotsholme boys' school; and the ex-army officer and Christian Socialist, Henry Hyde Champion. Bradley and Havelock Ellis struck up a friendship and exchanged letters. Bradley recorded that Ellis had sent her a set of some 'wonderful Socialistic papers.'[55] Her political engagement, however, centred on participation in social reform campaigns and support for women's suffrage, rather than socialism.

The Ruskinian Christian Socialist, Edward Deacon Girdlestone, provided Gore with a connection not only to Ruskin but to the Fellowship of the New Life and to Edward Carpenter. Ruskin lavished praise on Girdlestone's pamphlet, published in 1876, entitled *Society Classified: in reply to the question, "How far is*

---

53 E. T. Cook and Alexander Wedderburn (eds.), *The Works of John Ruskin* (London: George Allen, 1909, Volume XXX, 'The Guild and Museum of St. George'), p. 86; Members of Clifton College, *The History of Saint Agnes Parish* (Bristol: Clifton College, 1890), p.p. 2 & 5.

54 Emma Donoghue, *We are Michael Field* (Bath: Absolute Press, 1998), pp. 23 & 24.

55 Michael Field, *A Fellowship: The Letters of Michael Field* (Sharon Bickle (ed.), Unpublished PhD Thesis, Monash University, 2003, Vol. 2, p. 238), cited in Sharon Bickle, "Kick[ing] Against the Pricks': Michael Field's *Brutus Ultor* as Manifesto for the 'New Women". *Nineteenth Century Theatre & Film*, Volume 33, Issue 2, January 2006, p. 19.

the saying true that every one lives either by Working, or by Begging, or by Stealing?"[56] Ruskin wrote: 'It is the most complete and logical statement of Economic truth, in the points it touches, that I have ever seen in the English language'.[57] Ruskin's moral critique of *laissez-faire* economics undermined the hegemonic justification of the status quo and despite Ruskin's conservatism constituted a subversive force. It is difficult to exactly pinpoint what or who sparked Gore's attraction to socialism in offering the solution to the ills of capitalist society, but Girdlestone and Carpenter were certainly early influences.[58]

In 1879, the year after his wife Catherine had died, Girdlestone married Anna Friederike Thomas, from Nordlingen, Bavaria. They moved to Upper Park Street (now Southleigh Road) in Clifton, and established private tuition classes in a range of subjects from mathematics to music. He became heavily involved in the Land Nationalisation Society, becoming Vice President when Alfred Russel Wallace, who co-published the theory of evolution by natural selection with Charles Darwin, was the Society's President. Locally, in propagandising the Land Question, Girdlestone worked with Francis Gilmore Barnett, a Bristol solicitor and a radical Liberal councillor, whose brother was warden of the London settlement, Toynbee Hall, and Rev. William Hargreaves, who preached at Oakfield Road Unitarian Church, just round the corner from where Girdlestone lived.[59]

As well as the Land Question, Girdlestone was particularly concerned about what he had argued was the misdirection 'of *honest hearty labour*', in producing a disproportionate amount of luxuries, enjoyed largely by the middle and upper classes, compared with the necessaries of life. He raised this matter as early as 1876 in a paper read at the Weston-super-Mare Social Science Club, expressing his concern about, and the evils resulting from, the 'waste of labour', citing the question that Ruskin had put to Workmen and Labourers in *Fors Clavigera*, Letter 29: 'What are you making? Are you making Hell's articles or Heaven's, Gunpowder, or Corn?'[60] Girdlestone took Ruskin's ideas and a radical critique of labour and inequality into Christian Socialism. In the 1880s, he

56 E. D. Girdlestone, *Society Classified: in reply to the question, "How far is the saying true that every one lives either by Working, or by Begging, or by Stealing?"* (Weston-Super-Mare: Charles Robbins, 1876).

57 E. T. Cook and Alexander Wedderburn (eds.), *The Works of John Ruskin* (London: George Allen, 1909, Volume 28, *Fors Clavigera*, Letters 63, March 1876), p. 555.

58 S. Bryher, *An Account of the Labour and Socialist Movement in Bristol* (Bristol: 1929), Part 1, p. 42. Samuel Bale wrote under the pseudonym, Samson Bryher.

59 Rev. Hargreaves delivered a lecture, on 29 May 1883, advocating Alfred Russel Wallace's plan for the nationalisation of land. *Western Daily Press*, 31 May 1883.

60 E. D. Girdlestone, *Our Misdirected Labour considered as a grave national and personal question in regard to its amount, consequences & causes:* a paper read at a meeting of the Weston-Super-Mare Social Science Club. (Weston-super-Mare: Charles Robbins, 1876) p. 13.

wrote a tract entitled *Christian Socialism Versus Present Day Unsocialism*, which was well received by followers of the Fellowship of the New Life.[61] He argued that too great a portion of labour was employed on producing the conveniences rather than the necessities of life:

> Lavishers on luxury however often defend their expenditure by saying that, but for their extravagance, a number of operatives would be thrown altogether out of work! And true that is! And shameful that it can be true! ... It is however only in the same sense as a 'bull in a china shop' brings work to the potter is a public benefactor, that the consumer of luxuries is so![62]

Carpenter, who had introduced Girdlestone to the Bristol labour movement, also touched on this subject, questioning the wastefulness of living a luxurious life style in a paper read before the Fellowship in January 1886.[63]

Carpenter's early connection to Bristol had arisen through William Harrison Riley, the Republican propagandist, who constituted a link back to Chartism and planted the seeds of left discontent in Bristol. Between 1875-77, Riley, with his wife, had managed a Social Improvement Institute, a wholly temperance society, at 6 Brunswick Square, Bristol. In collaboration with John Sharland, who was the Honorary Secretary of the Institute, and his brother Robert, they helped to run educational classes, discussions and entertainment. In 1877 Riley left for Sheffield where in 1879 he met Carpenter. Ruskin had taken Riley on to manage Totley farm, one of his Guild of St. George projects. The venture collapsed. Ruskin and Riley fell out, and Riley and his family subsequently emigrated to the United States of America.[64]

However, through Riley Carpenter was to form a life-long friendship with Robert Sharland, and closely followed the development of socialism in Bristol. At the end of February 1884 Bristol socialists, taking their lead from Robert and John Sharland, formed the Bristol branch of the Democratic Federation. In October 1884 the Democratic Federation changed its name to Social Democratic Federation to become the first British Marxist Party of national significance.

61 K. Manton, 'The Fellowship of the New Life: English Ethical Socialism Reconsidered', *History of Political Thought*, Vol. XXIV. No. 2, p. 287-296.

62 E. D. Girdlestone, *Christian Socialism Versus Present Day Unsocialism* (Ireland: Limavady, 1887), pp. 100–1, cited in Manton, 'The Fellowship of the New Life: English Ethical Socialism Reconsidered', p. 288.

63 E. Carpenter, 'Simplification of Life' in E. Carpenter, *England's Ideal* (London: Swan Sonnenschein, 1887), first read before 'The Fellowship of the New Life', in January 1886.

64 Bryher, *An Account of the Labour and Socialist Movement in Bristol*, Part 1, pp. 14-15. Also see Rowbotham, *Edward Carpenter: A Life of Liberty and Love*, pp. 66-68.

Factionalism haunted the new Party, however, which was led by the autocrat Henry Mayers Hyndman, a former Tory radical. By the end of 1884 divisions within the organisation led to a split. In late December, the majority of the Social Democratic Federation Executive Council, including the artist and poet, William Morris, the philosopher Ernest Belfort Bax, Eleanor Marx-Aveling, and her partner, the atheist Edward Aveling, handed in their resignations and left the organisation. They attacked Hyndman for his ' "arbitrary rule" and tendency to "political opportunism tinctured with Jingoism." '[65] In January 1885, less then a week after their secession they formed the Socialist League.[66]

The split between the Social Democratic Federation and the Socialist League, which no doubt Gore observed with interest, was, however, not just about the dictatorial and arrogant manner of Hyndman, it also involved differences over political strategy. Hyndman determined that his party would contest elections on a programme that prioritised radical political reform to create a democratic state. He and his supporters believed this to be 'an important first step toward social reform' whereas the secessionists gave precedence, though not exclusively (the League contained parliamentary and anti-parliamentary members), to fighting for social reforms through anti-parliamentary tactics.[67]

This fallout among British socialists did not deter Gore. Early in the New Year Gore, drawing on the debating skills he had acquired at Christ's Hospital, publicly declared his thoughts on socialism. He contributed to a Clifton Literary Society debate on the motion, 'That this Society views with alarm the spread of Socialistic principles in England and on the Continent.' According to a contemporary account,

> The defender of the socialist propaganda was a young man who undertook it at very short notice, "though", as he wrote to a friend who was going to hear the debate, "I am a half hearted supporter, certainly a not very deeply read one". He soon afterwards became very enthusiastic and rapidly famous throughout the city – H. H. Gore.[68]

On the 27 February 1885, Gore contacted the recently formed Socialist League, ordering ten copies of *Commonweal*, the League's official organ, along with a request for copies of the League's manifesto and suggestions for forming a branch.[69] A week later, 5 March, he wrote to John Lincoln Mahon, a Scottish

65 E. P. Thompson, *William Morris: Romantic to Revolutionary* (London: Merlin Press, 1977), p. 379.
66 Thompson, *William Morris: Romantic to Revolutionary*, p. 359.
67 M. Bevir, *The Making of British Socialism* (New Jersey: Princeton, 2011), p. 124.
68 Bryher, *An Account of the Labour and Socialist Movement in Bristol*, Part 1, pp. 23-24.
69 Gore to the Socialist League, 27 February 1885, the International Institute of Social History, Amsterdam.

engineer and secretary of the Socialist League's provisional council, saying that, as he had already explained to the founder of the Socialist League, William Morris, while it was not possible to form a branch in Bristol it was likely that one could, if approved by the Socialist League, be established in Bath.[70] A radical republican tradition already existed in Bath through William Baster, a socialist who often attended radical gatherings in Bristol and had been involved with William Harrison Riley in the establishment of the Social Improvement Institute in Bristol. Baster had set up a similar institute called the People's Club in Bath.[71]

Gore's reason for ruling out the establishment of a Bristol branch of the Socialist League was predicated on fear. He explained that he and other potential members were sympathetic to the League, but felt averse to 'acknowledging their principles openly when they are socialistic'. He added that he himself 'being dependent' was 'absolutely forbidden to join your league.'[72] Gore no doubt suspected that he would lose his position as an articled clerk with Bramble and Watts if he were to join a socialist organisation and feared that his Conservative father would withdraw financial support.

Given the timing of Gore's letter to Mahon (5 March), it is most likely that William Morris had already broached the question of joining the Socialist League. For on the evening of 3 March, Morris had delivered a lecture on 'Art and Labour' at the Museum in Queens Road, Clifton, and on the following morning he took the opportunity to have breakfast with three socialist workers – a shoemaker, a clerk, and a wire worker.[73] A little later he addressed attendees of the Exhibition of Women's Industries at the Queen's Villa in Queen's Road.[74] On 11 March 1885, Morris reported to his daughter May that although he was well received in Bristol he was unable to get the socialists there to break from the Social Democratic Federation and join the Socialist League.[75] A possible reason for this could have been the letter Edward Carpenter had sent in January 1885 to his friend Robert Sharland expressing serious doubts about the wisdom of his leaving the Social Democratic Federation and joining the Socialist League.[76] Nonetheless, Morris thought his visit was not in vain as he was hopeful to

70 Gore to John Mahon, provisional council member of the Socialist League, 5 March 1885, the International Institute of Social History, Amsterdam.
71 William Baster was also a founder member of the Bristol Branch of Democratic Federation (March 1884), which was later to become the Social Democratic Federation. Bryher, *An Account of the Labour and Socialist Movement in Bristol*, Part 1, pp. 13-14, 19; *Western Daily Press*, 2 July 1874; *Bristol Mercury*, 10 April 1875.
72 Gore to John Mahon, April 1885, the International Institute of Social History, Amsterdam.
73 Bryher, *An Account of the Labour and Socialist Movement in Bristol*, Part 1, p. 28.
74 *Western Daily Press*, 4 March 1885.
75 William Morris to his daughter May Morris, 11 March 1885, P. Henderson (ed.), *The Letters of William Morris to His Family and Friends* (London: Longmans Green, 1950), p. 233-4.
76 Edward Carpenter to Robert Sharland, 22 January 1885, quoted in C. Tsuzuki, *Edward Carpenter: Prophet of Human Fellowship 1844-1929*. (Cambridge: Cambridge University Press, 1980), p. 58.

have a branch of the Socialist League in nearby Bath, a view confirmed by the contents of Gore's letter to Mahon.[77]

The question of establishing a branch in either Bristol or Bath rumbled on into the summer. Morris was due to lecture in Bristol on 21 July, and, Gore, in his correspondence with the Socialist League, was still intently seeking advice on forming a branch before Morris' visit, as 'he want[ed] to be a little more definite about our members before then.'[78] In the event, no branch of the Socialist League would be formed either in Bristol or Bath in 1885, or indeed 1886, although the Bath-based socialist, William Baster, was in correspondence with the Socialist League and took multiple copies of its official organ *Commonweal*.[79]

As autumn approached Gore's association with the Socialist League lapsed and he applied himself to his studies and training, so that he could eventually set up his own practice as a solicitor. Gore's allegiance to the Guild of St. George was also being side lined. Instead his search for ethical social action led him towards Christian Socialism and he joined the Guild of St. Matthew.[80]

Founded by the Reverend Stewart Duckworth Headlam in Bethnal Green in 1877 the Guild of St. Matthew had, from 1884, been publically espousing socialism. Radicalised by Henry George's influential *Progress and Poverty*, Headlam, an Anglo-Catholic socialist, advocated nationalisation of the land, progressive income tax, universal suffrage, and the abolition of hereditary peers.[81] In 1880 he appalled his fellow Anglicans by bravely defending the right of the Northampton MP and atheist, Charles Bradlaugh, to sit in Parliament, after he had been prevented from doing so because he refused to swear the oath of office on the bible. It would take Bradlaugh eight years of campaigning before he was able to get this exclusion decision rescinded.[82]

Headlam was not simply unconventional in defending the rights of secularists like Bradlaugh. He was renowned for his bohemianism and infuriated many Christians by living among the London poor as a 'slum' priest, his defence of ritualism, and love of music halls and ballet. At source,

77 William Morris to his daughter May Morris, 11 March 1885, Henderson (ed.), *The Letters of William Morris to His Family and Friends*, p. 233-4.
78 Gore to the Socialist League, 20 July 1885, the International Institute of Social History, Amsterdam. In this letter Gore reminded the Socialist League not to forget his request for 'suggestions for forming a branch of the SL' and that he wanted it 'at once'.
79 William Baster, (4 Nelson Place Bath) to the editor of *Commonweal*, 9 September 1886 & 3 October 1886, the International Institute of Social History, Amsterdam.
80 D. Sutcliffe, *The Keys of Heaven: The Life of Revd Charles Marson, Christian Socialist & Folksong Collector* (eBook, Nottingham: Cockasnook Books, 2010), Kindle file, location, 1355.
81 M. Burleigh, *Earthly Powers: The Clash of Religion and Politics in Europe from the French Revolution to the Great War* (New York: Harper Collins, 2005), pp. 385-6.
82 J. R. Orens, *Stewart Headlam's Radical Anglicanism: The Mass, The Masses and the Music Hall* (Illinois: University of Illinois Press, 2003), p. 42.

however, he occasioned their wrath by his endorsement of and backing for socialism. Headlam regarded the blending of Anglo-Catholicism and socialism as fundamental to the work of the Guild of St. Matthew fusing a moral commitment of collective responsibility with analysing the root causes of poverty. The Guild considered 'the English system of land tenure... along with the growth of the large capitalist' to be 'accountable for a great part of the squalor of our overgrown towns.'[83]

Nonetheless, the three stated objects of the Guild, to be found on the flyleaves of its pamphlets, did not include the word socialism. The Guild's objects were:

I. To get rid, by every possible means, of the existing prejudices, especially on the part of "Secularists," against the Church—Her Sacraments and Doctrines: and to endeavour "to justify GOD to the people."

II. To promote frequent and reverent Worship in the Holy Communion, and better observance of the teaching of the Church of England as set forth in the Book of Common Prayer.

III. To promote the Study of Social and Political Questions in the light of the Incarnation.[84]

It was the third object that was open to interpretation, and Headlam was never short in expounding the virtues of Anglo-Catholic socialism: 'we are Socialists because we are Sacramentalists, that our zeal for social reform is the outcome of our churchmanship.'[85] To the Anglo-Catholic socialists, the receiving of bread and wine during the Eucharist becomes the physical and spiritual body and blood of Jesus Christ, 'the social and political Emancipator, the greatest of all secular workers, the founder of the great socialistic society for the promotion of righteousness, the preacher of a revolution'.[86]

Headlam, however, took this a step further by proclaiming that the real presence of Christ was not only in the Eucharist but also outside the Church in the pubs, music halls and homes of the suffering poor and oppressed. His stress upon communion and sharing led him to regard the Eucharist as symbolising Christ's presence both within and outside the Church, spiritually and physically in daily life. In opposition to Protestant individualism, Headlam adopted an interrelating perspective that organically fused faith and social reform, calling

83 D. G. Ritchie, *The Moral Function of the State* (London: Guild of St. Matthew, a paper read before the Oxford Branch of the Guild of St. Matthew, 17 May 1877), p. 5.

84 'Guild of St. Matthew, Objects' in Ritchie, *The Moral Function of the State*, flyleaf.

85 S. D. Headlam, *The Catholicity of the English Church* (London: Guild of St. Matthew, 1898), p. 4, Bristol Selected Pamphlets, University of Bristol, Library.

86 P. d'A. Jones, *The Christian Socialist Revival 1877-1914: Religion, Class, and Social Conscience in Late-Victorian England* (Princeton: Princeton University Press, 1968), p. 161.

on the people to take 'spiritual strength and refreshment from Christ'.[87] He equated 'the enemies of Socialism and the upholders of privilege' with hostility to 'catholic doctrine and worship'.[88]

When his critics called on him to define whether his church was Roman or Protestant, and whether the priesthood dominated the conscience of the people, Headlam differentiated English Anglo-Catholicism from that of the Church of Rome. He specified, first, that as far as the Guild of St. Matthew was concerned their church was totally opposed to 'the Pope of Rome assuming jurisdiction over the Dioceses of England' and did not accept the Pope's decrees as binding; and, second, the priesthood 'instead of dominating the conscience, is ordained to *liberate* the conscience'.[89]

He regarded the structure of the Anglican Church as more democratic than Roman Catholicism. Dismissing protests against the ritualistic practices of the Anglo-Catholics, Headlam presented Sacramentalism as connected with material existence: 'The whole of the work of the Guild of St. Matthew would be useless if it were not our bodies, as well as our souls which are to be preserved unto everlasting life'. In contrast to the puritanism prevalent within the nonconformist and Evangelical Anglican circles, Headlam argued that in the taking of bread and wine communicants experience 'the outward and visible as well as inward and spiritual' uplifting presence of Christ.[90] The Church, he wrote, 'is bound by its nature to be communistic.'[91]

Headlam had detractors within the Guild, however. The Reverend Charles Marson, a former editor of the *Christian Socialist,* was critical of Headlam for confining his activities to High Anglicans. Towards the end of the year Marson, along with Alfred Howard, a Fabian socialist, and Gore planned the establishment of an undenominational Christian Socialist Society. The foundation of their Christian Socialist Society in April 1886 provided an organisation that non-sacerdotal Christian socialists felt they could join. [92] It held its first public meeting on 21 June 1886.[93] By then Girdlestone, with Gore, had orchestrated the opening of the first local branch of the Clifton and Bristol

87 Headlam, *The Catholicity of the English Church*, p. 8.
88 Headlam, *The Catholicity of the English Church*, p. 4.
89 Headlam, *The Catholicity of the English Church*, pp. 5-6.
90 Headlam, *The Catholicity of the English Church*, p. 7.
91 S. D. Headlam, *Laws of Eternal Life; being studies in the church catechism* (London: W. Reeves, 1897, first published, London: Frederick Verinder, 1888), p. 3.
92 Sutcliffe, *The Keys of Heaven: The Life of Revd Charles Marson, Christian Socialist & Folksong Collector*, Kindle file, location, 1343; Jones, *The Christian Socialist Revival 1877-1914: Religion, Class, and Social Conscience in Late-Victorian England*, p. 308; Orens, *Stewart Headlam's Radical Anglicanism: The Mass, The Masses and the Music Hall*, p. 105.
93 Jones, *The Christian Socialist Revival 1877-1914: Religion, Class, and Social Conscience in Late-Victorian England*, pp. 308 & 311.

Christian Socialist Society.[94] This small group was to play a significant part in the Bristol socialist movement.

On 22 June, the day after the first public meeting of the Christian Socialist Society in London, Gore took his Incorporated Law Society's final examination. The following month he received the news that he had passed.[95] He was now free to operate as a fully qualified solicitor and, most importantly, felt he had the security and confidence to give his time to openly advocating socialism.

On 7 August 1886, the *Bristol Mercury* published the first of what was to become a series of articles by W. A. Leonard, critically dissecting the beliefs expressed by campaigners for socialism.[96] Two further articles in the series followed, on 14 and 21 August, before Gore was called upon to respond to what he saw as an ill-informed critique of socialism, because it focused solely on the 1884 manifesto of the Democratic Federation. In his rejoinder, Gore disassociated himself from much of the state socialist position of the Social Democratic Federation, as well as Hyndman, who he described as a 'windbag'. He registered annoyance that Leonard seemed ignorant of the other versions of socialism propounded by the Socialist League, the Socialist Union, a group set up to foster unity, or the Fabian Society, which advocated gradual reform. In particular, Gore drew attention to the undenominational Christian Socialist Society, which, earlier in the year, he had helped to create.[97] He described this Society as consisting

of an earnest little band of workers, gentlewomen and gentlemen in the true sense of the words. They are fired with the enthusiasm of a faith in the spirit of love and self-negation, and they strive to slacken the course of competition, and enlarge the borders of the Kingdom of Heaven. They have only been associated for a few months, but there is much work in the future for them; and it is not without significance that Lawrence Gronlund, the author of "The Co-operative Commonwealth," wished to dedicate his new work on the French Revolution (Danton) to that society.[98]

Gore's Christian Socialism was part of a great ferment of debate occurring in the first half of the 1880s. The Christian Socialists' conviction that social

94 Bryher, *An Account of the Labour and Socialist Movement in Bristol*, Part 1, p. 42.
95 The Incorporated Law Society's successful candidates at the Final Examination held on the 22 and 23 June 1886, *The Times*, 10 July 1886.
96 W. A. Leonard, 'SOCIALISM. – 1.' *Bristol Mercury*, 7 August 1886.
97 Jones, *The Christian Socialist Revival 1877-1914: Religion, Class, and Social Conscience in Late-Victorian England*, p. 308.
98 Hugh Holmes Gore, 'SOCIALISM.' A Rejoinder, *Bristol Mercury*, 28 August 1886.

equality must be part of the Christian mission drew on Gronlund, an American living in London and occasional visitor to Bristol. They also absorbed Henry George's writings on land nationalization and his rejection of the assumption that poverty was inevitable. Edward Carpenter who linked spiritual and social transformation in his books and articles was also influential.[99]

The philosophical underpinning came largely from the work of Thomas Hill Green. Green's social philosophy called for an organic model of society and argued for a realignment of the relationship between society and the state. This involved a rejection of traditional liberalism's emphasis on individualism. Green's reworking of liberalism, under the influence of Georg Wilhelm Friedrich Hegel's Idealism, emphasised the individual's obligations to society at large. In this scenario, the freedom of the individual was seen as the end rather than the means, hence he argued that state intervention to tackle unemployment, poverty and social needs – the removal of obstacles to self improvement – would do much to ensure the well being of all, giving individuals the freedom to develop to their full potential.[100] Christian Socialists welcomed this, as it buttressed their contention that 'the proper function of the State is to reconcile the interest of each with the interests of all',[101] though in practice Green's followers were inclined to disagree over the extent and nature of state intervention. Moreover, Green's Hegelian Idealism did not allow for differing degrees of power attached to particular 'interests'.

The role of the state was similarly important in Henry George's solution to the 'want and suffering and anxiety among the working classes.'[102] He argued that the way to bring about a fairer, just and more equal society 'must be sought in the laws which govern the distribution of wealth.' His remedy was to 'make land common property'…as 'the unequal ownership of land necessitates the unequal distribution of wealth'.[103] Landowners had an inordinate amount of power and could compel their tenants to act in a particular way in respect to religion, education, dress and so forth.[104] George proposed a single tax on the land. He argued that *'[i]t is not necessary to confiscate land; it is only necessary to confiscate rent.'*[105] He explained that this would drive down its value to zero,

99 Jones, *The Christian Socialist Revival 1877-1914: Religion, Class, and Social Conscience in Late-Victorian England*, p. 308.

100 See M. Richter, *The Politics of Conscience: T. H. Green and his Age* (London: Weidenfeld and Nicolson, 1964), pp. 267-9.

101 Richter, *The Politics of Conscience: T. H. Green and his Age,* p. 49.

102 H. George, *Progress and Poverty* (London: The Henry George Foundation of Great Britain, 52nd Anniversary Edition, 1932), p. 9.

103 George, *Progress and Poverty*, p.234.

104 George, *Progress and Poverty*, p. 249.

105 George, *Progress and Poverty*, p. 288.

securing equal rights to the land, a form of land nationalisation. George did not look to the improvement of human nature to progress his cause as 'the advances in which civilisation consists are not secured in the constitution of man, but in the constitution of society', which are not 'fixed and permanent'.[106] George believed in the ideal of socialism, but however desirable it could not 'be manufactured – it must grow.'[107] This exerted an influence upon the Marxists within the Social Democratic Federation and was incorporated into the Christian Socialist and Fabian view of the permeation of socialist ideas into culture and the body politic.

Gronlund and his supporters, however, opposed George's case for a single tax on land to resolve inequality. They advocated the full socialisation of the means of production, including agricultural land, as the only remedy. In his extremely influential book, *The Co-operative Commonwealth in its Outlines: An Exposition of Modern Socialism*, Gronlund argued that 'it is certainly better to agitate for complete rather than partial Socialism.'[108] Turning to classical Marxism, Gronlund specified that workers, even if they had access to free land, still had to sell their labour power to the owners of the means of production, the capitalists, in order to live. Hence, they were still exposed to exploitation, or as Gronlund called it *'fleecing'*.[109] Gronlund, however, rejected the contention that conflict between the hostile classes, the bourgeoisie and the proletariat, over the fruits of labour would sooner or later result in a proletarian revolution, as the first step along the road to the establishment of a socialist society. He argued we 'cannot accomplish the progress of our race by leaps but must do it by growths.'[110] Like Henry George and the Fabians he believed in evolution rather than revolution.

Gore, along with other Bristol socialists and liberal progressives, was also drawn to the ethical socialism of Carpenter, which stressed self-realisation, as opposed to individualists who supported property rights and economic liberalism (*laissez faire*). Carpenter's disregard for socialist sectarianism allowed him to support all factions, and be held in high regard. During the 1880s and 1890s, he exercised a unifying influence upon differing socialist groupings in Bristol[111]

Gore's commitment to and understanding of socialism was still incipient in 1886. However, he did make an impact upon his opponent, Leonard, in

106 George, *Progress and Poverty*, p. 398.
107 George, *Progress and Poverty*, p. 228.
108 L. Gronlund, *Insufficiency of Henry George's Theory* (New York: New York Labor News Company, 1887), p. 8.
109 Gronlund, *Insufficiency of Henry George's Theory*, p. 11.
110 L. Gronlund, *The Cooperative Commonwealth in its outlines: An Exposition of Modern Socialism* (Boston: Lee and Shepard, 1884), p. 59.
111 Rowbotham, *Edward Carpenter: A Life of Liberty and Love*, pp. 126 – 7 and 166.

the debate on socialism played out in the local press, for on the 29 August, the day after the publication of Gore's rejoinder, Leonard wrote to William Morris seeking his recommendation on the most authoritative works to read on socialism.[112] Morris passed this correspondence to his son-in-law and Secretary of the Socialist League, Henry Halliday Sparling. Sparling sent Leonard the League's manifesto and other material. On 3 September 1886, Leonard contacted Sparling, thanked him for his courtesy, and revealed that he was unaware Morris was connected to the Socialist League. He went on to say he had written an article on socialism to which 'a rejoinder was made…and I have sent out a reply'.[113] Clearly, he took Gore's criticism seriously.

Gore, however, was not impressed by Leonard's response to his rejoinder. Despite claiming that he was sympathetic to some of the reforms advocated by socialists, Leonard, a critic of Henry George,[114] argued that equal division of work and wealth were not possible 'till man's nature itself is changed'.[115] He added a postscript:

> Since writing the above, I have had sent me direct the manifesto of the Socialist League; H. H. G. calls it a "carefully prepared manifesto."…I think we shall find on examination that its teachings are similar to those of the Social Democratic Federation, and which H. H. G. describes as "frothy."[116]

Leonard then went on to paraphrase from the Socialist League's manifesto: 'State Socialism must take the place of present civilisation'. Gore accused Leonard of grossly misrepresenting the Socialist League's position. He maintained that, as presented in its manifesto, the Socialist League was actually criticising those who were advocating state socialism.

> "State Socialism would be no better solution in dealing with the real evils of life than competitive co-operation for profit", which is useless (the league says).[117]

112 W. A. Leonard to William Morris, 29 August 1886, the International Institute of Social History, Amsterdam.
113 W. A. Leonard to H. H. Sparling, the Socialist League, 3 September 1886, the International Institute of Social History, Amsterdam.
114 See his article in the *Western Daily Press*, 26 April 1883.
115 W. A. Leonard, 'SOCIALISM – IV.' A Reply to a Rejoinder, *Bristol Mercury*, 4 September 1886.
116 W. A. Leonard, Postscript to 'SOCIALISM – IV.' A Reply to a Rejoinder, *Bristol Mercury*, 4 September 1886.
117 Hugh Holmes Gore, 'SOCIALISM. An Explanation', *Bristol Mercury*, 11 September 1886.

The manifesto actually stated:

> No better solution would be that of State Socialism, by whatever name it may be called, whose aim it would be to make concessions to the working class while leaving the present system of capital and wages still in operation: no number of merely administrative changes, until the workers are in possession of all political power, would make any real approach to Socialism.[118]

From the beginning, however, there were differences between the leading cadres of the Socialist League and dissension appeared. Its manifesto, issued in 1885, was cobbled together as a compromise between the different factions. As early as April 1886, Friedrich Engels, co-author of *The Communist Manifesto*, expressed his concern, as Morris' more nuanced critique of reformism and opportunism was beginning to be drowned out by the anarchists' anti-parliamentary faction. [119] Conflict between two separate camps, pro and anti-parliamentarian, was to seriously undermine the League's ability to operate as a united party and eventually lead to the ascendency of the anarchist communists in 1890.

Gore, however, chose to advance the debate with Leonard by accusing him of stubbornly refusing to broaden his critique of socialism due to his lack of knowledge of other socialist organisations. 'He still harps on Mr Hyndman, and this with poor reason.'[120] Two more articles written by Leonard on socialism were to appear in the *Bristol Mercury*, on 25 September and 2 October, but Gore declined to take up the offer of having the last word. In a letter to the editor of the *Bristol Mercury* he announced:

> I understood the subject of the articles was to be socialism. Mr W. A. Leonard has ceased to write on that subject, and is now writing about himself and Mrs Besant [she had recently joined the Fabian Socialists]. I have nothing further to add, except to thank you for kindly allowing a Socialist to tell the public something of the real principles of a Socialists creed.[121]

118 William Morris and E. Belfort Bax, 'The Manifesto of The Socialist League', *Commonweal*, *February 1885, pp. 1-2 cited on http://www.marxists.org/archive/morris/works/1885/manifst1.htm* accessed 24/08/2013.
119 E. P. Thompson, *William Morris: Romantic to Revolutionary*, p. 405.
120 Hugh Holmes Gore, 'SOCIALISM. An Explanation', *Bristol Mercury*, 11 September 1886.
121 Gore to the editor of the *Bristol Mercury*, 1 October 1886. Annie Besant would later take a prominent role in supporting the women and girls on strike at the Bryant and May match-making factory in Bow, London.

Gore's open debate with Leonard broke through the reticence he had indicated before he qualified in 1885 in advocating his socialist beliefs in public. His acceptance of Christian Socialist principles, along with his role in establishing the Clifton and Bristol Christian Socialist Society, with Girdlestone, set him on the path to become the first professed socialist to be elected to the Bristol School Board.[122] The programme of the Clifton and Bristol Christian Socialists, written by Girdlestone, was published in October 1886, soon after Gore's public debate with Leonard.[123] The group then launched a series of public meetings and lectures. Gore was an active presence in these events, either presiding or lecturing.

122 Jones, *The Christian Socialist Revival 1877-1914: Religion, Class, and Social Conscience in Late-Victorian England*, p. 311; Sutcliffe, *The Keys of Heaven: The Life of Revd Charles Marson, Christian Socialist & Folksong Collector*, Kindle file, location, 1359.
123 E. D. Girdlestone, *Thirty Nine Articles of Belief, Proposed as the Profession and Programme of Christian Socialists* (Bristol: J. W. Arrowsmith, 1886).

Chapter 3

Reputation Building

By the end of 1886, not only had Gore openly declared his support for socialism but he had also established his own solicitor's practice, operating from both his Clifton address, and 11 Clare Street in the centre of Bristol. It had proved a defining year for him. In 1887, as part of his transition from dependent to independent living, Gore planted himself in a working class area near to the heart of Bristol's industrial district. He was not attempting to set an example by moving to work and live in a slum area, among the poor, as Stewart Headlam had done in Bethnal Green. However, it did constitute a significant break from his time dwelling in a well-to-do district with his parents in a comfortable Clifton home.

From relative luxury Gore moved into an unfurnished apartment, with an oven grate and dresser, at 52 Franklyn Street, St. Paul's, overlooking St. Agnes' Park, not far from the centre of Bristol. It was a 'respectable' working class street and not the 'slum court' to which he would relocate in 1891.[124] The area was currently becoming densely populated with some households taking in lodgers and some houses divided into apartments.[125] James Ramsay MacDonald, later to become the first Labour Prime Minister (1924), had lived in this street for a brief period in 1885 after joining the Bristol branch of the Social Democratic Federation.[126]

Gore's move into the upstairs apartment of 52 Franklyn Street brought him into close association with Robert Sharland – a founder member of the Bristol Socialist Society – who occupied the rooms downstairs with his wife and son.[127] They had been living there for several years.[128] Sharland was a skilled wireworker – most likely the one that William Morris met in March 1885 – and a member of the Amalgamated Engineers' Union.[129] He was a man of broad cultural interests; an admirer of the American poet Walt Whitman; and a good

---

124 The economic and social historian Helen Meller records that Gore 'chose… to live in a slum court', but she does not provide a date, and does not mention that when Gore first moved out of Clifton he settled in Franklyn Street. See H. E. Meller, *Leisure and the Changing City, 1870-1914* (London: Routledge & Kegan Paul, 1976), p. 157.

125 See the Census Returns of England and Wales, 1891, Ancestry.com, courtesy of the National Archives of the UK, accessed 23 September 2013.

126 Bryher, *An Account of the Labour and Socialist Movement in Bristol*, Part 1, p. 30.

127 *Matthew's Bristol and Clifton Street Directory* (Bristol: John Wright, 1888, compiled late 1887). The directory mistakenly places Gore at number 32 but later editions place him at number 52. The 1891 Census of Returns of England and Wales also records him living at 52 Franklyn Street.

128 *Matthews Bristol and Clifton Directory, 1887-1892.*

129 See Bryher, *An Account of the Labour and Socialist Movement in Bristol*, Part 1, p. 18, 23-25.

friend of Edward Carpenter, who used to stay with him and his family when speaking in Bristol. Sharland had played a pivotal role in the decision of the Bristol branch of the Social Democratic Federation to break from the national body and establish its independence, as the Bristol Socialist Society, in the wake of the Social Democratic Federation's scandal of accepting "Tory Gold", in the November 1885 General Election campaign.[130]

Despite Gore and Sharland belonging to discrete socialist organisations, they were happy to reside under the same roof and relations between them appear to have been good. Regardless of the differences between Gore's Clifton and Bristol Christian Socialists and the Bristol Socialist Society over how they thought that socialism could be brought into being, close links were established between the two organisations. For instance, in April 1886 Girdlestone had contributed a pound's subscription to the Bristol Socialist Society 'which he hoped he could continue annually',[131] and Gore addressed a couple of their meetings – an open air one in August 1886 and a lecture on 'thrift' in January 1888.[132] The defining difference between them was that the Clifton and Bristol Christian Socialists rejected violent revolution in favour of moral persuasion, stressing the virtues of 'patience, hope and faith'.[133] The Bristol Socialist Society, while not excluding moral education, was not convinced that the transformation from capitalism to socialism could be accomplished gradually. This did not mean that its members advocated violent means, although they believed that such means might be inevitable if capitalism was to be overthrown.[134]

The rear of Gore's (and Sharland's) residence adjoined the grounds of the new St. Agnes' Parish Church. Consecrated in 1886 the Church appointed the socialist-leaning Reverend Thomas William Harvey as its first vicar. Harvey came to Bristol in December 1880 to take up the post of curate of the Clifton College Mission. Based at a former engineer's workshop in St. Agnes, this demanding position had previously been held by the Ruskinian, Reverend Rawnsley. Looked upon with a certain amount of suspicion at first, Harvey soon established respect from all sections of the community. Money was raised for a new Mission room, which opened on 10 May 1882, and a Workmen's Club and a Men's Mutual Improvement Society was formed debating subjects such as 'the action of the Sanitary Authority, Local Option, Trades Unions, Compulsory Insurance, and Elementary Education.'[135]

130 Bryher, *An Account of the Labour and Socialist Movement in Bristol*, Part 1, p. 24.
131 The Minutes of the Bristol Socialist Society, 22 April 1886.
132 The Minutes of the Bristol Socialist Society, 9 August 1886 and 25 January 1888.
133 Hugh Holmes Gore, SOCIALISM. A Rejoinder, *Bristol Mercury*, 28 August 1886.
134 The Minutes of the Bristol Socialist Society, 16 September 1886.
135 Members of Clifton College, *The History of Saint Agnes Parish* (Bristol: Clifton College) pp. 10-12.

Gore thus arrived into a community Harvey was nurturing which aimed at making 'it possible for the people of St. Agnes to achieve an independent cultural existence.'[136] Moreover, Harvey 'had a brief for a class not nearly enough considered by the Church – the intelligent artisan.'[137] He supported the labour movement, befriending John Gregory, a local poet-shoemaker, member of the Bristol Socialist Society, and Vice-President of the Bristol Trades Council. Unlike Gore, however, Harvey's radicalism did not extend to adopting an anti-monarchist position.

By 1887, Queen Victoria's Golden Jubilee year, Gore had abandoned any vestiges of loyalty to the crown inculcated by his old school and the Guild of St. George. He braved royalist sentiment and openly revealed his opposition to the monarchy through his active involvement in the Anti-Jubilee committee. Gore signed an Anti-Jubilee statement ridiculing the event as an attempt by the Tory and the Liberal parties to gain working class support by evoking patriotic feelings and actions, and called upon workers to protest 'against the evils of the present [capitalist] system, its waste and injustice on Jubilee day.'[138] He spoke at anti-jubilee public gatherings. At one open-air meeting, held at Avon Street, St. Philip's, on 17 June 1887, Gore contended that the jubilee jamboree

> would be a more appropriate occasion for a national rejoicing if they celebrated the passing of some great measure of reform which had been insisted on by the people, in spite of the strenuous opposition of those who were interested in sustaining a monarchy.[139]

The Anti-Jubilee protests climaxed in a demonstration held on 21 June in St. Philip's, attended by around 600 people. The authorities regarded their anti-patriotic protest as seriously subversive and over-reacted by calling out the troops. The third Battalion of the Gloucester Regiment duly marched directly towards the right flank of the rally 'with blast of trumpets and beating of drums drowning for the time the speaker's voice. Then a sudden order was given to fall into line across nearly the whole width of the open space', which, as intended, seriously disrupted the meeting, impeding citizens' rights to hold peaceful demonstrations. Unfazed by the crude attempt to sabotage the demonstration, protestors screamed, howled and groaned, until the military stood down.[140]

136 Meller, *Leisure and the Changing City, 1870-1914*, p. 154.
137 Colvile, H. C. A., *Thomas William Harvey: Prophet and Priest* (Bristol: J. W. Arrowsmith, 1918) p. 64.
138 Bryher, *An Account of the Labour and Socialist Movement in Bristol*, Part 1, p. 43.
139 *Bristol Mercury*, 18 June 1887.
140 Robert Sharland to the Editor of the *Bristol Mercury*, published 23 June 1887.

Angry at this effort to suppress protest, the Anti-Jubilee committee submitted a strong complaint through the local press about the bullish behavior of the military.[141] Nevertheless, despite this unsettling incident, overall the protest meetings against the jubilee humbug were successful.[142] Gore played a central part in articulating the socialist anti-monarchy position, as well as peacefully exercising the right to free speech. His actions brought him into closer association with the Bristol Socialist Society, but were at odds with the views of his Clifton and Bristol Christian Socialist colleague, Girdlestone, who, staying loyal to Ruskin's Guild of St. George code to 'obey all the laws of my country faithfully; and the orders of its monarch,' objected to those socialists showing hostility toward the Queen, and indeed demurred on the Christian Socialist position of supporting Home Rule for Ireland.[143] The vast majority of Gore's Bristol socialist and labour comrades, however, supported his anti-monarchist position.

In July 1887 Gore took on a newly qualified young man, Glanville Munro[144] as a partner in his practice which was now functioning solely from Clare Street.[145] Munro seems to have shared Gore's personal and political interests. He was the treasurer of the Redland Athletic Club and an active member of the Clifton and Bristol Christian Socialist Society.[146] This partnership with Gore, however, turned out to be short-lived. It was dissolved in February 1889 when Munro 'retired'.[147] Munro entered a disastrous downward spiral of self-destruction, setting up his own practice but quickly falling from grace after becoming bankrupt in November 1890.[148] In 1893, along with two others, he was charged with several cases of conspiracy in obtaining goods by deception by means of issuing cheques against unfunded accounts.[149] Munro was found guilty, and condemned to five years incarceration and struck off the rolls as a solicitor.[150]

In 1887 divisions among members of the Christian Socialist Society resulted in a failure 'to agree on a clear *political* program.' Differences of opinion widened between the contending factions about whether or not the Society

141 Robert Sharland to the Editor of the *Bristol Mercury*, published 23 June 1887.
142 The Minutes of the Bristol Socialist Society, 23 June 1887.
143 Jones, *The Christian Socialist Revival 1877-1914: Religion, Class, and Social Conscience in Late-Victorian England*, p. 319; Orens, *Stewart Headlam's Radical Anglicanism: The Mass, The Masses and the Music Hall*, p. 87.
144 G. D. M. Munro was among the successful candidates at the June final examination of the Incorporated Law Society, *Bristol Mercury*, 4 July 1887.
145 Matthew's Bristol and Clifton Street Directory (Bristol: John Wright, 1888, Compiled in 1887).
146 *Bristol Mercury,* 9 May 1887 and 12 December 1887.
147 *Birmingham Daily Post*, 13 February 1889.
148 *Bristol Mercury*, 1 November 1890 and 16 February 1891.
149 *Bristol Mercury*, 26 June 1893.
150 *Bristol Mercury*, 11 August 1893.

should adhere to a single political platform, since it had no such single religious creed. The Society was on the brink of collapse. An emergency meeting was held in September 1887, at which a motion was tabled calling for the Society's dissolution. Never one to shy away from a controversial issue, Gore seconded the motion, but, on the casting vote of the meeting's chairman, the Society survived to live on for five more years.[151] Gore accepted the decision, retaining his membership and his leading position in the Clifton and Bristol branch and set about raising the Society's profile by organising public meetings with eminent speakers.

By the autumn Gore had established himself as one of the leading voices in Bristol's labour movement and had formed a good relationship with the working class communities of St. Paul's, St. Jacob's, St. Philip's, the Dings and St. Jude's. Gore's charismatic style, debating skills and the force of his oratory, had attracted public attention. His clandestine homosexuality,[152] however, made him vulnerable, especially at a time when the practice of homosexuality, either in public or private, was being subjected to increased attention, following the introduction of the Labouchère Amendment of the Criminal Law Amendment Act of 1885.[153] The change in the law introduced a new offence of 'gross indecency', in private as well as in public,[154] although in practice it 'had little bearing on the pattern of arrests and prosecutions.'[155] However, it fostered an atmosphere of repression and fear. The Labouchère Amendment Act became commonly known as the 'Blackmailer's Charter', as it provided extortionists with an easier target.[156]

It may have been as a result of this Act that Gore was subjected to blackmail in a case brought before the Bristol magistrates on 31 October 1887. Thomas Sherwood Smith, Secretary of the Bristol and Clifton Permanent Building

151 Jones, *The Christian Socialist Revival 1877-1914: Religion, Class, and Social Conscience in Late-Victorian England*, p. 325.

152 A. Crawford, *C. R. Ashbee: Architect, Designer & Romantic Socialist* (New Haven: Yale University Press, 2nd edition 2005, first published 1985), p. 436 ftn. 63, Crawford notes that Hugh Holmes Gore 'seems to have been a homosexual'. Angela Tuckett, refers to Gore's homosexuality in A. Tuckett, 'Enid Stacy, The Nineteenth Century Political Radical and Activist for Peace, Social Justice and Women's Rights' (unpublished, edited edition: June 2012), p. 65, footnote 9, Working Class Library, Salford.

153 Hilliard, 'Unenglish and Unmanly: Anglo-Catholicism and Homosexuality', p. 182.

154 H. G. Cocks, *Nameless Offences: Homosexual Desire in the Nineteenth Century* (London: I.B. Tauris, 2003), p.30.

155 J. Bristow, 'Remapping the Sites of Modern Gay History: Legal Reform, Medico-legal Thought, Homosexual Scandal, Erotic Geography', *Journal of British Studies*, Vol. 46, No. 1 (January 2007), p. 122.

156 J. Weeks, *Coming Out: Homosexual Politics in Britain, from the Nineteenth Century to the Present* (London: Quartet, 1977), p. 22.

Society, and Vice Chair of the Keynsham Liberal Association, was summoned by Gore for first unlawfully 'demanding of the said Hugh Holmes Gore, with menaces, and without any reasonable or probable cause, certain money', in a letter sent on 21 October 1887; and second for unlawfully threatening 'to publish a false libel', concerning Gore, 'with the intent then and thereby to extort money, to wit, the sum of £15, from him.' The case was eventually settled out of court. Smith withdrew the allegations contained in the letter, and expressed regret for having written it.[157]

This was not in fact the first time that Smith had been charged with libel. In November 1877 he was accused of publishing false and scandalous libels concerning John Freeman Norris, a barrister-at-law, reviling him 'in the most violent manner'. Smith accepted his guilt, apologised and consented to be bound over, on the deposit of £100, not to repeat the libels or offend Norris in any way.[158]

Gore's reputation may have been left undamaged, but bringing this case to court must have been a difficult and testing time for him, mentally, spiritually, and emotionally. However, he found solace in his Christian and socialist beliefs and got on with the task of organising public meetings under the auspices of the Clifton and Bristol Christian Socialist Society. The main presenter at one of these meetings was Henry Hyde Champion, a former editor of the *Christian Socialist*. On 19 November 1887 Champion delivered a thoughtful speech, reflecting his emotional commitment to Christian Socialism. He predicted that in 'a few years time the preaching of socialist ideas would lead to a great religious revival.'[159]

Champion had achieved notoriety in 1886 when, along with other members of the Social Democratic Federation, John Burns, Jack Williams, and Henry Mayers Hyndman, he spoke from a socialist stand at a mass rally of the unemployed in Trafalgar Square. After the rally had finished, and the demonstrators had left the square, mayhem ensued — windows were smashed and shops looted, as socialist supporters and their unemployed allies, twenty thousand strong, made their way along Pall Mall. Champion, Burns, Williams and Hyndman were held responsible. They were arrested and appeared at the Old Bailey charged with uttering seditious words with intent to incite to riot.[160] The four-day trial was heard before Mr. Justice Cave, who was renowned for his fairness and impartiality, a rare quality among nineteenth century judges.[161] Champion

157 *Bristol Mercury*, 1 November 1887. The contents of the letter were not published.
158 *Western Mail*, 16 November 1877; *Sheffield Daily Telegraph*, 16 November 1877.
159 *Western Daily Press*, 21 November 1887.
160 J. Barnes, 'Gentleman Crusader: Henry Hyde Champion in the Early Socialist Movement', *History Workshop Journal*, No.60, autumn, 2005, p. 126.
161 See M. Daniell and R. A. Nicol, *The New Trade Unionism; its relation to the old; and the conditions of its success* (Bristol, Pamphlet: 1890), Appendix, pp. 16-20.

and Hyndman defended themselves, and an advanced radical, William Marcus Thompson, defended Burns and Williams. The jury found all the defendants not guilty. Although they thought 'the language of Champion and Burns was highly inflammatory' they acquitted them of any malicious intent.[162] When Champion came to Bristol he had just been expelled from the Social Democratic Federation for criticising its leader for advocating violent revolution.

More public lectures followed the one given by Champion and, as a consequence, by the middle of January 1888 the Clifton and Bristol Christian Socialist Society's financial account had fallen into a small deficit.[163] Nonetheless, the lecture programme continued. On 25 January Gore delivered a talk on 'Socialism and Thrift' at a well-attended meeting chaired by Robert Weare, a member of the Bristol Socialist Society.[164] This series of lectures spawned correspondence in the local press on the advantages of, and objections to, socialism and the problem of the unemployed. Gore, in his contribution, argued that the 'morality or ardent faith' of Christian socialism 'is more likely to guide men [sic] aright than the hesitating and erratic steps of expediency.'[165]

By expediency Gore was referring to examples given by previous correspondents as 'to whether a scheme [for the unemployed] will "pay."' From a Christian standpoint Gore argued that this objection was untenable 'as though to make a profit were the Christian as well as the commercial ideal.' George Eliot's words from her novel, *Romola*, were used to illustrate his point:

If you mean to act nobly and seek to know and do the best thing[s] God has placed within reach of man [men,] you must learn to fix your mind on that end[,] and not on what will happen to you because of it.

Gore remarked that 'this may be Hegelian, but it is also purely Christian ethics.'[166]

In May 1888, at the behest of his London-based Guild of St. Matthew friend, the Reverend William Edmund Moll, Gore was called upon to conduct the prosecution against Harry Frank Tracey, the senior curate of Romsey Parish Church, Hampshire, at a hearing in the local Town Hall. This was a particularly sensitive case. Tracey was charged with performing 'an unnatural offence' on

162 The Proceedings of the Old Bailey, London's Central Criminal Court, 1674 to 1913, Old Bailey Proceedings Online (www.oldbaileyonline.org, version 7.0, 18 June 2014), April 1886 (t18860405), accessed 18 June 2014.
163 *Bristol Mercury*, 18 January 1888.
164 *Western Daily Press*, 27 January 1888.
165 *Western Daily Press*, 24 February 1888.
166 *Western Daily Press*, 24 February 1888; George Eliot, *Romola* (London: Penguin, 1996, first published 1862-3). p. 582.

William Munn, a fourteen-year old boy. The hearing attracted considerable local attention but he had the support of his parishioners with whom he was extremely popular. Nonetheless the court committed him to take his trial at the Assize Court.[167] In the mean time Tracey faced a second charge of unlawfully and indecently assaulting thirteen-year old Edward Harlock, which came before the Romsey Borough Police-Court on 22 June 1888; again Gore appeared for the prosecution. However, after hearing the evidence the magistrates took less than ten minutes to clear Tracey of this charge. On leaving the court Tracey received a rousing reception. Gore, however, was booed and jeered all the way to the railway station.[168]

Just over a month later, on 30 July 1888 at the Hampshire Assize Court, the Grand jury threw out the charge hanging over Tracey of indecently assaulting William Munn, whose testimony was disbelieved.[169] It is difficult to say what impact these cases would have had on Gore. He was passionate about protecting vulnerable children, but it may well have reminded him that as a public figure he, too, could be open to false accusations, and would have to be extra careful in concealing his homosexual feelings at a time of hardening public attitudes. Thus, to enjoy the comradeship of like-minded men would have probably involved him in making clandestine arrangements.

In 1888 Gore joined radical liberals in anti-Coercion demonstrations following the imprisonment of John Dillon, an Irish nationalist parliamentarian, under the provisions of the new Criminal Procedure Act, or Coercion Act, for advocating the 'Plan of Campaign' amongst Irish tenant farmers. This campaign had organised collective resistance to those landlords who refused to reduce the rents of their tenants. Dillon was arrested in April 1888 for 'exhort[ing] the tenants of Lord Massereene in County Louth to join the Plan'.[170] On 20 June, he was sentenced to six months imprisonment. On his journey to Dundalk jail in County Louth, Ireland, he was 'cheered for half a mile by a sympathetic throng', illustrating the sharp divide which existed between the Irish people and their rulers.[171]

There was a strong reaction against the imprisonment of Dillon from Home Rulers. This feeling of injustice was heightened by the deterioration in Dillon's health, and the death, on 8 July, of the Irish nationalist, and tenant farmer, John Mandeville, from a throat infection brought on by the brutal treatment he had

167 *Western Gazette*, 25 May 1888.
168 *Western Gazette*, 29 June 1888.
169 *Western Gazette*, 3 August 1888.
170 F. S. Lyons, 'John Dillon and the Plan of Campaign, 1886-90', *Irish Historical Studies*, Vol. 14, No. 56 (Sep., 1965), p. 326.
171 *Pall Mall Gazette*, 22 June 1888.

received in Tullamore prison.[172] On Saturday 4 August 1888 at the Ropewalk, River Street, St. Jude's, a protest by Bristol Liberals against the imprisonment of Dillon attracted a 1,000 strong crowd. Dan Irving, representing the Bristol Operatives' Liberal Association, presided; among the speakers were Gore, Handel Cossham, Liberal MP for Bristol East, John Valentine, Irish Home Rule activist and chair of the Bristol branch of the Irish National League, and Robert Gray Tovey, a Bristol Town councilor and secretary of the Trades Council and the Bristol Labour League, an organisation campaigning for working class representatives in Parliament. Two resolutions were passed. One condemning Dillon's imprisonment, and a second moved by Gore stating:

We, the assembled citizens of Bristol, indignantly protest against the conduct of those of our Parliamentary representatives who by voice and vote have upheld the present Ministry in their method of government by trickery and force, and we assert that they misrepresent the wishes and lack the confidence of the large majority of the people of our city.[173]

In moving the proposition he said 'it was a relic from a barbarous age when men were put into prison, as Mr Dillon had been, for the expression of opinion, and such a practice was not fit for an enlightened age such as the present.' Tovey seconded the motion.[174]

By this time Gore had established close relations with Edward Carpenter who had also been involved in protests against the Tory-Liberal Unionist government's coercion in Ireland.[175] Carpenter had become an important figure for a group of younger men. Drawing on his natural communicative abilities, sincerity and sexual honesty, he was able to bring together radical left people with diverse views about how to effect the transformation of society. At his home, in the rural settlement of Millthorpe, near Sheffield, Carpenter also offered a warm welcome to many radicals wishing to talk over their personal and sexual anxieties with him. [176]

In October 1888, Gore travelled to Millthorpe to visit Carpenter. Residing there at the time was Cecil Reddie, a socialist teacher, who, like Gore, was sexually attracted to other men. Gore already knew Reddie who had been an

172 Lyons, 'John Dillon and the Plan of Campaign, 1886-90', p. 331.
173 *Bristol Mercury*, 6 August 1888.
174 *Bristol Mercury*, 6 August 1888.
175 Rowbotham, *Edward Carpenter: A Life of Liberty and Love*, p. 120. Edward Carpenter was a frequent visitor to Bristol and addressed many meetings including ones to the Clifton and Bristol Christian Socialist Society, Bryher, *An Account of the Labour and Socialist Movement*, Part 1, p. 42.
176 Rowbotham, *Edward Carpenter: A Life of Liberty and Love*, p. 105.

Dr. Cecil Reddie

assistant master at Clifton College in Bristol before he had left in April 1888, after experiencing a breakdown.[177] Also teaching at the College at the time of Reddie's tenure was another covert homosexual, Henry Graham Dakyns, a long-standing friend of Bristol born John Addington Symonds, whose father had been a Vice President of the College and had sat on its Council. Symonds, like his father, also had strong links with the college and had on occasions been called on to deliver lectures to the boys. Before his death in 1893 he would publish a monograph on Walt Whitman and strongly argue the case for the decriminalisation of sodomy.[178] Neither Reddie nor Gore had ever met Symonds but they would have been very aware of his presence and his work. Carpenter, however, met Symonds briefly in 1892 and following an exchange of ideas between himself, Ellis and Symonds in the course of their correspondence

177 A. Crawford, *C. R. Ashbee: Architect, Designer & Romantic Socialist*, pp. 20-21 & p.436, ftn. 63; P. Searby, 'Reddie, Cecil (1858-1932), *Oxford Dictionary of National Biography*, (Oxford: Oxford University Press, 2004; online edn, May 2005, accessed 15 July 1914).
178 C. Craft, *Another Kind of Love: Male Homosexual Desire in English Discourse, 1850-1920* (Berkeley: University of California, 1994) p. 32.

that year he was inspired to write his 1894 pamphlet *Homogenic Love and its Place in a Free Society*.[179]

Reddie had encountered Carpenter a few years earlier at meetings of the Fellowship of the New Life, and was familiar with ideas of 'combining the personal with the political.'[180] The Fellowship went on to encourage small-scale alternative projects and in 1889 Reddie established a progressive boys' school at Abbotsholme, Staffordshire, initially run on socialistic lines. Also staying with Carpenter when Gore arrived was Charles Robert Ashbee, the architect, designer and romantic socialist who had worked with Gore's contemporary at Bristol Grammar, Llewellyn Smith, in the social settlement, Toynbee Hall, in London's East End. In June 1888, Ashbee had established the School and Guild of Handicraft, where Llewellyn Smith took the boys' decoration class. Ashbee too was sexually attracted to men, although several years later he married Janet Forbes despite not being 'violently in love'.[181] Carpenter's aura, and the reassuring environment at Millthorpe, enabled these men to openly discuss their homosexual feelings, as well as their socialism.[182]

This intimacy between Carpenter, Ashbee, Reddie and Gore at their rendezvous in Millthorpe was a sexual-spiritual one because it was carried out in the conscious awareness of their sexual orientation and spiritual longing for comradeship with one another. It was based on friendship and trust and the sharing of ideas such as Reddie's plan to establish a new progressive boys' school.[183] While there was an acceptance of strong male friendships in Victorian Britain, the remote settlement at Millthorpe was unusual in that it provided an alternative way of living secluded from the prying eyes of journalists and social purists. There for a few fleeting days Gore could be completely at ease with his sexual orientation and socialist views.

179 Rowbotham, *Edward Carpenter: A Life of Liberty and Love*, pp. 185-189.

180 Rowbotham, *Edward Carpenter: A Life of Liberty and Love*, pp. 89-90.

181 From Janet Forbes Journal 1895-1906 quoted in Felicity Ashbee, *Janet Ashbee: Love, Marriage, and the Arts & Crafts Movement* (New York: Syracuse University Press, 2002), p. 24.

182 Searby, 'Reddie, Cecil (1858-1932), *Oxford Dictionary of National Biography*; Crawford, *C. R. Ashbee: Architect, Designer & Romantic Socialist*, pp. 20-21, 36 & p.436, ftn. 63.

183 See Rowbotham, *Edward Carpenter: A Life of Liberty and Love*, pp. 131-2.

Chapter 4

School Board Election, January 1889

On his return from Millthorpe Gore pursued his political mission with renewed vigour. Towards the end of 1888 he delivered a series of lectures to local Liberal Associations outlining some of the principles of his Christian Socialist beliefs, which helped to raise his political profile. His aim was to attract support for his ideas and values, beyond partisan socialist circles, with an eye on the forthcoming School Board election that was scheduled to take place in January 1889.[184]

School Boards were the public bodies that established and administered elementary schools locally in England and Wales between 1870 and 1902. The Forster Act of 1870 was the first of a series of Acts of Parliament introduced in the late nineteenth century to bring about publicly funded compulsory education for children aged between five and thirteen. As well as local taxpayers, parents had to contribute to the funding of their children's education unless too poor to do so. Women as well as men who met the property qualification could be elected by local ratepayers to serve on a School Board. In 1880 thirty three year old Emily Sturge, a Quaker, was elected to of the Bristol School Board becoming its youngest member. And although few were supportive of her 'entire programme' on 'Women's Rights'[185] it would have been her liberal and non-conformist religious views that mattered most to the electorate. Divisions along political, social and religious lines (religious teaching in Board Schools was restricted to non-denominational instruction) came to dominate disagreements among Bristol School Board members up to its dissolution in 1902 when, under the Balfour Act, newly-established Local Education Authorities took on the responsibility for elementary education.[186]

In January 1889 the Christian Socialists adopted Gore to stand as their School Board candidate. The Bristol and District Labour League was expected to follow suit. The Labour League, an all male institution, had been established in 1885 to promote direct labour representation on local governing bodies

---

184 Gore's lectures included 'Socialism in Theory and Practice' presented to the Bedminster Young Men's Liberal Association, 7 November, 1888; 'Christian Socialism' lecture given to the Easton branch of the Operatives' Liberal Association, 10 December, 1888; 'The Madness of Liberty' delivered to the Lower Easton branch of the Operatives' Liberal Association, 17 December, 1888. See the *Western Daily Press*, 9 November 1888; 12 December 1888; 19 December1888.

185 *Western Daily Press*, 15 January 1880.

186 See C. Gibson, *The Bristol School Board 1871-1903* (Bristol: The Bristol Branch of the Historical Association, 1997), pp. 1, 2, & 20.

and indeed ultimately the national Parliament. The majority of the League leaders had strong links with the Christian Socialists, although, as Samuel Bale, a contemporary of Gore, emphasised, the League 'had not yet accepted the principles of Socialism as a basis or object.'[187] Therefore, the League, in keeping with its aim of placing working men on all local representative bodies, decided to put forward its own Labour candidate for the School Board election, Thomas George Harding, 'a *bona fide* working man, [and] a member of the Trades Council'.[188] As the School Board consisted of fifteen members, each elector was entitled to that number of votes; and, if the elector wished, all fifteen votes could be cast for one candidate. Seizing this opportunity, those of Gore's supporters who resented Harding's nomination distributed a leaflet urging electors to use all their fifteen votes for Gore. [189] Gore could rely on backing from other quarters as well. Dan Irving, then the Chair of the Bristol Operatives' Liberal Association, noted in a letter to the editor of the *Western Daily Press* that many members of his Society had pledged their support for Gore, as well as for their own candidate William H. Elkins.[190]

In his election campaign, Gore was described as a 'non-political candidate'. This suggests that he stood as a non-party candidate. He was, however, the Clifton and Bristol Christian Socialist Society's nominee, enjoyed the support of the Bristol Socialist Society, and had a track record for publically propagating his socialist views.[191] Moreover, prominent members of the Christian Socialist Society spoke in his support at campaign meetings, including the Reverend Philip Peach, the vicar of Pawlett, in Somerset, and his friend the Reverend Charles Marson, rector of St. Mary's, Orlestone, Kent, and a founding member of the Christian Socialist Society.[192] A year earlier Marson had written to the Archbishop of Canterbury, Edward White Benson, asking whether Gore could be ordained as a deacon to assist him with his work at Orlestone, but this proved to be unachievable, as Gore did not have a university degree.[193]

Gore stood as a non-sectarian candidate and on a socialistic programme. If elected he promised he would fight fervently 'against the prosecution of

187 Samuel Bale writing under the pseudonym Samson Bryher in, *An Account of the Labour and Socialist Movement in Bristol* (Bristol: 1929), Part 2, p. 14.

188 See the *Bristol Mercury*, 6 December 1888 and the letter from John Gregory, secretary of the Labour League, published in the *Western Daily Press*, on 3 January 1889.

189 Bryher, *An Account of the Labour and Socialist Movement in Bristol*, Part 2, p. 13.

190 *Western Daily Press*, 21 January 1889.

191 Bryher, *An Account of the Labour and Socialist Movement in Bristol*, Part 2, p. 12.

192 Bristol School Board Election: 'The Candidature of Mr H. H. Gore', *Western Daily Press*, 8 January 1889.

193 Sutcliffe, *The Keys of Heaven: The Life of Revd Charles Marson, Christian Socialist & Folksong Collector*, Kindle file, location, 1624.

parents for non-payment of school pence' and seek its abolition. He advocated free school meals and secular education. 'He was against cramming humbug down children's throats' and considered 'teaching the Bible without note or comment was a most ridiculous thing.'[194] Committed to improving the health of the children, he proposed that a gymnasium should be *in situ* at each school. 'He was even in favour of dancing being taught to the children in the younger schools',[195] which had the approval of Marson, who had gained recognition for his zeal in promoting folksongs and Morris dancing.

During the election campaign Gore became involved in a fracas with a bailiff employed on the St. Anne's estate of Bristol solicitor, James Sinnott. This incident was recalled at an official inquiry, which began in Bristol in June the following year, to hear evidence over a claim to public rights of way running through St. Anne's woods, part of the St. Anne's estate, and the right to use the St. Anne's ferry crossing over the river Avon. This inquiry arose out of the application of the secretary of the Bristol and District Footpath Preservation Society, Richard C. Tuckett, to assert public rights of way through Sinnott's Estate and was taken out in response to a court injunction restraining Tuckett along with other members of the Preservation Society, or indeed the public, from using the disputed footpaths.[196]

The Footpath Preservation Society was inspired by John Ruskin and contained many respectable liberal supporters. However, Gore who was an active member and leading protagonist appears to have developed direct action tactics. During an early stage of the inquiry's proceedings the St. Anne's estate bailiff, Richard Adams, alleged that on one occasion in January 1889 Gore had led around sixty men on a walk in the woods along the disputed footpath leaving a trail of broken fences. On another occasion Adam's said 'he again met Gore with a gang of men' in St Anne's woods who 'instructed him to tell Mr Sinnott that they intended to come there every Sunday, and to knock down anything and everything which obstructed their way.'[197] However, Gore was not called as a witness in this inquiry which dragged on until March 1891 when

194 Bristol School Board Election: 'The Candidature of Mr H. H. Gore', *Western Daily Press*, 8 January 1889.

195 Bristol School Board Election: 'The Candidature of Mr H. H. Gore', *Western Daily Press*, 8 January 1889.

196 *Bristol Mercury*, 18 June 1890.

197 *Western Daily Press*, 19 June 1890. Adam's went on to testify that in April 1889 Gore and a band of men returned and removed the gates obstructing access to the footpaths. Moreover, he alleged that 'when he saw the party they were approaching the wall that divided the field from the mill house garden. He had seen men carrying things away. One was carrying a fir tree, and on witness remonstrating with him, he said he was going to take it home and plant it in the garden, and see if it would grow.'

Anti-Humbug.

Two objects have been accomplished by the recent Meetings in the Haymarket on the subject of

The Royal Visit

(1) The successful vindication of the people's right to hold Public Meetings in open spaces, where no obstruction is caused. (2) The maintenance of our right to be heard in the Town Council, against an arrogant attempt to refuse that right by the Mayor and his followers. One other thing has been proved, namely that there are

A large number of Citizens who are opposed to the farce that is being enacted in regard to this visit of Royalty.

The wide expression of sympathy and the active support rendered to the Committee, suggested to them the idea of

A COUNTER DEMONSTRATION,

But in consequence of there being no General Holiday announced, this idea has to be reluctantly abandoned, as the Committee and a great number of those who have supported them in their recent efforts will be at their daily work on Wednesday.

The Committee would, however,

Call upon you, their fellow-workingmen, who purpose attending this stupid show, to pause and consider what you are doing.

There will be an attempt by a set of toadies, having the same interest in you that a cat has in a mouse, to excite your enthusiasm by gay bunting, music and military display, for

The Prince and King Wathen?

Will you cheer for some millions a year being taken out of your pockets to support hereditary paupers? Will you cheer for the degradation to which you, your wives, and children, brothers and sisters are reduced by the present arrangements of society. Will you cheer for "**More Work and Less Pay.**" Will you cheer when children are crying for bread, for money being squandered as you see it? Will you cheer for the fearful ordeal and sufferings of the last two winters, whilst a worse is approaching. Will you cheer to be taunted that your want of work at such times, means "**you won't work?**" Will you cheer for all manner of insult and abuse, when in your distress, you approach those who are in authority?

Cheer these things and you lick the feet that kick you.

To cheer hereditary privileges (of which the Crown is the centre) is nothing less than a cry to be kept in your present condition.

The CLASSES know this and act upon it to keep you under.'

It is high time the MASSES knew it too, and acted accordingly.

Anti-Humbug Poster, original poster for a counter demonstration to the Royal visit in July 1889.

the Official Referee, Henry W. Verey, found for and in favour of Tuckett and the Footpath Preservation Society.[198]

These incidents did not harm Gore's standing with the electorate; in fact it may have enhanced his credentials as the January 1889 School Board election resulted in an astounding victory for the Socialists, and was a great tribute to Gore. He attracted 14,132 votes, the second highest in the field of twenty candidates. Harding, the Labour League's choice, was one of the five defeated candidates. He trailed in at the eighteenth position with 3,869 votes. A few days later, on the evening of 28 January, Gore's mentor, Edward Carpenter, arrived in Bristol to deliver a lecture on 'The Failure of Modern Commerce' at a meeting organised by the Bristol Socialist Society, perhaps in anticipation of Gore's success.[199] Gore presided. He received a hearty welcome and, before introducing Carpenter, he took the opportunity to thank the electorate of Bristol for their trust by returning him to the School Board the previous week.[200]

A fortnight later Gore was on the rugby field playing half-back for Bristol's second team against Gloucester.[201] He was in a buoyant mood. On 11 February 1889 he spoke at a conference convened 'to consider the question of forming a Sunday Society for Bristol'. The conference expressed the view that a Sunday Society could 'interest that part of the population which does not attend a place of worship in literary, historical, and scientific subjects, and to afford them opportunities of cultivating these branches of knowledge by listening to lectures on such subjects.'[202] With this idea in mind the Bristol Sunday Society was formed, and a management committee elected which included the Bristol Socialist Society member, Robert Weare. It proved to be popular, and was still functioning at the turn of the century.

In the summer, Gore once again demonstrated his anti-monarchy credentials. The Operatives' Liberal Association held an open-air meeting in the Horsefair, Bristol, in protest against the proposed grants of public money to the eldest son and eldest daughter of the Prince of Wales. The rally attracted a thousand people. Gore was one of the speakers backing a resolution put to the meeting which objected to the extension of Royal grants, the cost of which already 'constitute[d] a severe burden on the country for which there is no adequate return.' It was carried unanimously, after which it was agreed to forward the resolution to the Prime Minister, the leader of the Opposition, and to the Members of Parliament for Bristol.[203]

198 *Bristol Mercury*, 23 March 1891.
199 Committee Meeting Minutes of the Bristol Socialist Society, 20 January 1889.
200 *Western Daily Press*, 29 January 1889.
201 *Gloucester Citizen*, 11 February 1889.
202 *Western Daily Press*, 13 February 1889.
203 *Western Daily Press*, 13 July 1889.

Concerned about Royal privileges and how to combat them, Gore had turned his attention to see what lessons could be learned from the French Revolution, in what was its centenary year. On 24 July 1889, ten days after the one hundredth anniversary of the storming of the Bastille, he delivered a lecture on the 1789 Revolution to the Redfield branch of Operatives' Liberal Association. Unfortunately, there is no record of what he said, but it would not be long before Gore, rather than talking about a revolt, would witness rebellion closer at hand. On 20 August a strike by London dockers triggered a wave of industrial disputes that spread across the country, an event that came to be associated with the birth of new unionism.

Chapter 5

Bristol Town Council Election, November 1889

A generous gift of £30,000 from the Australian trade union movement strengthened the London dockers' resolve in their fight for six pence an hour (the dockers' tanner). This substantial contribution, provided by fellow trade unionists in Australia, changed the dynamics of this conflict, and the pace of donations received to aid striking dockers increased. Gore was among those who joined the rush of sympathy. On behalf of the Clifton and Bristol Christian Socialists he wrote to the ministers of religion in Bristol 'asking them to appeal to their congregations… to assist the London dock labourers.'[204] Shaken by the degree of public support for the dockers' cause, after five weeks the employers eventually gave way, conceding to most of the dockers' demands. Their victory inspired hopes for change beyond the trade union movement. On 16 September, a few days before the London dock labourers marched back to work in triumph, Gore delivered another lecture on the French Revolution, this time to the Lower Easton branch of the Operatives' Liberal Association.[205] Reaching out to radical liberals he expressed his confidence in the power of socialist ideas to attract new adherents.

The strike of previously casualised workers was one of the most memorable events in the history of the modern British labour movement. Through collective action the emergence of new unionism gave largely unorganised, unskilled and semi-skilled workers the means of presenting their political, social, and economic demands, including the eight-hour day. In September workers struck at the St. Vincent's galvanising works of John Lysaght and Company in St. Philip's Marsh. This was the first of many strikes to hit Bristol in the last few months of 1889.[206] Bristol's socialists came to their defence. Moral arguments for socialism combined with Marxist influenced analyses of the struggle between capital and labour in the workplace. Gore, along with his socialist friends Edward James Watson and Robert Weare, joined Albert Vincent, vice-President of the Bristol Trades Council, in advising and acting on behalf of the strikers. They successfully enrolled most of the men into the Gas Workers and General Labourers' Union, founded in March 1889 and led by Will Thorne,

---

204 *Western Daily Press*, 7 September 1889.
205 *Western Daily Press*, 19 September 1889.
206 For an account of the Bristol strike wave see M. Richardson, *The Bristol Strike Wave of 1889-90: Socialists, New Unionists and New Women: Part 1: Days of Hope* and *The Bristol Strike Wave of 1889-90: Socialists, New Unionists and New Women: Part Two: Days of Doubt* in D. Backwith, R. Ball, S. E. Hunt and M. Richardson (eds.), *Strikers, Hobblers, Conchies and Reds: A Radical History of Bristol 1880-1939* (Breviary Stuff Publications, 2014).

a campaigner for the eight-hour day and a member of the Social Democratic Federation. A blunt speaking Gore warned that '[t]hey must be prepared to endure a little hardship… [and] they must make up their minds to have no beer at public houses during the strike.'[207] Elected to head a deputation of strikers to put their case, Gore approached the representatives of the Company. They refused to open negotiations with him, however, on the grounds that he was an 'outsider'. The deputation withdrew and called another meeting at which, on Gore's advice, they agreed to suspend outside help for twenty-four hours.[208]

On Friday 20 September another deputation of Lysaght strikers approached their employer. This time the management agreed to meet, and after a short discussion acceded to all the men's demands with one minor exception 'that all work in the dipping shop would be inspected'.[209] Gore, at the victory meeting held that evening, heartily congratulated the men upon their success. His words suggest that at this time his position on the relations between capital and labour were relatively conciliatory and not that far removed from radical liberalism:

> He hoped that the struggle would teach them to combine more and more for the protection of their interests. He hoped, also, that they would not feel, because they had had a difference with their masters, any antagonism towards them, but [that] it should tend to strengthen their relations with the firm, especially as they had secured the advance.[210]

Self-help voluntarism, support of moderate trade unionism, and the encouragement of harmonious relationships between employers and employees were consistent with the politics of radical liberalism.

Gore was attempting to take the moral high ground, while supporting workers' struggles for material improvements that he considered to be realistically achievable. In late September the Bristol Socialist Society approached Gore and asked him if he would contest the St. Philip's South Ward in the Municipal elections that were due to be held on 1 November. He declined.[211] However, on the 7 October his growing popularity among electors in the working class district of St. Philip's South impelled a number of them to form a deputation to wait 'upon Hugh Holmes Gore to request him to allow his name to be put before the constituency as a candidate for a seat on the Town Council.'[212] Gore

207 *Western Daily Press*, 17 September 1889.
208 *Western Daily Press*, 19 September 1889.
209 *Western Daily Press*, 20 September 1889.
210 *Western Daily Press*, 20 September 1889.
211 Minutes of the Committee Meeting of the Bristol Socialist Society, 23 September 1889.
212 *Western Daily Press*, 8 October 1889.

agreed to their request on the understanding that he would run as a socialist.[213] Committee rooms were established at Louisa Street in the heart of St. Philip's.

He now had an election campaign to mount, one which involved the promotion of a socialistic programme for the welfare of the whole community. This had to be balanced with the continuation of his work in aiding workers in struggle. He often seemed tentative about his position in regard to fully supporting strikes, as he felt he needed to make a solid case in order not to unduly antagonise employers. One example of his caution arose in the case of men and women employed at the chocolate and cocoa making firm J. S. Fry and Sons, located in Union Street, Broadmead, near the centre of Bristol, founded by the devout Quaker, Joseph Fry.

In a pamphlet published in October 1889, twenty-nine year old Miriam Daniell, a formidable woman with great energy and drive, and twenty-one year old Robert Allan Nicol, an enthusiastic ex-medical student from Dunfermline, exposed the poor working conditions that existed at Fry's.[214] They were members of the Bristol Socialist Society. Their findings prompted the Bristol Trades Council and Bristol Socialist Society to cooperate in convening a gathering of Fry's workforce on 19 October to consider 'the desirability of organisation for the purposes of maintaining a fair standard of wage and honourable conditions of labour.'[215]

Large numbers of Fry's workers came, filling the meeting place to capacity. Daniell addressed the women and girls downstairs and Albert Vincent, vice-president of the Bristol Trades Council, the men and boys upstairs. After the speeches Fry's workers aired multiple grievances, venting their anger towards their employer for ignoring their complaints. Daniell and Vincent urged them to join the Gas Workers and General Labourers' Union, which in its short history had established a good record of actively encouraging women and men to join its organisation and seek improvements in their pay and conditions. Gore, however, eschewed backing wage increases at Fry's 'simply because he felt he was not justified in asking terms the employers could not concede.'[216] Yet within twenty-four hours of Daniell and Vincent's address, the company, as part of a deliberate and successful strategy in keeping the trade unions out, granted a pay rise, though only for its male employees.[217]

213 *Western Daily Press*, 8 October 1889.
214 M. Daniell and R. A. Nicol, *The Truth about Chocolate Factories of Modern White Slavery* (G. H. Wood Collection, Huddersfield University: October 1889)
215 *Western Daily Press*, 21 October 1889.
216 Robert Weare to the editor of *Western Daily Press*, 25 October 1889. See also Richardson, *The Bristol Strike Wave of 1889-90: Socialists, New Unionists and New Women: Part 1: Days of Hope*, pp. 108-9 and 119.
217 See Richardson, *The Bristol Strike Wave of 1889-90: Socialists, New Unionists and New Women: Part 1: Days of Hope*, p. 108.

Some local employers, who had been suspicious of Gore, came to call on his services to bring about amicable settlements to industrial disputes. For example, on 24 October, a few days after Fry's factory owners had defeated the attempt to unionise its workforce, the Port of Bristol employers sought Gore's assistance in facilitating an agreement between themselves and the Dock Labourers' Union to end the corn porters, deal runners[218] and dock labourers' strike. He played an important part in negotiating a settlement by telephone with the timber merchants in regard to the deal runners, completing what turned out to be a decisive victory for Bristol dock workers.[219]

On 26 October, following the dockers' great victory celebration on Clifton Downs, Bristol trade unionists and socialists formed a Strike Committee and Gore became a key member.[220] The Committee played a crucial role in supporting workers on strike and in building community backing. Its remit extended beyond the dockers. On 24 October a dispute involving around 1,700 cotton workers, mainly female, had erupted in the Great Western Cotton Works in Barton Hill. The women had taken part in the dockers' victory celebrations and were resolved to improve their pay and conditions. On the 29 October Gore accompanied Miriam Daniell, treasurer of the Strike Committee, in talks with the Managing Director of the Cotton Works, George Spafford. They attempted to squeeze concessions from him that would meet the strikers' approval. The concessions offered were minimal and came with a warning that unless the strikers returned to work at the old rates of pay the mill would close. Throughout this strike, which continued on until the end of November, Gore felt that the demand for an advance in wages, however justified, was unachievable. Indeed, whilst the eventual settlement secured some of the cotton workers' demands about conditions, it did not include any improvement in pay.[221]

Gore's position was not out of line with the general view of the Strike Committee. They tried to determine the merit and feasibility of industrial stoppages before offering support. Fear of factory closures or job losses meant that in some cases they did recommend workers should return to work on the employers' terms. This was the advice they had given to factory hands at the cotton works, but when workers voted overwhelmingly to persist in their strike the Committee rallied around to whip up public support.

218 Deal runners were skilled dock workers designated to unload timber from ships, a task that required them to run up and down narrow planking ramps carrying long lengths of wood.
219 *Western Daily Press*, 25 October 1889.
220 Minutes of the Bristol Workers' Organising Committee, 26 October 1889.
221 See Richardson, *The Bristol Strike Wave of 1889-90: Socialists, New Unionists and New Women: Part 1: Days of Hope*, pp. 117-8; M. Richardson, *The Maltreated and the Malcontents: Working in the Great Western Cotton Factory 1838-1914* (Bristol: Bristol Radical History Group, 2016), pp. 98-102.

Gore, however, belonged to the conciliatory wing of the Committee. He encouraged dialogue over conflict in differences between employers and employees. While not opposed to workers taking strike action against injustices, if he thought disputes were unwinnable, or might have a negative effect on other workers, Gore was prepared to use his position on the Committee to short-circuit democracy. His judgements were not always accurate.

On the 29 October, following a wildcat stoppage at the brushmaker companies, Greenslade's and Brison's, Gore, with James Vickery, chairman of the Bristol branch of the Gasworkers and General Labourers' Union, met with the representatives of the two companies. Not only did Gore and Vickery agree that all the women and girls who were on strike 'should return to work without any alteration in their wages or hours of labour' they also 'apologised for the abrupt manner' in which the women had walked out.[222] It was an unpopular decision but Greenslade's, who were carrying high stocks, had threatened to lockout all of its 500 hands, an eventuality which Gore and Vickery had wanted to avoid. A week later, however, sixty piecework men at Greenslades struck for an advance of ten per cent increase in pay. They successfully challenged the Company's lockout threat, signifying that Gore and Vickery had been over cautious. A settlement was reached with the men five days later.[223]

During the autumn of 1889 Gore was preoccupied with the forthcoming Council elections. Apart from holding a couple of meetings, one to endorse his candidature, and one open-air election hustings in the heart of St. Philip's South, Gore seemed content to place his election chances on his popularity in the area.[224] However, he enjoyed an added bonus for an issue that came to the fore just a couple of days before the election. On the evening of the 29 October, Gore's main opponent, the sitting councillor and Liberal Unionist, James Dole, attended a 'non-political' public meeting at the Shaftsbury Hall in St. Philip's in support of the Sugar Convention Bill. Because of its complexity this Bill may have appeared to the less-informed as an arcane issue but it was of great significance to Bristol citizens. The slow progress of the Bill, which had passed its first reading in parliament in April, was frustrating its (mainly Conservative) supporters – and those working in the refining industry – making it a live issue at the local elections.

Sugar refining had been one of Bristol's leading industries in the eighteenth century. However, by the mid nineteenth century, the industry in Bristol

222 *Western Daily Press*, 30 October 1889.
223 *Western Daily Press*, 8 and 12 November 1889.
224 *Western Daily Press*, 30 and 31 October 1889.

was in steep decline and by 1889, at the time of the election, only two sugar houses were left and only one of these, the Bristol Sugar Refining Company in Old Market, with around 150 employees, was operational. The other, Wills, Young and Company in Castle Street, had been seriously damaged by fire in the summer which put it out of action for six months.[225] Supporters of the Sugar Convention Bill maintained that this decline in Bristol and elsewhere in Britain was because sugar refined in European countries was supported by state subsidies, called bounties, which allowed their sugar to be sold at a considerably lower price than it could be produced in Britain. The passing of the Bill would allow first that 'any one of the signatory Powers to the Convention may prohibit the importation of bounty-fed sugar, and the second that any of the signatory Powers may impose countervailing duties',[226] with a hike in sugar prices being the most likely consequence.

In Bristol many radical liberals and socialists alike were inclined to oppose the Bill because dearer sugar would increase the costs to the confectionery industry.[227] J. S. Fry and Sons, the liberal and Quaker cocoa and chocolate manufacturers, and their employees, were particularly concerned. Opponents of the Bill maintained that it would lead to significantly more job losses in Bristol than the projected losses expected by Bristol's sugar refiners. Moreover, another reason for contesting the Bill, put forward by the Windmill Hill branch of the Liberal Operatives' Association in Bristol, was on the grounds that the working class would be the hardest hit by price rises, as they extensively consumed foods containing sugar.[228] Liberal Party members were divided over the matter. At a meeting held in Shaftsbury Hall, chaired by the Conservative Councillor James Inskip, Dole, the Liberal Unionist candidate, moved a resolution supporting the efforts of those determined to pass the Sugar Convention Bill, which the meeting approved.[229]

It was this outcome, argued the *London Daily News* correspondent, 'which decided the working men to vote against him [Dole] and to return Mr. Hugh Holmes Gore'.[230] The result of the 1889 Council election for the St. Philip's and

225 K. Morgan, 'Sugar Refining in Bristol', in K. Bruland and P. O'Brien, *From Family Firm to Corporate Capitalism: Essays in Business and Industrial History in Honour of Peter Mathias* (Oxford: Clarendon Press, 1998), pp. 157-8; *Western Daily Press*, 10 June 1889 and 24 July 1889.
226 Baron H. D. Worms, the Under Secretary of State for the Colonies, Hansard, Sugar Convention Bill, HC Deb 11 April 1889 vol. 335 cc303-26. http://hansard.millbanksystems.com/commons/1889/apr/11/sugar-convention-bill accessed 13/10/13.
227 *Western Daily Press* 6 May 1889.
228 See the resolution passed strongly condemning the proposed Sugar Convention Bill at the Windmill Hill branch of the Liberal Operatives' Association, *Western Daily Press* 6 May 1889.
229 *Western Daily Press*, 30 October 1889.
230 *London Daily News*, 4 November 1889.

St. Jacob's South Ward was H. H. Gore (Socialist)[231] 1,293, J. Dole (Liberal) 465, and W. H. Cowlin (Conservative) 13. The *Western Daily Press* pronounced that 'even the most ardent of Mr Gore's admirers could scarcely have anticipated so decided a victory as was proclaimed'.[232] The young victor was hoisted on to the shoulders of a few 'sturdy men' and carried triumphantly through the streets of St. Philip's to his committee room in Louisa Street.[233] While it is unlikely that his election victory rested solely on Dole's position on the Sugar Convention Bill, no doubt some disgruntled Liberals did plump for Gore when they saw their candidate supporting the Conservative Party line.[234]

In the weeks following the election Gore's free time was taken up with his involvement on the Strike Committee, particularly in raising funds and campaigning in support of the cotton workers. For instance, on 25 November 1889 Gore, along with Miriam Daniell, attended a meeting of the Radstock (Somerset) miners called to consider an advance in wages and to advocate the eight-hour day. After the main business Daniell gave 'an eloquent address' appealing for donations to help the women and men on strike at the Great Western Cotton Works in Bristol. Gore supplemented her talk by highlighting the success they had had in organising women into a branch of the Gasworkers' union.[235] Samuel Henry Whitehouse, the miners' agent for the district, is quoted as saying 'he was proud to have the son of a magistrate's clerk advocating the cause of their Bristol friends. He hoped they would get subscriptions at the pits for them.'[236]

Gore and other strike committee members had already become the subject of many hostile letters published in the local press for siding with the cotton strikers. A particular concern of some correspondents was Gore's public request that the directors of the Cotton Works forego their five and a half per cent dividend in order to increase the wages of their employees; one correspondent challenged him to 'give all his profits to the strikers' fund', adding pointedly 'I should like to know if he gives his time and professional services free?'[237]

231 While the *Western Daily Press* categorised Gore as an Independent candidate, and Alfred B. Beaven, *Bristol Lists: Municipal and Miscellaneous. (Bristol Times and Mirror*: 1899) recorded Gore as a Unionist Socialist, in this election he stood simply as a socialist.
232 Western Daily Press, 2 November 1889.
233 *Western Daily Press*, 2 November 1889.
234 *London Daily News*, 4 November 1889.
235 *Western Gazette*, 29 November 1889.
236 *Western Gazette*, 29 November 1889.
237 *Western Daily Press*, 15 November 1889.

Chapter 6

Children in Need

Gore's commitment to the cause of working people and ethical socialism influenced both his work as a solicitor and his personal involvement in several philanthropic projects. His professional work included representing the Society for the Prevention of Cruelty to Children in court. First established in July 1884 as the London Society for the Prevention of Cruelty to Children, in 1889 it dropped 'London' from its title and replaced it with 'National', reflecting a growing awareness of children's sufferings. It soon became a countrywide body with 32 branches operating across England, Wales and Scotland, employing fifteen inspectors, paid for from subscriptions and donations. The growth of the Society helped in the passing of the 1889 Prevention of Cruelty to and Protection of Children Act, the first Act of Parliament to criminalise the ill treatment of children in Britain.[238] Gore personally felt strongly about Children's welfare, not only as a paid professional but also as an elected member of the School Board, a role in which he learned that there was a strong correlation between cruelty to children and the social and environmental circumstances of deprivation.

Gore represented the Society for the Prevention of Cruelty to Children in one of the first cases under the new Act to be brought against parents, (or other persons), for the callous treatment of a child. The Act asserted the rights of children and raised complex issues about the relation of the state to the family and working class families in particular. Because of the newness of the Act, this particular case attracted much public attention. On the 5 December 1889 Henry and Anne Lines, the parents of William Lines, a boy under the age of ten, appeared in court charged with unlawfully sending their son out on a public street in Bristol to sell newspapers. Standing in the dock they looked a sorry sight, disheveled and emaciated, as a police constable gave evidence stating that on Wednesday 4 December, around half-past seven in the evening, he had come upon William Lines, a young boy, selling the *Evening News* in West Street, Old Market. 'He had no shirt and his clothes were all tatters. It was intensely cold, and the boy looked frozen.' In their defence the boy's parents said that they were destitute, and following a plea from their son, they had allowed him out to sell newspapers in order to earn some money to put some bread on the table and a fire in the grate.[239]

---

238 M. Flegel, '"Facts and Their Meaning": Child Protection, Intervention, and the National Society for the Prevention of Cruelty to Children in Late Nineteenth-Century England', *Victorian Review*, Vol. 33, No. 1 (Spring 2007), p. 94.
239 *Western Daily Press*, 6 December 1889.

At the second Court hearing it came to light that although the father, Henry Lines, had been put out of work as a consequence of the Great Western Cotton Mill strike, he had been fortunate enough to find occasional employment as a mason's labourer, at 22s a week. He had also been in receipt of strike pay and soup tickets. According to the prosecution, the true facts were that Henry Lines spent most of his money on beer. When two School Board officers called at his house to discuss his child's welfare they had found him drunk and incapable, lying in front of a fire. However, as the defendants had pleaded guilty they were dealt with leniently and were discharged with a severe reprimand and a warning that if they were brought before the courts again on similar charges it would be likely that they would receive a custodial sentence.[240]

The more heartbreaking cases of cruelty to children were those that involved physical violence. Elizabeth Stone, a middle-aged woman, was charged with an aggravated assault upon her ten-year old stepdaughter Alice Stone. Gore prosecuted on behalf of the Society. He presented evidence showing that Alice had been severely beaten on her back by her stepmother, who had also, on a separate occasion, pushed her stepdaughter onto the hot bar of the fireplace grate, which resulted in a nasty burn to the forearm. The healing process was slow due to the filthy condition in which the child was kept and consequently when, sometime after, a doctor was called upon to examine the child he was still able to ascertain the cause of her injuries.[241]

Prone to bouts of drinking Alice's stepmother often became violent, leading her to habitually hit and scream at Alice. This brutal behavior had come to the attention of the School Board officer who, before the Act for the protection and prevention of cruelty to children had been passed, often had reason to caution Elizabeth for maltreating Alice. Thus, because of her bad record of domestic violence, Elizabeth Stone was sent to prison for six months. Alice was sent away to a school in Coventry.[242]

Cases of child neglect and mistreatment brought before the Bristol Courts increased following the introduction of the 1889 Act. Gore was greatly respected for his role as prosecutor for the Society for the Prevention of Cruelty to Children, although a minority continued to resent what they viewed as the state meddling in people's 'private' affairs. Before 1889 reformers had been reluctant to tamper with parents' freedom of action in the family home. 'Children were considered the chattel of their parents, and interference with parental treatment of children

240 *Western Daily Press*, 6 January 1890.
241 *Western Daily Press*, 10 May 1890.
242 *Western Daily Press*, 10 May 1890.

was considered tantamount to an attack on private property.'[243] Hence, child protection legislation was seen as an incursion into the family life, especially among sections of the working class.

In the Victorian period children aged fourteen and under constituted one-third of the population[244] and the family played the most important part in the socialisation of their children. Parents' values and behaviour provided a template for their children to follow. By the late nineteenth century the industrial working class had, to a significant degree, accepted the legitimacy of managerial authority in the workplace. This conformity to authority helped shape working class attitudes to obedience and authority in the home.[245]

When it came to child labour there was a serious cultural clash between the poorer working class and middle class reformers.[246] Victorian working class families tended to be large and were often dependent on children to make up the family wage to anything like subsistence level. The need for children's earnings generally made those parents living on or below the poverty line hard taskmasters and resistant to outside interference.[247] Indeed, the pressure on children to contribute towards the family wage 'was a key factor that inspired a number of traditions of resistance, such as social crime and subsistence truancy.'[248]

A minority of working class men and women were committed to education and self-improvement. An alliance of radical workers and middle class reformers campaigned for the extension of education. The introduction of the 1870 Forster Education Act was the first of a number of Acts of Parliament passed before the end of the nineteenth century making education compulsory for children between the ages of five and thirteen. While some liberal campaigners believed that formal education could reduce social discord, disagreement emerged over the values children should be taught. A long-standing battle for control existed between non-conformists and Anglicans over schools.[249] The radical working

243 For an account of the introduction of child legislation in late Victorian England see Behlmer, G. K., *Child Abuse and Moral Reform in England, 1870-1908* (California: Stanford University Press, 1982).

244 J. Walvin, *A Child's World: A Social History of English Childhood 1800-1914* (London: Penguin, 1982), p. 11.

245 See E. Roberts 'The Family' in J. Benson (ed.), *The Working Class in England 1875-1914* (London: Croom Helm, 1985), p. 2; M. L. Kohn, 'Social Class and Parent-Child Relationships: An Interpretation', *American Journal of Sociology*, Vol. 68, No. 4 (Jan., 1963), pp.471-473.

246 Walvin, *A Child's World: A Social History of English Childhood 1800-1914*, ftn 5, p. 30.

247 L. A. Tilly and J. Scott, *Women Work & Family* (London: Routledge, 1989, first edition was published in 1978 by Holt, Rinehart and Winston, New York), p. 113.

248 S. Humphries, 'Radical Childhood in Bristol 1889-1939' in I. Bild (ed.) *Bristol's Other History* (Bristol: Bristol Broadsides, 1983), p. 31.

249 P. McCann (ed.) *Popular Education and Socialization in the Nineteenth Century* (London: Methuen, 1977), p. xiii and p. 113.

class was also suspicious of political and religious indoctrination.[250] Gore's approach was to foster a critical consciousness.

Gore's humanitarian–philanthropic socialism influenced his personal life. He gave some of his time to running Sunday morning adult classes and organising evening events at a former ragged school in Sidney Alley, Kingsland Road, St. Philip's. Many of its attendees worked close by at the Lysaght's plant in Silverthorne Lane, and lived in the surrounding streets.[251] Gore saw education as a source of developing enlightened discourses. Moreover, he recognised that values of fellowship and endeavour were transmitted socially and culturally not just through formal learning. His favoured cause was running the popular Dings' Boys' Club, whose headquarters was established at the former ragged school. He liked to show his friends what he had achieved at the club. Edward Carpenter paid a visit to the Dings' club in July 1891 when he came to deliver a talk to the Bristol Socialists on his recent journey to India.[252]

In the early 1890s a Scottish socialist, John Bruce Glasier, also went to see Gore at his club because he wanted to persuade him to become more visible nationally. In recalling the occasion a few years later, Glasier offered a vivid impression of why the Dings' club was so important to Gore. He remembered

spending the night with him. We were supping on fried fish from a neighbouring shop. The boys sat around and after supper and prayers were read, off went the boys to their hammocks, whilst I sat and tried to induce Gore to come out more prominently. "No!" said he "I will stick to the boys." Those boys are rapidly growing into men, they will soon have the political destinies of east Bristol, in their hands, and Gore's reward will be exceedingly great.[253]

Gore's club was one of many similar contemporary projects that sought to tackle the social needs of children in deprived areas. Stimulated by concerns

250 B. Simon, *Studies in the History of Education 1780-1870* (London: Lawrence & Wishart, 1960), pp. 354-367.
251 *Western Daily Press*, 18 September 1889; St. Philip's and St. Jacob South, Bristol, Census 1891, Ancestry.com, courtesy of the National Archives of the UK the National Archives, London, England, accessed 29 September, 2014.
252 Minutes of the Bristol Socialist Society, 17 July 1891.
253 *The Labour Leader*, 6 April 1895, p. 2. Interestingly, forty five years later John James Milton, the Labour Lord Mayor of Bristol, one of Gore's boys, recalled his boyhood days at the Dings' Club: 'I always held the view that the Dings' Club was the best in Bristol', *Western Daily Press*, 27 September, 1938, Local World Limited, Courtesy of The British Library Board. Perhaps Gore's socialist teachings did have some impact.

about juvenile crime and fears of gangs as well as anxieties about immorality they sought to offer recreational and educational alternatives. In Bristol religious philanthropic groups and individuals had established centres in the working class areas of St. Philip's, St. Jude's and St. Jacob's, providing youth groups designed to recruit boys and girls. The Churches, charities, and public schools all developed networks within these communities.

Within a hundred metres or so of the Dings' Club was a well regarded, and much larger, church boys and girls' club, the Shaftesbury Crusade. Its meetings and activities were held at the Shaftesbury Club and Institute on Kingsland Road. St. Philip's Coffee Company Limited owned the Shaftesbury Club building. It had opened on 10 February 1888, after several 'leading' citizens took stakes in the company so that it could be used for community activities in an industrial area blighted by poverty. The non-denominational Club contained a large hall, able to seat up to 400 persons; a smaller hall; billiard rooms; skittle alleys and a large coffee bar. While 'The hall belonged to no sect or party',[254] the minister of Redland Park Congregational Chapel, Reverend Urijah Rees Thomas, a forty-nine-year-old bachelor, Chairman of the Bristol branch of The Society for the Prevention of Cruelty to Children, Vice President of the Bristol School Board, and member of the Clifton branch of the Anti-Vivisection Society, grasped the opportunity offered by the Club's premises to found the Shaftesbury Crusade. Tapping into the energy of the Redland Park Young People's Guild, he was able to attract volunteers to help in establishing the Crusade's social activities. Focusing on the area's youth, boys and girls' clubs, sport's clubs, gymnastics, first aid and Bible classes were developed, some of which proved to be popular.[255]

Urijah Rees Thomas was chairman of the Bristol and West Liberal Association nevertheless Gore's concern for children's social needs led him to cooperate with him, despite their differing political positions. As members of the Bristol Children's Help Society they worked together on the Barton residential summer camps in Somerset. In August 1890, in the third week of the camp, Thomas was captain and Gore his deputy for one contingent of boys. On entering the camp, the boys would remove their clothes, which would be taken away, cleaned and disinfected, and slip into the blue serge suits provided. On a typical day, the boys would rise from their hammocks at 7:30 in the morning and wash and dress before downing a hearty breakfast of porridge, followed by tea and bread and butter with jam or treacle. Then they would go out on an all day ramble in the countryside, near Winscombe, on the western

254 *Western Daily Press*, 16 February 1888.
255 Meller, *Leisure and the Changing City, 1870-1914*, pp. 164 & 170; D. M. Thomas, *Urijah Rees Thomas: His Life and Work* (London: Hodder & Stoughton, 1902).

edge of the Mendip hills, taking a packed lunch with them and not returning to base until six in the evening.[256]

Through the Dings' Boys' Club, Gore was able to develop a closer, less formal personal fellowship and social awareness among working class boys. He took great pride in producing the first edition of the *Dings' Club Song Book*, which was released on Whit Sunday 1891. In this first edition Gore referred to Clifton College, a public school founded in Bristol in 1862, as a model for the Dings' Club to follow. He declared that the idea underpinning the Dings' Club activities was to be a 'Clifton College Minor (C.C.M.), a fellowship of gentle boys, and later gentle men, living in the Dings. May this Song Book help us all to become brave, true, and warm-hearted gentle men.'[257] His close friend, the architect, Charles Ashbee, designed the motif on the front cover. His illustration showed five Cherubs holding a banner emblazoned with the words 'song book'. This type of design may appear somewhat bizarre to modern eyes but Cherubic figures and naked fairy folk were not uncommon in this period[258] and Ashbee repeated similar motifs in later work.[259]

Ashbee followed the Dings' club activities with interest: Not only did he contribute the design for the cover but on his occasional visits to the club he also helped teach the boys singing.[260] He believed in the extension of working class education and his own homoerotic emotions strengthened his commitment to personal service. Along with his friend Carpenter he adopted the Whitmanic image of 'comradeship'. In a letter to his future wife Janet Forbes he summed up how he saw this:

> Comradeship to me so far—an intensely close and all-absorbing personal attachment, "love" if you prefer the word… for my men and boy friends, has been the one guiding principle in life…Some women would take this, and perhaps rightly, as a sign of coldness to their sex, and they would shrink from a man who revealed himself thus…*That* depends upon the woman.[261]

256 *Bristol Mercury*, 20 August 1890.
257 Hugh Holmes Gore (Compiler), *Dings' Club Song Book* (Guild & School of Handicraft: 1894, first published 1891).
258 For instance see 'Emily Gertrude Thomson' in S. W. Thomson, *Manchester's Victorian Art Scene and its Unrecognised Artists* (Manchester: Manchester Art Press, 2007) Chapter 14.
259 See the decorative initials drawn by Ashbee for *The Prayer Book of King Edward VII* in F. MacCarthy, *The Simple Life: C. R. Ashbee in the Cotswolds* (London: Lund Humphries, 1981), illustrations between pages 88 -89.
260 Holmes Gore, *Dings' Club Song Book*.
261 Letter from Charles R. Ashbee to Janet Forbes, 2 September 1897 quoted in Felicity Ashbee, *Janet Ashbee: Love, Marriage, and the Arts & Crafts Movement* (New York: Syracuse University Press, 2002), p. 25.

This ideal of comradeship was consciously democratic in the sense that it crossed class boundaries.

The *Dings' Club Song Book* was published by Ashbee's Guild and School of Handicraft, founded in 1888 to train young working class men in skilled crafts. Included in the book were works written by William Morris, *Marching On* and *The Message of the March Wind*. Although Gore's aim was to enable working class boys to acquire the ideal of public school fellowship, he clearly intended boys to become conscious of inequalities. Two verses from *The Message of the March Wind* highlight the contrasting positions in the social order held by the privileged boys from Clifton College and the working class members of the Dings' Club.

> Of the rich men it telleth, and strange is the story
> How they have, and they hanker, and grip far and wide;
> And they live and they die, and the earth and its glory
> Has been but a burden they scarce might abide.

> Hark! the March wind again of a people is telling;
> Of the life that they live there, so haggard and grim,
> That if we and our love amidst them had been dwelling
> My fondness had faltered, thy beauty grown dim.[262]

Gore sought to raise the boys' social awareness amid the club activities, and this distinguished the Dings' Club from Reverend Thomas' Shaftesbury Crusade Club which aimed simply to help the boys rather than stimulate them to question society.

Taking its cue from the Children's Help Society, the Clifton College Mission Committee decided to run its own annual summer camp at Berrow, near Burnham-on-Sea, Somerset. It encouraged Clifton College boys to lend a hand in order 'to show that at the time when they are about to enjoy a long holiday they are not forgetful of the hard working boys of Bristol who desire and need, but almost never get, a week's holiday.'[263] The camp was run along more disciplined lines than the one at Barton, nevertheless there was much fun to be had. In August 1891 Gore took a group of boys from the Dings' Club to the camp. They adapted quickly, demonstrating their prowess in many of the sporting activities on offer. These activities included a cartwheel race won by

---

262 William Morris, *Poems by the Way Love is Enough* (London: Longmans, Green and Co, 1896), first published December 1891. Morris' poems, *Marching On* and *The Message of the March Wind* were included in Gore's Dings' Song Book.
263 *Western Daily Press*, 13 August 1891.

Dings' Club Song Book, 1894.

a boy from the Dings' Club who completed an impressive thirty revolutions. Moreover, the Dings' boys gave a clog-dancing recital, an art that survived from earlier in the century in the streets of St. Philip's. In the evenings, the boys, with great enthusiasm, chanted sonnets from Gore's song book set to the music of well-known tunes. Before retiring to bed they sang 'the Evening Hymn',[264] possibly Henry Purcell's *An Evening Hymn*.

> Now that the Sun hath veil'd his Light,
> And bid the World good Night;
> To the soft Bed, my Body I dispose,
> But where shall my Soul repose?
> Dear God, even in Thy Arms, and can there be
> Any so sweet Security!
> Then to thy Rest, O my Soul! And singing, praise
> The Mercy that prolongs thy Days.
> Hallelujah![265]

In many ways the boy's experience of the camp resembled the routine and order Gore himself had known at Christ's Hospital.

Gore's active engagement with the Dings' Club caused him to move out of Franklyn Street sometime in 1891 and take up residence at the Clubhouse in Sydney Alley, a slum area.[266] The occupations of his immediate neighbours indicate that he had moved to a poor working class district. His street provided rented accommodation for working class families dependent for their living on a wide range of jobs. The 1891 census returns record that Gore would have rubbed shoulders with people such as James Bailey, a sea mariner, his wife Harriet, and their eight children; Thomas Pussey, a gas works haulier, his wife Elizabeth, and their seven children; and Harry Hillier, a machine driller, his wife, Emma, a haulier, and their five children. His neighbours' manner of living, speaking, acting, dressing and behaving would have been very different from what Gore would have experienced in Clifton.[267] Bruce Glasier recollected that Gore 'just quietly went about his work, took up his residence in St. Philip's, looked to the street urchins, helped those around him, and indeed – seemed to effectually efface himself.'[268]

264 *Western Daily Press*, 13 August 1891.
265 http://artsongcentral.com/2007/purcell-an-evening-hymn/ accessed 28 July 2015.
266 *Matthew's Bristol and Clifton Directory*, (John Wright: 1892, compiled late 1891).
267 *Census Returns of England and Wales 1891*, Ancestry.com, courtesy of the National Archives of the UK, accessed 29 September 2014.
268 *The Labour Leader*, 6 April 1895, p. 2.

The same charismatic oratorical force that enabled Gore to defend clients and inspire strikers no doubt helped him as a club leader. But essentially he was personally popular because of the time given and enthusiasm he brought to the Dings. This was acknowledged at a ceremony on New Year's Day, 1892, when he was presented with a framed copy of Millet's *Angelus* in recognition of his 'excellent work' in managing and bringing success to the Club in the previous year. Dr. John Withey, who presented the picture, said that he 'had watched with deep interest Mr Gore's passage from boyhood to manhood, and he trusted a long career of usefulness lay before him.'[269]

Gore set out at the Dings' Club to equip the boys with a cultural awareness in an entertaining way and frequently called on fellow socialists to give a helping hand. For instance, his younger brother, Arthur, also a solicitor, and Gore's friend, the socialist Edward James Watson used their artistic talents in acting and music to direct vignettes, such as the trial scene in *The Merchant of Venice*.[270] And Edward Ernest Bowen (1836-1901), Harrow schoolmaster and song writer, friend to the working classes and trade unions, but an opponent of Home Rule,[271] supplied a football composition for the 1894 edition of *Dings' Club Song Book*.

Dings' boys were also encouraged by Gore to develop self-confidence through learning craft skills. As in Ashbee's Guild of Handicraft School, during the winter months evening classes were provided in woodcarving, metal work, brasswork and leather. In June 1893 a combined sale of their work, along with that of the members of the King Arthur Boys' Club, St. Francis, Ashton Gate, marshalled by Gore's curate friend, the Reverend Arthur Easton, took place at All Saints' Hall, Clifton. Among the items on offer were candlesticks, flower vases, fireguards, leather bookbindings, shelves, tables, letter racks, tea trays, pen trays and alms dishes.[272]

Gore's Boys' Club flourished despite competition from the larger, and better equipped, Shaftesbury Crusade and other religious clubs. Gore was establishing roots in the community. He would have been known in the area for his School Board work, as well as for his active support of militant unionism. The political lines were clearly drawn. Gore had been a member of the strike committee that had backed the women and men's claim for an advance in wages during the Great Western Cotton Mill strike of 1889, whereas Thomas, along with fellow members of the Bristol Ministers' Fraternal Society, had refused to back

269 *Western Daily Press*, 2 January 1892.
270 *Western Daily Press*, 7 May 1892. Arthur Holmes Gore was killed in the First World War at Gallipoli, Turkey, on the 12 August 1915.
271 W. C. Lubenon, *The Cambridge Apostles, 1820-1914: Liberalism, Imagination, and Friendship* (Cambridge: Cambridge University Press, 1998), p. 188.
272 *Bristol Mercury*, 17 June 1893.

the cotton workers' demands, arguing that the company could not afford even a small increase in their wages bill. Undoubtedly, some of the strikers living in the Dings' area would have been hostile to Thomas taking the side of their employer.[273]

Gore's active role in the boys' club coincided with a deeper engagement in the socialist movement in Bristol. Since the start of Bristol's strike wave, in September 1889, the members of the Clifton and Bristol Christian Socialists had come to feel that working cooperatively with the Bristol Socialist Society would offer 'greater opportunities for usefulness.'[274] This kind of fluidity was typical of local socialist activism which did not always mirror metropolitan organisational divisions.

273 For an account of this strike see Richardson, *The Bristol Strike Wave of 1889-90: Socialists, New Unionists and New Women: Part 1: Days of Hope*, pp. 111-19.
274 E. D. Girdlestone, "Christian Socialism in England', *The Dawn* (Andover – Harvard Theological Library, p. 16, first published by Progress Publishing Company, Cambridge, Massachusetts: May 1890).

Chapter 7

1890 Parliamentary By-Election Debacle in Bristol East

It was not uncommon, particularly locally, for radical activists to belong to more than one political organisation, though sometimes this gave rise to controversy. Despite joining the Bristol Socialist Society in the winter of 1889-90, Dan Irving, who had lost a leg in an accident while working as a foreman shunter for the Midland Railway Company, kept his membership of the Bristol Operatives' Liberal Association alive.[275] Irving retained some loyalty to the Liberals arguing that as there was not an independently organised Socialist or Labour party, socialists should work within the Liberal party to secure representation of working men committed to socialistic polices, such as the eight-hour day and land nationalisation.[276] Edward James Watson, Gore's Christian socialist colleague, expressed the views of the opposing camp, maintaining that workers should have nothing to do with the Liberal party given its lack of enthusiasm about labour concerns; 'whilst the Liberals were shilly-shallying the workers would be slaving and starving.'[277]

The upsurge in new unionism nationally exposed a clash of interests because many of the employers were part of the Liberal establishment. In the spring of 1890, as the Bristol strike wave of the preceding autumn and winter months subsided, divisions over the socialists' relationship to the Liberal party were accentuated. The Liberal Party had traditionally been the Party that represented the rights of organised workers, but increasingly the failure of Liberalism to represent working class interests shifted some leading socialists and trade unionists into supporting independent labour representation.

From the 1850s a working arrangement between trade unions and the Liberal Party had assumed a formal institutional framework, and December 1867 saw the creation of the Bristol Operatives' Liberal Association.[278] Along with other radical working men's political clubs it constituted a vehicle through which social reforms could be grafted onto the Liberal Party's policies. In the 1880s, this consensual arrangement proved resilient despite of the revival of socialist ideas, the emergence of new unionism, and the concomitant weakening of paternalism, which loosened the ties of loyalty between workers and their employers.[279]

275 Bryher, *An Account of the Labour and Socialist Movement in Bristol*, Part 2, p. 10.
276 Richardson, *The Bristol Strike Wave of 1889-90: Socialists, New Unionists and New Women: Part 2: Days of Doubt*, p. 137.
277 E. J. Watson letters to the editor of the *Bristol Mercury*, 11 March 1890; *Bristol Mercury*, 13 March 1890.
278 *Western Daily Press*, 5 December 1867.
279 J. Saville, *The Labour Movement in Britain* (London: Faber and Faber, 1988), p. 19.

In January 1890 east Bristol Liberals began making provisions for fighting the next General Election. While the election was not thought to be imminent, on 22 January, at a meeting of his constituents in Redfield, Handel Cossham, the sitting Liberal Gladstonian MP, and owner of Kingswood and Parkfield Collieries, urged his supporters to prepare for one. And as part of this preparation, the Redfield and Lower Easton branches of the Operatives' Liberal Association, who had convened this meeting, used the occasion to launch a recruitment campaign inviting 'working men' to join the Association in order to strengthen the Liberal Party's links with the working class.[280]

Just six weeks later, on 2 March, Cossham, along with mine owners across the country, was faced with a demand from the National Miners' Federation for a ten per cent increase in miners' pay. The prospect of a national miners' strike loomed. In response to this threat, Cossham, who employed around 1,000 men, many of whom were his constituents, proposed a two-stage increase in miners' wages at his collieries, promising an immediate advance of five per cent and another five per cent on 1 July, which put pressure on other colliery owners to settle on similar terms.[281] William Whitefield, the Bristol district's miners' agent, and a friend of Gore, who represented the Bristol Miners' Association on legal matters, accepted this initiative.[282] Within twenty-four hours all the colliery owners on the Somerset and Gloucester sides of Bristol agreed to concede on the same terms as Cossham. They were the first areas in the country to follow Cossham's example thereby averting damaging strikes.[283]

Buoyed by this victory, Gore, in an astute move, proposed that if Handel Cossham was prepared to support the radical Liberal MP, Robert Bontine Cunninghame Graham in his attempt to introduce the Eight Hours Bill for miners in the House of Commons, then he would not be opposed by an independent labour candidate at the next General Election.[284] This proposal, however, was overtaken by events. The sudden death of Cossham on 23 April triggered a parliamentary by-election in Bristol East. On hearing the news, the Workers' Organising Committee, which was established in January 1890, called on its members to come together that evening to consider who they might put forward to fight this election. At this meeting it was resolved that the parliamentary seat should be contested by a working man. While Dan Irving and William Whitefield's names were put forward, Whitefield emerged as the favoured candidate. Backed by Gore, Watson, and the committee of the

280 *Bristol Mercury*, 23 January 1890.
281 *Bristol Mercury*, 12 March 1890.
282 Gore was also the treasurer of the Bristol Miners' Association.
283 *The Times*, 17 March 1890.
284 *People's Press*, 29 March 1890.

Bristol Miners' Association, Whitefield secured the support of the Organising Committee, and the Bristol Trades Council to run on an independent labour candidate ticket.[285]

Dan Irving appealed to the meeting of the east Bristol Operatives' Liberal Association held on 28 April 1890 to get behind Whitefield and not put forward its own candidate. However, by an overwhelming majority the Association rejected his request and selected Sir Joseph Dodge Weston, Chairman of the Great Western Cotton Mill, to run.[286] Weston's standing as a promoter of liberal principles made him the ideal parliamentary candidate to follow in the footsteps of Handel Cossham. He had had experience as an MP for Bristol South (1885-6) under William Gladstone's premiership. Moreover, following the defeat of the first Irish Home Rule Bill in 1886 he became a loyal supporter of Gladstone's campaign to reinvigorate support for Irish self-government within the United Kingdom. Nonetheless, two days after Weston's selection a hopeful boost to Whitefield's candidature arrived. Gore received a telegram from Michael Davitt, the Irish Republican and social campaigner, backing Whitefield:

> I am heartily in support of the labour candidate, and all working men in Ireland will wish Mr Whitefield's return. It would be a graceful and politic act for the Liberal party to adopt the candidate first in the field, and thereby help to remove from the minds of the toiling masses everywhere the feeling that their cause has only a make belief support from those who make no effort or sacrifice to increase the number of labour representatives in the House of Commons.[287]

Despite Davitt's clear approval of Whitefield's commitment to Irish Home Rule and his unequivocal support for Whitefield's pro-labour credentials, the east Bristol Liberal Association was in no mood to change its mind and remained firm on its decision to endorse Weston. Deeply disappointed by this decision, Irving dropped his support for working within the Liberal Party to secure labour representation and called for the formation of an independent labour party.[288]

Upset by the rebuff, Whitefield set about campaigning only to find that the reception he received among the voters of east Bristol was lukewarm. On 1 May 1890 Whitefield and his election agent, Gore, addressed around fifty

285 Workers' Organising Committee Minutes, 23 and 24 April 1890.
286 *Bristol Mercury*, 29 April 1890; *Western Daily Press*, 30 April 1890.
287 *Western Daily Press*, 1 May 1890.
288 *Western Daily Press*, 3 May 1890.

Lysaght workers outside their factory at St. Philip's but failed to get their support. 'Four or five hands were held up for Mr Whitefield, and nearly twenty against, the rest of the company not responding to the call.'[289] A much better reception to Whitefield was given later that day at a meeting held outside the Great Western Cotton Mill. Gore presided and the vast majority of the workers present endorsed Whitefield's candidature, with only one man voting against.[290] That evening, at the third campaign meeting near the Kingsland Road railway bridge, Gore played on the fact that Weston was one of the directors of the cotton mill, in which he had a large shareholding. Shareholders, he said,

> 'were getting 6 per cent, for their capital, and could not see their way to better the position of those employed at the works, while he would remind them that during the strike William Whitefield helped to keep the girls (A voice: "Come to principles").'[291]

A resolution pledging support for Whitefield was put to the meeting but while it was carried a significant minority of around eighty voted against.

The campaign had got off to a faltering start, which caused disarray among labour activists, leading to Gore becoming embroiled in a dispute over whether Whitefield should continue with his candidacy. At the Bristol Mayday demonstration on the 3 May Tovey, secretary of the Bristol Trades Council, announced, somewhat prematurely, that Whitefield's candidature had been withdrawn due to his ill health. 'Every delegate that he (Mr Tovey) had met that day and the night before had advised that action.'[292] This news was not well received by Gore who, speaking on another platform, said that

> the working men acted as fools to themselves. They had shown no enthusiasm with Mr Whitefield, who had pleaded their cause during the past week. They would probably return a man who from nothing had grown wealthy. Where did it come from? They knew that Sir Joseph Weston had kept down the wages of his working men (*sic*), and by their labours he had become more than rich, while they were just where they were 30 or 40 years ago, and they would remain such until they returned to Parliament a working man.[293]

289 *Bristol Mercury*, 2 May 1890.
290 *Bristol Mercury*, 2 May 1890.
291 *Bristol Mercury*, 2 May 1890,.
292 *Western Daily Press*, 5 May 1890.
293 *Bristol Mercury*, 5 May 1890.

Gore's statement that little enthusiasm was shown for Whitefield echoed the sentiments of the local press, who were not surprised by the turn of events 'because of the hollowness of support behind him [Whitefield]'.[294]

Gore worked himself up into a rage and what he uttered next from the platform of the May Day demonstration on Durdham and Clifton Downs would lead him to be seen by some contemporaries as a Tory.[295] In a fit of pique Gore allowed his personal feelings to cloud his better judgement by calling on labour supporters to vote for the anti-Home Rule Conservative candidate, James Inskip, which drew vocal opposition from the crowd. This call went against the Guild of St. Matthew's record of supporting the Home Government branch of the Irish National League,[296] founded by Charles Stewart Parnell in 1882, and undoubtedly would have infuriated Michael Davitt. Tovey, who had shared a platform with Gore in a protest against Dillon's imprisonment in August 1888,[297] was irate. He wrote a letter to the editor of the *Bristol Mercury* in which he assured the public that Gore's advice was only his personal view and not that of the Trades Council, and other labour organisations in the city.[298]

Gore, clearly rattled by the lack of support for Whitefield, suspected that the Bristol Trades Council and the Workers' Organising Committee, both of whom had nominated Whitefield, had withdrawn their backing because of their disenchantment with Whitefield's performance at campaign meetings. At the election committee meeting held on the following day, Sunday 4 May, a deputation from the National Amalgamated Sailors' and Firemen's Union put forward an alternative candidate, Joseph Havelock Wilson, as a replacement for Whitefield. However, in the absence of Whitefield's election agent, Gore — and the unknown whereabouts of Whitefield — the matter was adjourned to the following evening.[299]

Demonstrating confusion and disarray over the whole election matter, a proposition was put forward at the Sunday meeting to officially inform the local press of Whitefield's retirement and to supply them with reasons for it. This proposition was defeated 'on the ground that the area covered by Mr Whitefield

294 Editorial in the *Bristol Mercury*, 5 May 1890.
295 See W. John Lyes reference to a Liberal MP who 'regarded Gore as a Tory' in 'The 1895 By-Election in Bristol East', *Transactions*, Volume 130, p. 291.
296 'Rev. S. Headlam on Irish Organisation', *Freeman's Journal*, 28 November 1887.
297 *Bristol Mercury*, 6 August 1888.
298 R. Tovey, president of Bristol Trades Council, to the editor of the *Bristol Mercury*, 3 May 1890, and published on 5 May 1890.
299 Election Committee Minutes, Sunday 4 May 1890, in Workers Organising Committee Minutes Oct. 1889 – July 1890 (mistakenly, in the minute book, the date is given as Sunday 5 May 1890).

in the few speeches he had made was not sufficiently large and important to test the feeling of the constituency.'[300]

The following evening the adjourned meeting recommenced with Gore present. He informed those gathered that he had consulted with the Bristol Miners' Association and they felt 'that they had no alternative but withdraw Mr Whitefield from the contest …after what was said by Mr Tovey [to the rally] on Durdham Down.'[301] Gore, clearly unhappy at the turn of events, proceeded to say that Whitefield, who was of a nervous disposition, had become increasingly anxious due to the lack of support from those who he thought to be his closest friends, not only those in Bristol but elsewhere. The Committee brought the matter to a close by passing a resolution confirming Whitefield's unavoidable retirement as a candidate due to his ill health. Havelock Wilson's candidature was then considered but rejected, because the Committee were not sufficiently acquainted with the candidate to warrant spending any more of working people's money on an election with precious little campaigning time left, and, in all probability, little hope of winning.[302]

Despite being rejected by the Election Committee, Havelock Wilson acquired the backing of Bristol Trades Council, and Tovey was one of its members who rallied in Wilson's support. Gore, therefore, may well have had some cause to be suspicious of Tovey's intentions when Whitefield's retirement was declared at the May Day demonstration. Wilson, who later became the national leader of the Sailors' and Firemen's Union, was not well received by Bristol's voters capturing only about eight per cent of the vote. James Watts Treasure, a railway engineer, and a member of the Bristol Socialist Society – a supporter of Wilson – reported that on 'returning home after the declaration of the poll, the shoemakers and colliers simply buried us with turf and stones. All the glass of the cab was broken, and we were glad when we reached quieter quarters.'[303]

This brought an end to this sorry affair. Members of the Clifton and Bristol Christian Socialist Society, however, felt it right to thank Whitefield for the part he had taken in the election. They 'unanimously resolved to forward him a letter of condolence regretting that his health had broken down,' and asked him to accept a volume of Ruskin's works as a token of their appreciation.[304]

300 Election Committee Minutes, Sunday 4 May 1890.
301 Election Committee Minutes, Monday 5 May 1890.
302 Election Committee Minutes, Monday 5 May 1890.
303 Bryher, *An Account of the Labour and Socialist Movement in Bristol,* Part 2, p. 27.
304 *People's Press,* 17 May 1890.

Chapter 8

Days of Doubt

The realisation that the Bristol working class were not yet ready for a clear political alternative to the Liberal Party was a sobering experience for the socialists. One consequence was that they shifted ground and sought to build a broad labour movement spanning socialists, trade unionists and Liberal radicals around a programme of reforms, particularly the eight-hour day, a demand adopted by many European socialists.[305] Soon after the May 1890 local election a meeting was called by the Dock, Wharf, Riverside and General Labourers' Union to stimulate interest in union organising and support for the Bristol Trades Council's role in bringing all classes of workers together in one body. It attracted a loose coalition of progressive Liberal radicals, independent labour supporters and socialists, including Gore. They aimed to create a climate in which workers could participate and develop a consciousness of a wider class solidarity which could lead towards political change and social reform. Francis Gilmore Barnett, a solicitor and a radical Liberal councillor, who chaired the meeting, said he hoped the outcome of this unity would be 'a labour parliament in Bristol' representative of both men and women. Its purpose would be to 'see if the conditions 'of labour could be improved'; and 'allay friction that existed'. He trusted that it 'would be ready to hold out the hand of conciliation'.[306]

For Bristol socialists by June 1890 the days of hope stimulated by the militant outburst of new unionist strikes, involving men and women from a wide range of craft and non-craft industries, had turned to days of doubt. The employers' counter-offensive had revealed divisions within the working class leading to increasing scepticism about whether trade union militancy *per se* could bring about a more equal and just society. Among those searching for alternative strategies was Robert Allan Nicol, who had been appointed as the Bristol District Secretary of the Gasworkers and General Labourers' Union, and the effervescent Miriam Daniell, who acted as spokeswoman for the Bristol cotton workers. In 1890 Nicol and Daniell co-authored a pamphlet entitled *The new trade unionism; its relation to the old; and the conditions of its success* in which stated that 'the disastrous strikes witnessed in the past six months' had demonstrated 'the futility of organisation not founded on any great spiritual idea'.[307] They were particularly concerned about the narrow focus of unions

305 Rowbotham, *Edward Carpenter: A life of Liberty and Love*, p. 135.
306 *Western Daily Press*, 22 May 1890.
307 Daniell and Nicol, *The new trade unionism; its relation to the old; and the conditions of its success*, p. 7.

on immediate short term material gains, rather than working with the labour movement as a whole to seek the emancipation of the people. Trade unions, they felt, could not bring about any permanent improvement in workers' lives if they continued to focus exclusively on looking after their own interests, though 'in the hands of capable leaders' unions could prepare the way for the socialist transformation of society.[308]

A religious form of expression was common parlance. For example 'new union' leaders, Tom Mann and Ben Tillett, expressed their ideal Cooperative Commonwealth could only be attained by 'a real religious fervour thrown into the grand work of organising the workers'.[309] Gore too, stressed the significance of a spiritual awareness combined with educational means in the making of socialists. He wanted the spirit of social solidarity to permeate the body politic.

By June 1890 confidence in the ability of workers to make either economic gains or to bring about radical change had diminished. Trade union activists in Bristol, whether influenced by socialist, labour or Liberal Party politics, started to move away from militancy towards a more moderate accommodating agenda. They returned to the strategy of the old craft unions, pursuing their goals through consensus and agreement, an approach based on the assumption of interdependence between capital and labour.

While the explosion of strikes during 1889 and early 1890 had taken Bristol employers by surprise forcing some of them to come to the negotiating table, others had quickly adopted antagonistic measures of revenge. After several months of industrial disruption, the Bristol Chamber of Commerce, accepting that a change had occurred in capital-labour relations, showed a willingness to cooperate. Discussions commenced between delegates from the Bristol Trades Council and the Bristol Chamber of Commerce about formulating a draft scheme for a Board of Conciliation and Arbitration. After a summer of meetings, in October 1890 a Bristol Board of Conciliation and Arbitration was launched for voluntary use in the settlement of labour disputes.[310] It was the paradoxical outcome of militant new unionism. The acceptance of arbitration by the employers was an acknowledgement that the strength displayed by trade unions and their members in the wave of strikes during the previous winter could not be ignored.

308 Daniell and Nicol, *The new trade unionism; its relation to the old; and the conditions of its success*, p. 13. For the story of the fascinating lives of Daniell and Nicol see S. Rowbotham, *Rebel Crossings: New Women, Free Lovers, and Radicals in Britain and the United States* (London: Verso, forthcoming Oct. 2016).
309 Tom Mann and Ben Tillett, *The 'New" Trades Unionism. A reply to Mr. George Shipton* (London: Green & McAllan, 21 June 1890), p. 15.
310 *Rules of the Bristol Conciliation and Arbitration Board, for the Adjustment of Disputes between Capital and Labour*, Established 1890, Bristol Record Office.

Though Gore inclined to the idealist approach to politics, fostered by the philosophy of T. H. Green, his experiences during the strike wave of 1889 to 1890 had brought him round to the views of the Bristol Socialist Society. He saw the relationship of capital and labour as defined by conflicting interests. Nevertheless, he felt that these opposing interests of capital and labour could be regulated through compromise and mutual respect.

Gore had not been directly involved in the establishment of the Bristol Board of Conciliation and Arbitration and he continued to support union organising as a means of building the representative voice of labour. In early November he chaired a meeting of railway workers under the auspices of the General Railway Workers' Union at Shepherd's Hall, Old Market. In his opening remarks Gore touched upon the employers' counter-offensive against union organisation, but suggested that if only employers would bury their prejudices and accept or even encourage union organisation, they would see greater harmony between capital and labour.

> [He] noted the tendency to combination among masters; not to break the back of competitive trade— would that it were so— not to organise labour, but for the sole purpose of destroying trade unionism, and thus to reduce the rate of wages for the unskilled labourer. So much the more need for strengthening the union. If masters only looked far enough, and unprejudicially enough, they would see that trade unionism offered a possibility of organising labour and of redeeming the condition of workers, and making life no longer a scramble and battle, but joyful and peaceful.[311]

Gore recognised that Bristol's political and economic elite could no longer ignore a socialist influenced labour movement. Providing a political voice through greater labour representation on the Town Council had become increasingly important. But this was to prove difficult in a Council dominated by wealthy manufacturing employers, merchants and professionals.[312] Gore was well aware of this and put his energy, with others in the labour movement, into the election campaign for the labour candidate for St. Paul's Ward, William Baster, which was launched in November 1890. However, Herbert Ashman, a Liberal and owner of a leather merchants and importers company won the election on 12 December with a large majority.[313] While Baster was

311 *Western Daily Press*, 4 November 1890.
312 D. Large, *The Municipal Government of Bristol 1851-1901* (Bristol: Bristol Record Society, 1999), p. 12.
313 *Bristol Mercury*, 25 November 1890.

unsuccessful, securing only seventeen per cent of the vote, he had at least kept labour on the political map.[314]

A few months later, however, labour suffered a huge setback. In March 1891 Tovey, the first labour candidate to have been elected to serve on Bristol's Town Council, tendered his resignation as a councillor for the St. Paul's Ward because he was finding it increasingly difficult to cope with holding down a full-time job and carrying out his duties as a councillor. Speaking from the floor of the Council chamber, Gore was magnanimous in moving the acceptance of Tovey's resignation, despite the discord that had existed between them concerning Gore's call to labour supporters, at the Bristol East parliamentary by-election in May 1890, to vote for the Conservative candidate.

> Mr Tovey's work in the Council for the past three years had been such as was perfectly conscientious and consistent with the views he was sent to represent. He had discharged his duties faithfully…

Gore then took the opportunity to point out the injustice that only men of independent means could afford to undertake the public duties of a councillor, arguing that working men, without having some form of remuneration, were severely handicapped from doing so.[315]

At the same Council meeting Gore moved a resolution calling for the insertion in Council contracts of an 'anti-sweating' clause targeted to 'prevent the abuses arising from sub-letting'.[316] His aim was to get the Council, as employers of labour, to pay 'fair' wages – by this he meant the trade union rate. Gore had long stood for paying union rates to workers who were *indirectly* as well as directly employed by the Council; union rates of pay for construction workers employed on building and maintaining schools had been included in his manifesto when he was first nominated to stand as a candidate for the School Board.

In pressing for increasing state regulation through contract compliance, Gore was pushing an agenda that was not only supported by radical liberals and socialists, but also by the House of Lords' 'Sweating' Committee, whose recent report about Government contract work had been passed by the House of Commons in February 1891. The adoption of the fair wages resolution made it a requirement of the Government, in all government contracts, to bind their

314 S. Jordan, K. Ramsay and M. Woollard, *Abstract of Bristol Historical Statistics, Part 3: Political Representation and Bristol's Elections 1700-1997* (University of the West of England: 1997, Series Editor P. Wardley), p. 146.
315 *Bristol Mercury*, 11 March 1891.
316 *Bristol Mercury*, 11 March 1891.

contractors to bring the work under the purview of the Factory Act and not to pay less than a specified minimum rate of wages approved by the Government department concerned. Under pressure from radicals and socialists, some local authorities also adopted these measures in varying forms.[317] In 1890, for instance, Clementina Black, representing the Women's Trade Union League, successfully persuaded the London County Council to implement a fair wages scheme, which also included women in the clothing industry.[318]

Not only was Gore pressing for more public control over working conditions, he defended free speech in municipal facilities. On this issue he was in alliance with local radicals. Demands for freedom of speech were consistent with the individualistic emphasis upon liberty, characteristic of traditional liberal radical thinking. During 1891 Gore and his radical associates began a campaign for the right to hold meetings in Bristol's public pleasure parks. The local Council had adopted by-laws outlawing activities it deemed undesirable and had prohibited delivering 'any public address in any part of the pleasure grounds', unless, after a formal application, the Sanitary Authority saw fit to grant otherwise.[319] Drawing on his solicitor's skills, Gore attacked the Council's position and demanded that the clauses be debated in the Council chamber, one by one. The Mayor refused, and put the motion to accept them in total without discussion. Gore strongly objected, professing 'I will not have it.' When the vote went ahead, and the by-laws were passed, Gore gave notice that at the next Council meeting he would call for the rescinding of these laws. He also stated that he intended to inform the Local Government Board of the undemocratic way the matter had been handled within the Council that day.

Open-air meetings were held at the Rope Walk and Windmill Hill, at which simmering anger towards the Council was evident in the demand that public parks should be as free as Clifton Down for public assemblies. Letters strongly objecting to the Council's passing of what amounted to penal laws were published in the local press. The pressure on the council to change its position grew rapidly.[320] A committee was formed with the sole purpose of working to secure the unrestricted right to hold public meetings in large parks,

317 Barbara McLaren, *The sweating system: summary of the evidence given before the Committee of the House of Lords* (The Executive Committee of the Women's Liberal Federation: 1890), LSE pamphlets; *Bristol Mercury*, 11 March 1890; Jenny Morris, *Women Workers and the Sweated Trades: The Origins of the Minimum Wage Legislation* (Aldershot: Gower, 1986), p. 172.
318 S. Rowbotham 'Strategies against sweated work in Britain, 1820-1920' in S. Rowbotham and S. Mitter (eds.), *Dignity and Daily Bread: New forms of economic organizing among poor women in the Third World and the First* (London: Routledge, 1994), p. 178.
319 *Western Daily Press*, 9 May and 24 June1891.
320 *Western Daily Press*, 1 and 3 July 1891.

electing Gore as its secretary.[321] Despite the committee's efforts and the public outcry, on 14 July, at a specially convened meeting the Town Council rejected the motion to rescind the resolution, reconfirming the public parks' by-laws it had passed on 23 June.[322] But the Council conceded that meetings could take place in the public parks of Eastville or Windmill Hill provided that prior notice was given. This concession divided opinion and for a while the agitation against the council flagged.

On 31 July the Committee of the right to hold of free public meetings in the city's parks elected a new executive Committee to fight its cause and William Whitefield, the Miners' agent, invoking the agitation in London for the working class vote, threatened direct action. He announced that there 'were two or three thousand miners living around one of the parks and the Council might pass what resolutions they pleased but they would hold their meeting. If the Hyde Parks of Bristol were shut against them, then down with the railings.'[323]

The fight was then taken to the streets. The first of many rallies colonised a space not far from Lawford's Gate Prison, Old Market, which had been rebuilt following its destruction by fire in the 1831 Bristol riots. Attracting a large crowd, speakers at the meeting had just begun to spell out the attempt by reactionaries sitting on the Town Council to bridle the rising demand for more democratic rights, when the long arm of the law appeared and ordered those assembled to disperse. They regrouped nearby, on the corner of Midland Road, and passed a resolution, to be sent to the Council, expressing their conviction for the unfettered right to convene public meetings in Bristol's pleasure parks.[324] The campaign went on for several months until, on 13 October, the Council succumbed to pressure and offered a compromise far reaching enough to satisfy the protesters. It agreed to allocate specific spaces in Bristol's pleasure parks for the holding of public meetings. A significant victory, in which Gore played a key role, had been won.[325]

Earlier in the year Gore's Clifton and Bristol Christian Socialist Society had transmuted into the Bristol and Clifton Fabian Society, with some of its members, like Gore, taking up dual membership with the Bristol Socialist Society.[326] Gore had been associated with the Fabians since the mid 1880s.

321 Minute book of the 'Right of meetings in public parks, 1891'.
322 *Western Daily Press*, 15 July 1891.
323 Minute book of the 'Right of meetings in public parks, 1891', 31 July 1891.
324 *Western Daily Press*, 13 August 1891.
325 *Bristol Mercury*, 14 October 1891; Minute book of the 'Right of meetings in public parks, 1891', 14 October 1891.
326 A letter from the new organisation first appeared in the *Western Daily Press*, on 12 May 1891.

He approved their acceptance of reforms based on social investigation and by 1891 had shifted away from his earlier distrust of accepting the need for State intervention. By this time many Fabians had become disenchanted with the emphasis of Sidney Webb, a leading light in the Fabian Society, on permeating the Liberals and were entertaining ideas of an independent labour party. This tallied with Gore's own efforts in Bristol.

On 13 July 1891 Gore was proposed and accepted into the membership of the Bristol Socialist Society.[327] Unlike the middle class Clifton and Bristol Christian Socialist Society, the Bristol Socialist Society was mainly a working class and lower middle class organisation with its origins in Republicanism and radical liberalism. The dramatic experiences of the 1889 to 1890 strike wave and the successful School Board and Town Council election campaigns led Gore to work very closely with them. While the theoretical sources of his socialism differed from theirs, this active connection fostered strong bonds.

327 The Minutes of the Bristol Socialist Society, 13 July 1891.

Chapter 9

Mining Tragedy

Unlike the radical liberals who emphasised individualism, philosophically and politically Gore viewed individuals as socially interconnected and believed that they found realisation not in isolation but through an organic collectivity. He sought an ethical underpinning for his rejection of a selfish individualism and endorsed altruism.

On Saturday 10 October, a few days before the settlement was reached on the holding of public meetings in Bristol's pleasure parks, Gore outlined his views on the Christian ethics of socialism in a lecture delivered at Redland Park Hall, leaving it to the individuals in his audience 'to justify or deny, on consideration.'[328] He quoted from George Eliot's historical novel, *Romola,* which was clearly very significant in forming the altruistic ethics underpinning his beliefs:

It is only a poor sort of happiness that could ever come by caring very much about our own pleasures. We can only have the highest happiness such as goes along with being a great man, by having wide thoughts and much feeling for the rest of the world as well as ourselves.[329]

Gore was similarly impressed by Edmund Burke's critique of the implications of individual rights in the French Revolution. With Burke he was concerned that the focus on self and individualism would eventually destroy community, make it 'crumble away, be disconnected into the dust and powder of individuality'.[330] Gore regarded striving for riches and personal advantage as the *raison d'être* of individualism, and the separate self. In his address on ethics Gore argued that 'from the Christian standpoint', this constituted a form of sinning that must be renounced in order to 'realise the universal self.'[331]

The influence of the Christian socialist Bishop of Durham, Brooke Foss Westcott (1825-1901), is also apparent. Gore drew on one of Westcott's sermons:

The essence of sin is selfishness in respect of men. And self-assertion in respect of God, the unloving claim of independence, the arrogant isolation of our interests.[332]

328 *Western Daily Press*, 12 October 1891.
329 George Eliot, *Romola*, p. 582; *Western Daily Press*, 12 October 1891.
330 Edmund Burke, *Reflections on the Revolution in France* (London: Penguin, 2004), p. 194.
331 *Western Daily Press*, 12 October 1891.
332 Brooke Foss Westcott, *The Victory of the Cross Sermons preached during Holy Week, 1888, in Hereford Cathedral* (London: Macmillan, 1888), p. 22; *Western Daily Press*, 12 October 1891.

Westcott was convinced that more was needed than broadcasting pithy phrases 'as guides to life'. In order to overcome the evils of those seeking 'to get a benefit out of their neighbour' wealth had to be distributed fairly and justly. He envisaged that a new kind of co-operative state that could reduce selfishness:

> We wait for the next stage in the growth of the State, when, in full and generous co-operation, each citizen shall offer the fulness of his own life that he may rejoice in the fulness of the life of the body.[333]

The philosophical Idealism, which exerted an extensive influence upon liberal social reformers and many socialists alike, assumed the existing state could be transformed into a future ideal and be divested of the values of dominant interests.

Gore also argued was that it was necessary to accept legislation which would advance social cohesion. He stressed this was not to support an autocratic state but to counter the power of particular individuals to impose their will on others. Like many of his contemporaries, Gore hoped his ideal state would be an ethical force capable of rebalancing the consequences of social inequality.

Precedents for state intervention in industry already existed through the Factory Acts (1844, 1847, 1850, 1856) and the Factory and Workshop Acts (1870, 1871, 1878). Moreover, a gradual expansion of democracy had been won during the nineteenth century through the reform acts (1832, 1867, 1884). Gore saw participation in elections as a means of bringing pressure to bear upon the local state to temper the selfish and exploitative behaviour of some employers, who resorted to 'sweating' workers. With the aim of bringing about a fairer and more cooperative society, Gore combined campaigning for policies and legislation with his ethically motivated quest for a 'truer, deeper, more loving, and more spiritual life' under socialism.[334]

The unethical consequences of the selfish preoccupation with profits were highlighted in the summer of 1891 when tragedy struck the Malago Vale Colliery in West Street, Bedminster. On 31 August a gas explosion occurred deep underground in the new Argus shaft while examiners and timber men were carrying out routine checks, as they did every Monday morning, to ensure that it was safe for the day shift to proceed. Ten miners were killed and three severely injured. Gore was called upon to represent the Bristol Miners' Union and the relatives of the deceased at the Coroner's hearing. The hearing concluded that

333 Address of the Rt. Rev. Brooke Foss Westcott to the Church Congress in Hull, England, 1 October 1890, in 'Appendix' to Philo Woodruff Sprague, *Christian Socialism: What and Why* (E. P. Dutton: 1891), p. 195.
334 *Western Daily Press*, 12 October 1891.

a gas explosion had caused the miners' deaths and blamed a worker. A roof fall had let a trapped pocket of gas escape, which was 'fired by contact with a naked light carried by a workman, contrary to the regulations of the mine.'[335]

However, there was a story behind the miners' apparent disregard for safety. Many miners objected to using safety lamps because they were burdensome. They had to be carried rather than worn on their headgear, and they produced a weaker light than unprotected lamps. Hence miners could not produce as much coal with a locked lamp as they could with an open unprotected lamp. As they were on piece work their earnings were reduced, though the company hotly contested that this was the case, as they had built in an allowance to the piece work rate.[336]

Reflecting the overwhelming view of his members, William Whitefield, the miners' agent, said that where employers had made the use of locked lamps mandatory, as they had done in places seen to be at risk in the Bedminster and Malago 'Great Vein' workings, 'they were not willing to pay for the increased difficulty in getting the coal'. [337] The Great Vein workings had needed a great deal more propping than other pits; but prior to the Malago Vale Colliery tragedy, unprotected lights had been permitted in the places it was deemed as safe.[338]

As an outcome of this disaster, the company introduced the use of locked lamps (safety lamps) in all of its workings. The company, however, refused to consider the miners' application for an extra two pence a ton to meet the loss and inconvenience of employing closed lights. The result was a strike, which was to last sixteen months.[339] Gore fully supported the stoppage and the unions' attempts to improve miners' pay and conditions, which mine owners had stubbornly resisted. Inevitably, tensions rose and tempers frayed. The long strike set in motion older forms of direct resistance in which women played their part alongside the formal structures of trade unionism.

During the following months Gore was called upon to represent striking miners and their families in the courts, concerning incidents of alleged assault and intimidation. One of these cases concerned two redoubtable women who were found guilty of assaulting a non-striker, one had covered him with flour and mud, and the other, egged on by a crowd of onlookers hooting and shouting

335 *Western Daily Press* 15 September 1891. See also D. M. D. Stuart, *The Origin and Rationale of Colliery Explosions* (Bristol: John Wright, 1895), pp. 88-95.
336 *Bristol Mercury*, 18 November 1891.
337 *Bristol Mercury*, 20 November 1891.
338 *Western Daily Press*, 1 September 1891.
339 *Report on Strikes and Lockouts of 1892 in the United Kingdom: Boards of Conciliation and Arbitration*, Cmd 7403 (HMSO: 1894), p. 188; Western *Daily Press*, 17 November 1891; *Bristol Mercury*, 30 January 1893.

'kill and skin him', had pushed 'a tambourinist ring over his head'.[340] Such acts of humiliating and shaming blacklegs by women were a common feature in strikes and protests.[341] Moreover, the tambourine suggests the women were also making the hullabaloo known as 'rough music', which showed disapproval.[342]

Gore's interest in and his devotion to the cause of Bristol's working class had increased his popularity since he was first elected to the School Board in January 1889. However, the tenure of office of the Board members, including Gore, was due to end in January 1892. Unsurprisingly, given his high repute, a joint meeting of the Bristol Socialist Society and the Clifton and Bristol Fabian Society held on the evening of 20 November 1891 decided by a majority to adopt Gore as their Socialist candidate to contest the forthcoming Board election.[343] As the Election Day approached there was a flurry of activity. In the penultimate week before the election the socialists held twenty-six open-air meetings to promote their candidate. Although not all the socialists had supported Gore's candidacy, they all turned out to help and give weight to the campaign, including Robert Sharland, Edward James Watson and James Watts Treasure.[344]

During the election campaign a potentially damaging incident occurred. On 8 January 1892, the miners' agent William Whitefield, who was also running as a labour candidate in the School Board election, received a telegram from Gore informing him that the Malago Vale Colliery had gone into liquidation. Whitefield went public with the news only to find it was not true. The strike at the Malago colliery was in its tenth week, so the announcement could have been interpreted as a deliberate slur on the company. Both Gore and Whitefield were forced to publicly apologise in three newspapers for this 'serious mistake'.[345] Fortunately for them it did little or nothing to affect the election outcome. Of the twenty-two candidates contesting fifteen seats Gore, running under the Christian Socialist banner, secured second place with 12,370 votes, and Whitefield won labour's only seat with 7,650 votes.[346]

340 *Bristol Mercury*, 26 January 1892.
341 See E. P. Thompson, *Customs in Common* (London: Merlin, 1991), pp. 233-36.
342 E. P. Thompson, 'Rough Music Reconsidered', *Folklore*, Vol. 103, No. 1 (1992), pp. 3-26.
343 *Bristol Mercury*, 2 December 1891.
344 *Western Daily Press*, 18 January 1892.
345 *Western Daily Press*, 21 January 1892.
346 *Bristol Mercury*, 23 January 1892.

Chapter 10

Walsall Anarchists' Trial

The anti-parliamentary wing of the left did not share Gore's preoccupation with electoral politics. The anarchists clustered around Peter Kropotkin's newspaper *Freedom* and by the early 1890s anarchists had also become the dominant tendency in the Socialist League.

In 1890 the Socialist League was split between parliamentarians and anti-parliamentarians with Gore's former mentor, William Morris, standing in the middle. The differences intensified until the anarchists — united in rejecting the capitalist economy, state control, and social hierarchy — prevailed. Morris left the League in November 1890. In his farewell article he criticised both groupings:

> There are two tendencies in this matter of methods: on the one hand is our old acquaintance palliation, elevated now into vastly greater importance than it used to have, because of the growing discontent, and the obvious advance of Socialism; on the other is the method of partial, necessarily futile, inconsequent revolt, or riot rather, against the authorities, who are our absolute masters, and can easily put it down.

> With both these methods I disagree; and that the more because the palliatives have to be clamoured for, and the riots carried out by men who do not know what socialism is, and have no idea what their next step is to be, if contrary to all calculation they should happen to be successful. Therefore, at the best our masters would be our masters still, because there would be nothing to take their place. *We are not ready for such a change as that.*[347]

The provocative language of the anarchists evoked outrage in the press. The *Evening News* showed particular enmity towards anarchists recounting stories about them 'plotting acts of sedition, on the run, or on trial.'[348] There was certainly a rhetoric of violent direct action. For example In October 1891, the anarchist editor of the Socialist League's *Commonweal*, David Nicoll, called on workers to help themselves to food, clothing and shelter in order to stave off hunger and destitution.

347 *Commonweal*, 15 November 1890; also cited in Quail *The Slow Burning Fuse*, pp. 96-7.
348 H. Shpayer-Makov, 'Anarchism in British Public Opinion 1880-1914', *Victorian Studies*, Vol. 31, No. 4 (Summer, 1988), p. 496.

[I]f the capitalists and their government send police and soldiers to bludgeon and butcher you let them take care of their lives and property for both will be in danger. Dynamite and revolvers are cheap, and these assassins who butcher the poor and starve their children, may yet learn that workmen's arms can strike these murderers even though they may be carefully guarded in their splendid mansions.[349]

However, Nicoll's inflammable language was consistent with the anarchist's long-standing policy to only use violence as a means of self-defence.

While the British anarchist movement 'did not rule out the selective use of violence' or the use of violence as a means of self-defence, 'the British movement overwhelmingly adhered to law-biding tactics.'[350] A former employee in the political department of Scotland Yard, Detective-Sergeant Patrick McIntyre, recollected that

the general aim of the English Anarchists was not assassination. Their ideas were based on Communist principles. Such men as Tom Cantwell and [Ted] Leggett talked somewhat wildly at their various meeting-places, but the more sensible amongst them only smiled. I have heard one or two members preach the most violent doctrines imaginable, but it was a case of 'words [that] speak louder than actions.'[351]

Then on 31 December the poet John Barlas was brought before the Westminster Police-court charged with endangering lives by firing a five-chambered pistol by the House of Commons' Speaker's residence, in the Palace of Westminster, between 8 and 9 o'clock that morning. A police constable witnessed the event. He said that on approaching the defendant Borlas turned and handed him the gun and pronounced

I am, an Anarchist, and I intended shooting you; but then I thought it a pity to shoot an honest man. What I have done is to show my contempt for the House of Commons.[352]

The case was widely reported in the press. The more conservative newspapers announced an anarchist outrage. But most dismissed Barlas as insane. He

349 *Commonweal: A Revolutionary Journal of Anarchist Communism*, Vol. 7, No. 285, 17 October 1891, p. 1.
350 Shpayer-Makov, 'Anarchism in British Public Opinion 1880-1914', p. 490.
351 *Reynolds' Newspaper*, 14 April 1895.
352 *Exeter and Plymouth Gazette*, 1 January 1892.

appeared in court a week later accompanied by a number of friends, including a contemporary of his at New College Oxford, the poet Oscar Wilde, and Gore's associate the Christian socialist Henry Hyde Champion.

Broken of heart, bankrupt in purse, and dizzy in the head, he [Borlas], after gallantly but vainly struggling to reach the ideal dreamed about at Oxford, wakes up to find himself famous at last, but in the hands of the police and on his way to a lunatic asylum.[353]

Less than a week after the Barlas incident six men were arrested and jointly charged with plotting to manufacture a bomb with the intention of committing a violent act. It was a challenging proposition for the small band of supporters of the accused were divided and the political atmosphere febrile. Early that January Edward Carpenter called upon Gore to direct the legal defence of one of these men, a man Carpenter knew personally, Fred Charles, *aka* Slaughter. Carpenter organised one of the two accounts established to raise funds for the defence in what became known as the Walsall anarchist trial; the other was started by the militant and uncompromising editor of *Commonweal* David Nicoll. Agreement to merge the two funds could not be reached, causing confusion and tension.

David Nicoll.

This friction manifested itself in the appointment of the defence teams. Briefed by Gore, the instructing solicitor, William Willis appeared for Charles' defence; William Marcus Thompson, instructed by J. N. Cotterell, for Victor Cailes, Jean Battola and William Ditchfield; Mr Maw for Joseph Deakin; and Mr G. Ross for John Westley.[354] Gore's team had had their bail application for Charles turned down twice, but on 9 March 1892, after financial guarantees set higher than the other defendants in the case, it was finally approved. Edward James Watson, then a trainee solicitor at Gore's legal practice and a member of the Bristol

353 *Sheffield Independent*, 8 January 1892.
354 *Birmingham Daily Post*, 10 February 1892.

Socialist Society, deposited £500 as surety for Charles, as did Fred Henderson, Charles' brother-in-law, a socialist poet and a member of the Socialist League. However, Nicoll's concern was that Gore and his team would not put up 'a hard enough defence.'[355]

A division emerged over what constituted the best grounds. Nicoll believed it was politically necessary to expose the role of the police spies and *agents provocateurs*. The advanced radical barrister, William Thompson, did contest police infiltration in his defence of Cailes, Battola and Ditchfield.[356] However, because the trial was conducted amidst an international panic over anarchist 'terrorists', Gore, and the barrister he engaged, William Willis, advocated a narrower defence and refused to pursue the claim that the accused were set up by the police. Willis, a barrister noted for representing the best interests of his clients,[357] argued that pressing the issue of infiltration by a police spy would be tantamount to admitting that the accused *had* actually been contemplating using violence in Britain, while Carpenter held that there was already so much potentially damaging written material exhorting violence in anarchist publications that directly confronting the police would be fatal to the interests of the accused.[358] In the climate of increasing international hostility towards anarchists, and an extremely antagonistic Judge, it was exceedingly difficult to mount a defence that would get a sympathetic hearing.

Another potentially damaging factor was that the defence must have been aware that Charles had lectured on socialism in Chicago in 1886 and had been 'a warm friend of [Michael] Schwab and [Samuel] Fielden'.[359] Along with seven other trade union activists with anarchist beliefs, Schwab and Fielden had been accused of throwing a bomb at the police during a protest meeting near Haymarket Square on the evening of the 4 May 1886, killing one policemen and wounding six others. They were accused even though Schwab had left before the meeting began and Fielden was just concluding his speech a few feet away from the police Captain, William Ward, when the bomb was thrown into the police ranks. The trial of the suspects had taken place amidst media hysteria about anarchism and resulted in highly questionable verdicts. All were found guilty.

355 J. Quail, *The Slow Burning Fuse* (London: Paladin, 1978), p. 117
356 Quail, *The Slow Burning Fuse*, p. 117; On William Marcus Thompson see Yvonne Kapp, *Eleanor Marx, Volume II The Crowded Years 1884-1898* (London: Lawrence and Wishart, 1976) p. 228.
357 J. B. Atlay, 'Willis, William (1835–1911)', Rev. Eric Metcalfe, *Oxford Dictionary of National Biography*, Oxford University Press, 2004 [http://www.oxforddnb.com/view/article/36936, accessed 27 Jan 2014]
358 See Edward Carpenter's letter to the editor of *Freedom*, 25 November 1892, LSE Selected Pamphlets, (1892).
359 *San Francisco Call*, Vol. 71, No. 41, 10 January 1892.

Joseph Thomas Deakin.

Three were imprisoned, four executed and one committed suicide the day before he was due to be hung.[360] They became known in the anarchist and socialist movements as the Chicago Martyrs, and the Haymarket affair led many socialists like Charles towards anarchism in Britain.

Increasing attention to anarchist operations by the world's press also played a part in heightening public panic in the lead up to the commencement of the Walsall anarchist trial in 1892. It was the confession of one of the accused which made the defence of the Walsall anarchists especially hard. On the 16 January, a Walsall anarcho-socialist, Joseph Deakin, the first of six to be arrested and charged, signed a confession statement. He believed that two of his comrades, Fred Charles and William Ditchfield, fellow members of the Walsall Socialist Club, had betrayed him, as he had heard them admitting their guilt to police interrogators from his cell in the middle of the night. Later he said that the police duped him by mimicking the voices of Charles and Ditchfield causing him to panic. The statement connected three Socialist Club members Charles, Ditchfield and a brush manufacturer, John Westley, with French anarchist, Victor Cailes and Italian refugee shoemaker, Jean Battola, in the bomb plot.[361]

A Frenchman, Auguste Coulon, inexplicably melted away. He was a member of its North Kensington branch of the Socialist League and Secretary of the International Anarchist School run by Louise Michel, heroine of the Paris Commune of 1871. It was he who had initiated the 'plot'. Accusations

360 This section draws on the work of P. Avrich, *The Haymarket Tragedy* (Princeton: Princeton University Press, 1984), pp. 225 & 271, and T. Messer-Kruse, *The Haymarket Conspiracy* (Illinois: University of Illinois Press, 2012, Kindle edition). These two authors take opposing views of the Haymarket affair. Avrich argues that although the accused had advocated violence when it came to the crunch it proved to be rhetoric or plain bluster. In contrast, Messer-Kruse contends that while the accused may not have thrown the bomb, the evidence points towards a conspiracy, the intent being to provoke a police assault in order to spark a violent uprising.
361 Quail, *The Slow Burning Fuse*, Chapter six 'The Walsall Anarchists'.

that he acted as an *agent provocateur* in the pay of the police inspector William Melville would be confirmed when official papers were released a century later.[362]

Posing as an extreme and violent anarchist Coulon had befriended Charles, who had fallen on hard times, providing him with financial assistance. Charles moved to Walsall in search of work but, grateful for Coulon's generosity, had kept in contact with him. Through this connection Coulon was able to put the French refugee Cailes in touch with Charles in Walsall. A little later Coulon induced his next-door neighbour, Battola, to send a sketch of a bomb to Cailes in Walsall. After checking its validity with Coulon, who confirmed in writing that it was 'all right', he passed it on to Charles. The sketch, which was found in Charles' possession on his arrest, and Coulon's blessing connected them all with the conspiracy. Coulon promptly vanished and of course was never charged.[363]

The trial closed on 4 April. Charles, Cailes, Battola and Deakin were found guilty of conspiracy to murder. Deakin was sentenced to five years penal servitude, the others to ten. Westley and Ditchfield were acquitted. Judge Hawkins, in his summary, made the connection to the United States and France by indicating the trial had revealed that Charles, Cailes and Battola were working closely with 'their kinfolk, the American dynamitards', and Parisian anarchists.[364] *The Times* commented in its report that the 'punishment inflicted on the prisoners who were found guilty, if not exemplary, was at all events severe.'[365] The indictment of the anarchists extended to other sections of the left. The final sentence of *The Times* article maintained that since the Haymarket affair the public mood across the world had shifted against the anarchists and to all those on the 'left': 'the very men who petitioned the President of the United States to amnesty the Chicago Anarchists a few years ago are voting today for a new anti-Anarchist law.'[366]

In the event neither of the defence teams' strategies proved particularly effective, though Thompson saved Ditchfield, and Ross secured Westley's release. Gore's team's attempt to get the jury to acquit Charles on a legal technicality failed. Willis, in closing the defence, pointed out that none of the defendants had in their possession anything 'that would cause an explosion, or aid in causing an explosion'. This important fact was disregarded. His later attempt to excuse the behaviour of the defendants was contorted:

362 Michael Hassett, 'Melville, William (1850–1918)', *Oxford Dictionary of National Biography*, Oxford University Press, Sept 2010 [http://www.oxforddnb.com/view/article/101260, accessed 26 Jan 2014]
363 Quail, *The Slow Burning Fuse*, p. 109.
364 *Birmingham Daily Post*, 5 April 1892.
365 *The Times*, 5 April 1892.
366 *The Times*, 5 April 1892.

[H]owever mistaken, these people are much to be pitied, because by the neglect of political rulers themselves this organisation has come into existence which, perhaps, in its onward movement, if change does not come, may threaten to inflict all mankind with evils.[367]

As John Quail observes, this hardly amounted to 'what was supposed to be a conciliatory defence.'[368]

In contrast, there is little doubt about Gore's commitment in defending Charles. Gore's close comrade and legal associate, Edward Watson, put up £500 surety for the defendant: More personally, six months after the trial had ended, 8 October 1892, Gore presented his friend, Harry Thomas, with a copy of the second edition of Fred Henderson's socialist/anarchist verses, *By the sea and other poems*, in honour of Fred Charles.[369] Henderson, who was Charles' brother-in-law, dedicated it to 'my friend, Frederic Charles, who is now undergoing ten years' penal servitude for his alleged part in what is known as the Walsall Anarchist Conspiracy.'[370]

The severe sentences levied on the Walsall anarchists shocked many in the labour movement. On the 6 April 1892, Bruce Glasier wrote to his Scottish Socialist League comrade, James Brown, expressing his anguish: 'I am appalled at the result, the sentences are – even on the assumption of the prisoners guilt – ferocious in the extreme.'[371] However, the injustice did not make him adhere more closely to anarchism. The whole event had destroyed Glasier's 'hope in Revolutionary action' in Britain and pushed him in a reformist direction – 'I am back a parliamentarian.'[372]

Gore, although upset at Charles' sentence, resolutely carried on with his socialist propaganda work. He presided over a Bristol May Day meeting held in the Horsefair; and in an indirect reference to the Walsall affair he repudiated individual acts of terror as inappropriate in efforts to overthrow the capitalist system in Britain. Committed to parliamentary methods and convinced of the need for reforms, Gore nevertheless saw the relationship between capital and labour as conflictual. He argued:

367 *Birmingham Daily Post*, 4 April 1892; Quail, *The Slow Burning Fuse*, p. 120.
368 Quail, *The Slow Burning Fuse*, p.120
369 Nothing further is known of Harry Thomas, but he must have been a significant figure in Gore's life at this time given that the front paste-down of the book bears the inscription: "Harry Thomas / from his friend / Hugh Holmes Gore / (in mem. Fred. Charles). / Octr.8th 1892". See Robert Temple Booksellers bibliographical archive, http://www.roberttemplerarebooks.co.uk/Hrkiv9.htm#t1, accessed 28 January 2014.
370 Fred Henderson, *By the sea and other poems* (London: Fisher Unwin, 1892, second edition), p. 5.
371 John Bruce Glasier to James Brown, 6 April 1892, Glasier Papers, Sidney Jones Library, University of Liverpool.
372 John Bruce Glasier to James Brown, 24 March 1892, Glasier Papers.

Fear and terror were things absolutely necessary to make the masters change their position in this matter [caring little or nothing for their employees], and in some foreign lands, he regretted to say, fear and terror had to be produced by force, which in England they had not to use. He did not ask them to sympathise with everything their foreign brethren did; but he asked them to remember that their aim was the same – making the masters see they would have to disgorge their wealth. The workers failed because they distrusted each other and because they had not sufficient enthusiasm – persevering enthusiasm.[373]

373 *Western Daily Press*, 2 May 1892.

Chapter 11

Elections, Strikes, and the Law

Following the May Day labour demonstrations, Gore turned his attention once again to the Malago colliery disaster. On 25 May he attended a fund raising event at Bedminster Down School for the widows and children of the men who were killed in this tragedy. His younger brother and fellow socialist, Arthur Holmes Gore, provided the comedy act in an evening of entertainment. In June, the adjourned inquest into the disaster resumed with Gore representing the Miners' Union. The jury returned a verdict of accidental death. Neither the workers nor the Company were found culpable.[374]

By this time Gore had accepted a call to act as the election agent for Major Eustace Gresley Edwards, the thirty-eight year old independent labour candidate, in the impending July 1892 Dover Parliamentary Election.[375] A giant of a man, standing nearly seven feet, Edwards had given up his army commission to fight for the labour cause.[376] The Christian Socialist Guild of St. Matthew sponsored his candidature. His programme included support for measures such as the legal eight hours' working day, payment of members of all public bodies, national and municipal industries, progressive taxation of land values, graduated taxation of incomes, local direct popular veto and control of the drink traffic, and Home Rule for Ireland. This advanced programme attracted radical liberal, as well as labour, voters.[377]

Edwards, a High Anglican, attended the Holy Trinity Church at Dover where the Guild of St. Matthew member, Reverend George Sarson, was the resident priest.[378] Sarson crusaded vigorously for Edwards during the election campaign, and appeared with him on the platform at mass meetings. Sarson had been a close personal friend of Stuart Headlam and had produced a paper with him for the Church Congress of 1877 on 'The Church's Mission to the Upper Classes', but in 1891 they clashed over what educational policy the Guild of St. Matthew should adopt 'which threatened the very existence of the Guild.'[379] However, despite the resulting difficulty and discord in his relationship with Sarson, Headlam, encouraged by Gore, came to Dover during the election

---

374 *Western Daily Press*, 10 June 1892.
375 *Dover Express*, 1 July 1892.
376 *Dundee Evening Telegraph*, 12 September 1891.
377 *Dover Express*, 1 July 1892.
378 *Dover Express*, 22 April 1892.
379 Jones, *The Christian Socialist Revival 1877-1914: Religion, Class, and Social Conscience in Late-Victorian England*, p. 103.

campaign and addressed a public meeting on the Land Question.[380] Other speakers attracting large audiences in the campaign included James Ramsay MacDonald and the Fabian and Irish playwright, George Bernard Shaw.[381]

Gore proved to be a competent election agent in a contest that Edwards was expected to lose by a wide margin. However, in a two-horse race, (previous elections had gone by uncontested), Edwards secured a respectable thirty per cent of the vote though losing to the sitting Conservative MP George Wyndham. It was a remarkable result against a man embedded in the powerful Irish landed gentry, (his uncle the second Lord Leconfield owned 44,000 acres in counties Clare and Limerick, while the seventh earl of Mayo, proprietor of 7500 acres in Kildare and County Meath, was his cousin).[382] Coincidentally, Wyndham also happened to be the cousin of Lord Alfred Douglas, who had, by the time of Wyndham's re-election to Parliament, become the lover of the Irish writer and poet, Oscar Wilde.[383]

With the onset of autumn, Gore began to channel his efforts into the oncoming Bristol municipal election. On 28 September 1892, in a letter to the editor of the *Western Daily Press*, Gore set out his stall in regard to the development of the Port of Bristol, a subject which had long been the concern of ratepayers. He was in agreement with the majority view on the Town Council that in order for Bristol to remain a viable commercial port it had to make provision for larger steam ships to discharge their cargo at the river's mouth (Avonmouth), six miles from Bristol, as the river's course into Bristol was too narrow and treacherous for large ships to navigate. A significant amount of financial investment was required to expand Avonmouth docks, and Gore argued this would have to come from Bristol ratepayers.

Avonmouth had yet to be included within the boundaries of Bristol and therefore its rate payers were not liable to contribute. Moreover, private landowners stood to gain considerably from the construction of a twenty-acre dock from the hike in land values and increased revenue they would receive in rents.[384] The Council's proposed scheme, observed Gore, would leave Bristol 'entirely in the hands of the local landlords,' and any profits accrued would 'be annexed by the owners of the property at Avonmouth.'

380 Report of the Annual Meeting of the Dover Labour Electoral Association, *Dover Express*, 10 February 1893.

381 *Dover Express*, 1 July 1892.

382 Alvin Jackson, 'Wyndham, George (1863–1913)', *Oxford Dictionary of National Biography*, Oxford University Press, 2004; online edn., Jan 2008 [http://www.oxforddnb.com/view/article/37052, accessed 4 July 2014]

383 R. Ellmann, *Oscar Wilde* (London: Penguin, 1988), pp. 362 and 428.

384 *Western Daily Press*, 20 and 29 September 1892.

Gore proposed, therefore, that the City of Bristol purchase the land necessary for the expansion of Avonmouth docks, as he felt that the scheme would then be advantageous to all Bristol citizens rather than the landowning few.[385] This was one of the matters he raised when, on 29 September, he addressed a meeting of the Bristol Operatives' Liberal Association where the question of the representation of St. Philip's South Ward on the Town Council in the forthcoming Council elections was discussed.[386]

Gore, the retiring socialist councillor, had been invited to attend this meeting to state his case for re-election, again on a socialist ticket. As well as outlining his position regarding the Avonmouth dock scheme, Gore touched on the housing problem, one that had been too easily dismissed by the Town Council. He advocated that the Council should buy land and build dwellings at affordable rents to replace the worst tenements, which were to be found in the St. James' and St. Jude's areas of the City.[387] Bristol's acute housing problem had been highlighted the year before by the Bristol Fabians' tract entitled *Facts for Bristol*, published in May 1891, which revealed how thousands of Bristol families were crammed together in 600 courts amid appalling circumstances. The houses in these courts held an average of four persons to each room and living conditions were almost unbearable. Inadequate ventilation, sanitation, and water supplies, along with poor light and overcrowding, were public health concerns, which, according to the Fabian report, should have been addressed 'by the Town Council under the Artisans' Dwellings Acts to provide decent accommodation for the poor citizens.' The report went on to state that at 'least a thousand of Bristol's citizens have no better home than common lodging houses, of which there [were] 54 registered, with 1,128 beds.'[388]

While Gore's audience at the Operatives' meeting was broadly in accord with his views on the housing crisis, several speakers from the floor voiced their dismay over Gore's action in voting to increase the salary of the Chief Constable, Edwin W. Coathupe. Gore argued that to retain Coathupe, who, he said, had done an excellent job during his tenure as Chief Constable, a salary

385 *Western Daily Press*, 29 September 1892.
386 *Western Daily Press*, 30 September 1892.
387 However, It was not until after Gore had left the City that the Council began to erect its first dwellings, tenement blocks in East Bristol, which were completed in 1907, see M. Dresser, 'People's Housing in Bristol 1870-1939' in I. Bild (ed.), *Bristol's Other History* (Bristol: Bristol Broadsides, 1983), p. 148.
388 *Facts for Bristol,* Fabian Tract No. 18 (London: Fabian Society, May 1891), p. 5. This tract could be obtained from Gore's Christian socialist friend Paul Stacy, who was secretary of the Clifton and Bristol Fabian Society, 18 Cotham Road, Bristol. His sister Enid, a teacher at Redland High School, and a socialist, also lived at this address in 1891.

commensurate with other Council officials should be paid. Gore may have been influenced by Coathupe's cooperation, during 1889-90, with strike organisers at demonstrations and in street processions, a policing strategy that had enabled events to proceed relatively smoothly and which the organisers had 'warmly acknowledged'.[389]

As Gore had anticipated, he gained backing for his candidature from both the Clifton and Bristol Fabian Society and the Bristol Socialist Society.[390] But despite Gore's robust defence of his record in the preceding three years, he failed to secure the unambiguous support of the St. Philip's South branch of the Bristol Operatives' Liberal Association, who opted not to 'take any action with reference to Mr Gore's re-election' to the Town Council in November.[391] The Barton Hill branch of the Operatives' Liberal Association plumped for supporting William Henry Cowlin,[392] owner of a well-known local building and construction company. Nevertheless, ten days later, at a public meeting held in the heart of working class Barton Hill, Gore received a warm welcome and secured a pledge from the majority of those assembled that they would 'use every legitimate effort' to get him re-elected.[393]

Just before the election campaign had got underway, a major labour dispute broke out at Sanders' confectionery works in Redcliff Street, near the city docks. Following a one day strike on 5 September 1892, the majority of the 300 women and girls employed at Sanders' sweet factory joined the Gas Workers and General Labourers' Union and presented their employer with a list of demands, including the removal of the lengthening of the working day by one hour, which the company had imposed on them.[394] Two weeks later Sarah Edwards, one of the women involved in the dispute, was dismissed. Sackings of other union members followed over the next couple of weeks and younger and cheaper hands filled their vacated positions. [395] Unrest in the factory boiled over, and on 5 October a significant minority of women and girls still working for Sanders' stormed out demanding the re-instatement of their comrades.[396]

389 *Bristol Mercury*, 13 January 1890.
390 *Western Daily Press*, 13 October 1892.
391 *Western Daily Press*, 30 September 1892.
392 *Western Daily Press*, 13 October 1892.
393 *Western Daily Press*, 22 October 1892.
394 *Western Daily Press*, 19 October 1892.
395 As recorded in the *Western Daily Press*, 25 October 1892.
396 The number of women on strike is unclear but the numbers claiming union strike pay in the following weeks totalled more than 100. *Western Daily Press*, 8 and 25 October 1892.

Immediately, hostilities broke out between strikers and non-strikers.[397] That evening one of the non-strikers was waylaid by a group of women and struck in the face. Annie Smith, a striker, was arrested and charged with intimidation and common assault against Rebecca Porter who had filled Smith's vacated position in the factory. Two days later the case was brought before local magistrates. Gore conducted Smith's defence. Smith pleaded guilty to common assault but denied the charge of endeavouring to force Porter to join the strike by intimidation. Gore, having decided not to call witnesses, took the opportunity in defending his client to pull off a propaganda coup by exposing Sanders as a sweatshop employer. With a straight face he said:

> He was surprised that any employer of labour should dare to ask girls to work for such a sum as 3s per week. These facts he had mentioned because he wanted the magistrates to see that the poor girl had passed through great hardship.[398]

The magistrate ruled this as irrelevant. He told Gore to confine himself to the question of assault but it was too late, in the presence of the local press Gore had skilfully seized the opportunity to spread the word that the striking sweet women were up against a ruthless employer.[399] Such audacity added to his reputation as the 'people's solicitor'.

Soon after a strike committee was established to organise and direct the support for the Sanders' women. The twenty-four year old Enid Stacy, a close Christian socialist comrade of Gore and a member of the Guild of St Matthew, agreed to take on the role of Honorary Secretary of the Committee. Stacy came from a cash poor but 'culturally rich' socialist family.[400] As well as belonging to the Bristol Socialist Society she was also active in the Clifton and Bristol Fabian Society. In this organisation she worked closely with Gore, her younger brother Paul and Caroline May, a radical liberal and an energetic member of the Bristol Association of Working Women. Enid Stacy toiled tirelessly to bring the

397 For accounts of this dispute see Bryher, *An Account of the Labour and Socialist Movement in Bristol*, Part 2, pp. 32-38; S. Mullen, 'Sweet Girls and Deal Runners' I I. Bild (ed.) *Placards and Pin Money; Another Look at Bristol's Other History* (Bristol: Bristol Broadsides, 1986), pp. 112-126; R. Ball, *The Origins and an Account of Black Friday, December 23rd 1892*, in D. Backwith, R. Ball, S. E. Hunt and M. Richardson (eds.), *Strikers, Hobblers, Conchies and Reds: A Radical History of Bristol 1880-1939*, pp. 153-4.
398 *Western Daily Press*, 8 October 1892.
399 *Western Daily Press*, 8 October 1892.
400 A. Tuckett, 'Enid Stacy, The Nineteenth Century Political Radical and Activist for Peace, Social Justice and Women's Rights' (unpublished, edited edition: June 2012), Working Class Library, Salford, Chapter one, p. 1.

strike to a successful conclusion. Predictably, along with other strike committee members they were accused of being outside agitators and were blamed for bringing strikers into direct conflict with the police who were under strict orders to protect 'free labour' brought in to replace the positions vacated by the strikers and sacked workers.[401]

On 26 October a 1,000 strong rally held outside Sanders' factory ended in clashes between the police and the demonstrators. It marked an abrupt change in police strategy from 1889-90. In a highly charged atmosphere, police bellicosity served only to make the protesters more determined to confront and barrack strike-breakers. Several arrests followed and the detainees were brought before the local magistrates court to answer charges of breach of the peace, incitement and assault. In turn the protesters brought a charge of violent assault against one police constable, nominating Gore to conduct the prosecution on their behalf.

The first case to be heard, on 27 October, was the charge levelled against the French activist Gaspard de la Croix, that of being drunk and disorderly, and inciting the mob. Gore conducted the defence and, although 'he complained that prejudice had been introduced into the case',[402] La Croix was found guilty and sentenced to twenty-one days' imprisonment.[403] During the hearing, Superintendent Cann, called by the prosecution as a witness, revealed that La Croix was not the only person running around whipping the crowd up into a frenzy. He announced that it was his intention to bring charges against Gore's colleague, Edward James Watson, for similar offences.

The next day Gore and his supporters, including Watson, were out campaigning again for his re-election to the Town Council. His continued support of the local labour movement had gained him trust among the working class of St. Philip's; a factor which, according to the local press, greatly assisted his success in the 1 November election. Gore, now a popular figure, secured 1,008 votes, a margin of victory of 579 over his Liberal opponent William Henry Cowlin, although he was absent from the count leaving Watson to move a vote of thanks to the presiding officers for conducting the election.[404]

Within a few days of his election victory Gore was back in court conducting the defence of three Sanders' women strikers for disturbing the peace, and one charged with assault. The former were bound over to keep the peace and the latter was given a choice of paying a 10s fine plus costs or receiving a seven-day prison sentence. At the same hearing, but with a different defence solicitor,

401 Ball, *The Origins and an Account of Black Friday, December 23rd 1892*, pp.155-6.
402 *Bristol Mercury*, 28 October 1892.
403 *Bristol Mercury*, 5 November 1892.
404 *Western Daily Press*, 2 November 1892.

Edward James Watson and Harold Brabham, the secretary of the Bristol branch of the Gas Workers and General Labourers' Union, were bound over for breaches of the peace and for inciting others to assault and resist arrest.

Immediately following this trial, Gore donned the hat of the prosecuting solicitor in pursuance of a case against a police constable accused of assaulting two young female protestors, alleging that he had knocked the girls' heads together in a violent manner and wrestled them to the ground. Gore opened the prosecution with a cutting remark. In a sardonic tone he said that 'he knew it was generally assumed that magistrates sat for the purpose of acquitting policemen —'. The presiding magistrate cut Gore off in mid-sentence, rebuking him for making such a slanderous claim. The defence solicitor, too, registered his outrage at such a sensation-seeking allegation. Gore responded tongue-in-cheek, 'I was going to say that I knew that would not be the case in this instance.'[405]

Incensed, the defence solicitor retaliated accusing one of the witnesses, William Oxley, a member of the strike committee,

of being a professional agitator; by his personal appearance it would be seen he was not one of those people who earned his living by the sweat of his brow like an ordinary clicker [a stitcher of leather uppers to the sole of a shoe][406] or workman but went walking about the streets getting money off these little girls, and — [407]

Infuriated by this insinuation, Gore tossed his head back, picked up his papers, and stormed out of court; consequently the trial was brought to a quick conclusion. The case against the constable was dismissed. However, there were to be repercussions. Oxley called on Henry Wansbrough, the defence solicitor in this case, for a public withdrawal of the accusation he had made against him during the proceedings. After a number of public exchanges in the local press he eventually managed to extract a half-hearted retraction from him.[408]

In the meantime, disturbances between police and blacklegs on one side, and striking workers and their supporters on the other, intensified after deal runners were locked out, on 5 November, because of their refusal to accept piece working. The Shipping Federation brought in blackleg labour to unload

405 *Bristol Mercury*, 5 November 1892.
406 Oxley had been a clicker in a boot and shoe factory before becoming an insurance agent, which was his occupation when he appeared in court.
407 *Bristol Mercury*, 17 November 1892: Also see Ball, *The Origins and an Account of Black Friday, December 23rd 1892*, p. 158, and Mullen, 'Sweet Girls and Deal Runners' in I. Bild (ed.) *Placards and Pin Money; Another Look at Bristol's Other History*, pp. 123-4.
408 Bryher, *An Account of the Labour and Socialist Movement in Bristol*, Part 2, pp. 36-38.

timber cargoes. Regular confrontations between the police and the deal runners ensured the courts were kept busy. On Sundays locked out deal runners joined forces with Sanders' strikers in Sunday parades and meetings, which attracted thousands of supporters. At one of these gatherings, Gore declared he

> had come to the conclusion that the magisterial bench was packed with employers and their relations and friends, whose interest they always consulted, that the police were systematically used as paid hirelings of the classes, instead of impartial servants of the community, their legal advocates being paid out of our money to befoul the character of honest working men; and that the authorities being deaf to appeals, the working-classes are left absolutely without means of redress.[409]

Whether Gore's comments were seen as duplicitous, given that he voted to increase the Chief Constable's salary, is not known. But any doubts that Gore overstated his depiction of local state officials were soon quashed. On Black Friday, 23 December 1892, around 200 Dragoon Guards and Hussars, reinforced by local police and county constables, were summoned and deployed to break up a 20,000 strong labour demonstration called in support of deal runners locked out by their employers. The Dragoons charged towards the demonstrators with their helmets glistening and lances drawn scattering them in all directions.[410]

Mayhem ensued; dozens of civilians and police were injured. Among those hurt was William Redwood, a *Western Daily Press* journalist and a member of the Westbury Liberal Association. He was knocked to the ground but managed to scramble back to his office at the corner of St. Stephen's Street and Baldwin Street, badly bruised and covered in mud.[411] Harry Bow, an eye-witness, recorded an account of Black Friday in his diary, including sketches of scenes 'from the military invasion of Bristol'. Excited by the nights events he said:

> may I never smell [gun]powder again & its (*sic*) quite without precedent & licks all others hollow & twas (*sic*) like a garrison town with so many troops about & like a 2nd edition of the famous Bristol Riots of 1831 too, and sharp affrays & rushes occurred at several other parts of the town also.[412]

409 *Bristol Mercury*, 5 December 1892; see also Ball, *The Origins and an Account of Black Friday*, p. 164.
410 *Western Daily Press*, 24 December 1892.
411 Review of Samson Bryher's *An Account of the Labour and Socialist Movement in Bristol*, *Western Daily Press*, 28 July 1931.
412 The Diary of W. H. (Harry) Bow, 1892, Bristol Record Office.

THE MARCH OF THE WORKERS

FRIDAY, DEC. 23rd,

THERE WILL BE A

BIG LANTERN PARADE

OF THE

Locked-Out Deal Runners,

Sanders' White Slaves,

And the **GENERAL ORGANIZED TRADES.**

The **PROCESSION** will assemble at the **GROVE,** at 7 p m. sharp.

FINISHING WITH

A MONSTRE MEETING

In the **HORSEFAIR.**

The Christmas Bells are ringing, the sky is clear and bright;
Your masters pray for peace, but are compelling you to fight.

Away with Politics.   **Labour to the Front.**

Lantern Parade, original poster for the 'Black Friday' march.

Letters of protest were sent through the medium of the local press. For instance, the Bristol Liberal Reform Club passed a resolution strongly condemning 'the dastardly conduct of the authorities for instructing the military and police to charge the peaceful and orderly meetings of citizens held in the Horsefair this evening.'[413]

On 2 January 1893, at the quarterly meeting of the Bristol Town Council, Gore, who had been one of the main speakers on Platform Two at the Horsefair and had left the area just minutes before the Dragoons attacked, called on the Council to

> request the Home Office to appoint a Commissioner to inquire into and report as to the cause which induced the magistrates to obtain the presence of the military on the 23rd December; as to their justification in making such request; as to the conduct of the police and military on the 23rd December in relation to the disturbance on that day; and generally as to the action of the magistrates prior to and in relation to the disturbance on that day.[414]

However, when Gore's resolution was put to the Council it was lost lost by forty-two votes to eleven.

Over the next few months Gore was regularly called upon to defend strikers and their supporters, usually on charges of intimidation or assault, and he participated in many of the weekly parades and demonstrations organised by the strike committee. He criticised the magistrates for not only going against the advice of the Public Prosecutor but for bringing a charge against Ben Tillett, the Bristol born General Secretary of the Dock, Wharf, Riverside and General Labourers' Union. The accusation was that he:

> unlawfully did incite certain people then and there present to unlawfully assemble and unlawfully commit a riot in the said city and county of Bristol on the twenty-third day of December.[415]

Ironically, it was Gore's father, Thomas, who read out the charge in his position as the magistrates' clerk. Hardly any material has survived on Gore's personal relations with his family but Gore's views and his associates must have fuelled familial disputes.

413 *Western Daily Press*, 24 December 1892.
414 *Bristol Mercury*, 3 January 1893.
415 Cited in Ball, *The Origins and an Account of Black Friday*, pp. 178-9; *Western Daily Press*, 10 January 1893.

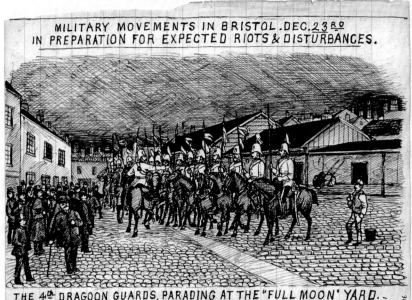

MILITARY MOVEMENTS IN BRISTOL.DEC.23RD
IN PREPARATION FOR EXPECTED RIOTS & DISTURBANCES.

THE 4TH DRAGOON GUARDS, PARADING AT THE "FULL MOON" YARD. –
FOR ACTIVE SERVICE AGAINST THE MEETING IN THE HORSEFAIR.

SCENES FROM THE MILITARY INVASION OF BRISTOL.DEC.23RD

A LIVELY AND WARLIKE SCENE IN WINE STREET. THE DRAGOONS
ON GUARD TO PREVENT THE PROCESSION FROM PASSING THROUGH IT.

Scenes from the Military Invasion of Bristol, December 23rd 1892, The Diary of
W. H. (Harry) Bow, 1892.

MILITARY MOVEMENTS IN BRISTOL ON DECEMBER.THE 23 RD DURING THE BIG LABOUR DEMONSTRATION.

A TROOP OF THE 20 th HUSSARS. PATROLLING AT THE BLIND ASYLUM. IN READINESS TO GO INTO ACTION AGAINST THE MOB. IF REQUIRED. " THEIRS NOT TO MAKE REPLY, THEIRS BUT TO DO AND DIE," TENNYSON.

Some weeks later, Sunday 29 January, Hugh Holmes Gore revealed at the usual weekly demonstration that the Public Prosecutor had refused to be a party to Tillett's prosecution. He went on to call for the removal of the existing magistrates, who he said were men of property and opposed to organised labour, demanding that they should be replaced by working men.[416]

Amusingly, just a week or so before, Gore had appeared before the court, on the other side of the dock, charged with trespassing and committing wilful damage to a farmer's fence on 31 December 1892. On that day Gore had taken a group of boys out on a recreational walk near Duchess' Pond at Stapleton near Bristol. During the walk he strayed from the footpath onto private land. William Baker, a dairy farmer, and tenant of the Duke of Beaufort, who owned the land, remonstrated with Gore who, ignoring his outcry, directed his boys across an open field towards a boundary hedge singing 'We'll hang Charley Wathen [the Liberal Unionist Lord Mayor of Bristol] on a sour apple tree'. On reaching the edge of the field Gore and his group clambered over the four-foot high hedge, spoiling it in the process. He refused to apologise for his action, defiantly declaring that he would do it again, though he offered to pay the farmer half-a-crown in damages. The court ruled that although a technical offence had been committed

416 *Bristol Mercury*, 30 January 1893.

they would not convict, but instead ordered Gore to pay half-a-crown in damages plus court costs.[417]

Gore's public displays of defiance could not be put down just to belligerence and show, natural to the rough and tumble world of electioneering. He was not afraid to put himself out on a limb in support of his friends and his beliefs. On 25 January 1893, he wrote a letter to the editor of *The Oxford Magazine* criticising a review of a new edition of Edward Carpenter's *Towards Democracy*, which contained several passionate love poems about working class male lovers. He objected to the reviewer's 'hostility and bitterness' and his failure to 'appreciate the finer tones and subtler symphonies of a poet.' Gore was particularly angry that the review failed to acknowledge Carpenter's courage in appearing at the Walsall anarchist trial as a character witness for one of the accused, Fred Charles.[418] In court Carpenter had declared himself an anarchist, a brave if foolhardy admission.[419] Moreover, in his letter, Gore said that in his close association with Charles, in the weeks leading up to the trial, he had come to realise that Carpenter's depiction of Charles 'as a gentleman generous to a fault' was indeed accurate.[420]

In court Gore was able to enthral a jury and enchant listeners in the public gallery with his rhetoric and theatrics, an ability which ran in the family – his younger brother Arthur turned to the stage to earn a living in the mid 1890s. He even tried his charm on magistrates. On one occasion, after his friend William Whitefield, the miners' agent for the Bristol district, had been sentenced to 14 days hard labour for being drunk and disorderly and assaulting the police, Gore pleaded with the magistrates to reconsider their sentence, as nearly a thousand unemployed men were waiting on Whitefield to pay out unemployment benefit from union funds. 'He offered to undergo the sentence for Mr Whitefield, if such arrangement could be made.' Of course he knew full well that would not have been possible.[421] The court rejected Gore's plea and refused to remit the sentence of hard labour.

417 *Western Daily Press*, 20 January 1893.
418 *The Oxford Magazine*, 1 February 1893.
419 See Rowbotham, *Edward Carpenter: A life of Liberty and Love*, p. 166.
420 *The Oxford Magazine*, 1 February 1893.
421 *Royal Cornwall Gazette*, 22 June 1893.

Chapter 12

Starnthwaite Home Colony: Searching for Utopia

Utopian ideas and small utopian projects flourished towards the end of the Victorian period. Capitalism had begun to falter from the 1870s encouraging ideas of demise. While one response was to create organisations and parties, thinkers and writers on the left envisaged imaginative alternatives.[422] In 1891 Oscar Wilde considered that

> A map of the world that does not include Utopia is not worth even glancing at, for it leaves out the one country at which Humanity is always landing. And when Humanity lands there, it looks out, and, seeing a better country, sets sail. Progress is the realisation of Utopia.[423]

William Morris shared a similar vision. His hopes for a more cooperative and communal society are expressed in his *tale A Dream of John Ball*, set during the time of the peasants' revolt of 1381. Morris makes use of John Ball's voice to express an idea of how socialism would foster truly human relationships: 'fellowship is heaven and the lack of fellowship is hell: fellowship is life, and the lack of fellowship is death'.[424] Morris believed in the need to imagine what might be. In his futuristic *News from Nowhere*, serialised in *Commonweal*, Morris outlined a vision of what this 'new day of fellowship' could look like.[425] He imagines life without wage slavery, money, poverty, politics, marriage and the tyranny of property rights.

The utopian vision of the future — the term comes from the book published by Sir Thomas More in the sixteenth century[426] — refers to an ideal society, one that may or may not be realisable. But in the late nineteenth century this desire to live in a more just, equal and harmonious community was taken literally by small bands of anarchists and socialists and small-scale experiments

---

422 M. Beaumont, *Utopia Ltd. Ideologies of Social Dreaming in England 1870-1900* (Chicago: Haymarket Books, 2009, first published by Brill Academic Publishers, The Netherlands, 2006) p. 12.

423 Oscar Wilde, 'The Soul of Man Under Socialism' in *The Complete Works of Oscar Wilde* (London: Book Club Associates) P. 1089.

424 William Morris, *A Dream of John Ball and a King's Lesson* (London: Reeves and Turner, 1888), p. 29.

425 William Morris, *News from* Nowhere (London: Reeves and Turner, 1892), p. 305.

426 Thomas More, *Utopia* (*Libellus vere aureus, nec minus salutaris quam festivus, de optimo rei publicae statu deque nova insula Utopia*) (First published in Latin in 1516).

in building model utopian communities enjoyed a mini-revival. Cynics, like George Bernard Shaw viewed them with caustic scepticism:

> When they were managed by men who had made fortunes, like Robert Owen, in private commerce, they made a hopeless mess of communism. And when the managers were all amateurs they split at once into the few born bosses who could manage, and the idealists who thought they were going to have a happy paradise, and take it easy.[427]

Nevertheless communities of various kinds continued to proliferate. While some sought to demonstrate that alternative ways of living were possible in the here and now, others addressed specific practical problems in capitalism. One such communal experiment was created by the Unitarian minister of Market Place Chapel, Kendal, Reverend Herbert Mills. He belonged to the Home Colonisation Society. He proposed the formation of a Home Colony in Starnthwaite to provide the unemployed with 'regular and useful work'. Arguing in 1889 that the key to success was for the Colony to be self-sustaining, he insisted they should produce 'not so much for sale as for the use of the workers, their foreman and director.'[428] In May 1888 Mills had outlined his plan at a specially convened conference in Bristol. Gore and the labour councillor Tovey were present at this meeting and, therefore, had some inkling of what Mills' venture was about.[429]

Mills launched his scheme at Starnthwaite in the Lake District in 1892 with the purchase of a cornmill, including all the necessary equipment for its operation, a sawmill, joiner's shop, a blacksmith's shop, three dwelling houses, a hayloft and a stable. However, he needed more land to expand his colony in order to sustain the self-employment of between thirty and forty people but the authority of the Home Colonisation Society was required to proceed with his plan. Mills estimated that the cost of the neighbouring land would be around £3,000 and he told the committee that he had already secured commitments of £2,000 from supporters. This convinced them to give him the go ahead.[430]

Mills recruited the Bristol socialist Katharine St. John Conway as his secretary. She was given the responsibility for selecting entrants to the community at Starnthwaite from a field numbering more than one hundred.

427 Cited in W. H. G. Armytage, *Heavens Below: Utopian Experiments in England 1560-1960* (London: Routledge and Kegan Paul, 1961), p. 430.
428 H. V. Mills, *Poverty and The State or Work For The Unemployed* (London: Kegan Paul, Trench & Co, 1889), pp. 185-187.
429 *Bristol Mercury*, 3 May 1888.
430 Meeting of the Home Colony Society 31 March 1892, *Pall Mall Gazette*, 1 April 1892.

Arthur Holmes Gore, Postcard Portrait.

She took on eighteen, including Gore's brother Arthur. Her former Bristol socialist comrades, Dan Irving and Enid Stacy, were also among the chosen ones, the latter, according to Mills, 'begged for several weeks to be admitted, alleging that she was permanently unemployed',[431] which happened to be true as she had lost her job as a teacher at Redland High School because of her socialist activities and involvement in the Sanders' confectionery strike.[432]

Dan Irving, one of the first to join the Colony in the summer of 1892, was given the foreman's position. Enid Stacy arrived in early 1893. More recruits followed. However, the aim of self-sufficiency could not be realised. Mills, unhappy about how Irving had been managing the colony, summarily asserted his authority and usurped Irving from his post. Irving was given notice to surrender his position and the colonists were told that they must sign up to a

431 L. Thompson, *The Enthusiasts: A Biography of John and Katharine Bruce Glasier* (London: Victor Gollancz, 1971), p. 76.
432 E. Malos, 'Bristol Women in Action, 1839-1919' in I. Bild (ed.) *Bristol's Other History,* p. 119.

new set of rules. A new foreman, Thomas Wilson, was taken on before Irving's notice had actually expired; a majority of the colonists refused to recognise him as their legitimate foreman, and remained loyal to Irving. On 28 March, Mills dismissed Richard Binfield and Edward Childs for insubordination, ordering them off the premises. They left but tried to regain entry a little later. They faced stiff resistance, however, and were forced to make a tactical retreat. They called for assistance from other colonists who were situated on an adjoining site. Dan Irving, Walter Neville, Samuel Pusk and John Moore came to their assistance and broke their way into the building causing some damage in the process. Police were called and charges were brought against all six men.

Angered by this turn of events, Stacy, together with John Moore and Dan Irving, told a 2,000 strong meeting in Kendal Market Place how they had been deceived by Mills.[433] At a well-attended public meeting in Accrington, Stacy denounced Mills 'as an autocrat, who had made rules which sixteen out of twenty-one adults [working at the Colony] had refused to sign.'[434] She went on to say that they were led to believe they were entering a commune but Mills had turned out to be an absolute dictator. The experimental colony had been supported by Robert Blatchford, then editor of the socialist newspaper, *The Clarion*, but when he learned about the true nature of the regime at Starnthwaite, he apologised to his readers 'for having given a puff to "The Westmoreland Open-air Workhouse."'[435]

Stacy and Irving summoned Gore to represent the colonists who were accused of maliciously damaging property belonging to the Home Colonisation Society. He argued that Irving's notice to relinquish his foreman's position had not expired when the break-in, which Irving had authorised, took place and was therefore '*bone-fide*'. Consequently, any damage caused had not been done maliciously. Unconvinced by Gore's arguments the magistrates found the defendants guilty, fining them a shilling each and costs.[436]

This was not the end of the matter, however. The convicted men, along with Enid Stacy, returned to Starnthwaite and forcibly took possession of the Mill and some farm buildings. On hearing this news Mills attempted to gain entry but failed. The next day, Tuesday 11 April, he returned with reinforcements — his solicitor, and twelve strong unscrupulous men hired from the nearby market town, Kendal. They smashed their way in and forcibly dragged the occupants out, along with their belongings. Strong words were exchanged for

433 Tuckett, 'Enid Stacy, The Nineteenth Century Political Radical and Activist for Peace, Social Justice and Women's Rights' (unpublished, edited edition: June 2012), Chapter Four, Working Class Movement Library, Salford.
434 *Bristol Mercury*, 4 April 1893.
435 *Manchester Evening News*, 8 April 1893.
436 *Liverpool Echo*, 10 April 1893; *Lancaster Gazette*, 15 April 1893.

several hours before the ejected colonists retreated to the relative tranquillity of Kendal town to gather their thoughts.[437] They set up a defence fund with Enid Stacy as its secretary. In a letter to the editor of *The Christian Weekly* she wrote 'We, the ex-colonists, fifteen in number (including five children), are asking [for] the sympathy and support of those who declare their belief in justice'.[438] It proved to be a long drawn out affair. Irving pursued Mills through the courts for several months in an endeavour to get compensation. The Starnthwaite case was not finally settled until the following year when Mills handed over £75 in damages to Irving, but both Mills and Irving had to share the court costs of more than £300.[439]

Despite her former close association with the Bristol socialists (Irving and Stacy) Katharine St John Conway supported Mills' decision to evict them. She continued to carry out her role as the secretary of the Home Colony at Starnthwaite for several weeks after the ejections.[440] However, despite the animosity between Conway and Irving reconciliation eventually materialised with the assistance of George Bernard Shaw and John Trevor, founder of the Labour Church.[441] Nearly six months later, on 23 September 1893, the tension between them had eased to the extent that Conway and Irving forbearingly shared a platform at an Independent Labour Party public meeting held in Edinburgh.[442] In the mean time, Conway had left Bristol and married the Scottish socialist, Bruce Glasier.

Murmurings abounded in Bristol socialist circles on the revolt at Starnthwaite. The involvement of Gore as the defence solicitor, and the fact that not only Irving and Stacy but Gore's brother Arthur had also spent some time at the Colony,[443] occasioned much small talk about the rights and wrongs of the conflict.[444] Nonetheless, by September the awareness that the estranged parties

437 *Liverpool Mercury*, 12 April 1893.
438 *The Christian Weekly*, 6 May 1893.
439 Thompson, *The Enthusiasts: A Biography of John and Katharine Bruce Glasier*, p. 77.
440 At an open-air meeting of the Lancaster Fabian Society, held on 12 June 1893, Katharine St John Conway, who addressed the meeting, was cited as the secretary of the Home Colony at Starnthwaite, *Blackburn Standard*, 17 June 1893.
441 Tuckett, 'Enid Stacy, The Nineteenth Century Political Radical and Activist for Peace, Social Justice and Women's Rights' (unpublished, edited edition: June 2012), Chapter Four, Working Class Movement Library, Salford.
442 *Edinburgh Evening News*, 25 September 1893.
443 Percy Widdrington, Chair of the Saffron Walden Divisional Labour Party to Comrades and Friends, in memory of Enid Widdrington (née Stacy), 24 July 1924, Angela Tuckett Papers, Working Class Movement Library, Salford, Manchester.
444 Laurence Thompson suggests that St John Conway may well have been worried that 'stories from the Bristol people' concerning the incident at Starnthwaite could have reached Edward Carpenter, see Thompson, *The Enthusiasts: A Biography of John and Katharine Bruce Glasier*, p. 82.

MUNICIPAL ELECTION

St. Philip's North Ward.

Bristol & District Trades Council Labour Electoral Association.

Labour Candidate.

A PUBLIC MEETING

(Under the auspices of the above) will be held at the

MISSION HALL, MINA ROAD,

ON

FRIDAY NEXT, OCTOBER 6th,

WHEN

Mr. JOHN SHARLAND

WILL ADDRESS THE MEETING.

Supported by Councillors—

F. GILMORE BARNETT, Dr. CUNNINGHAM, HUGH HOLMES
GORE, Rev. B. W. JACKSON.

Messrs. F. SHEPPARD, (Labour Candidate for St. Paul's Ward)
J. DAVIS, W. LEWIS, and other well known speakers.

Chair to be taken at 8 p.m., by

MR. S. SENNINGTON.

Working Men, attend in large numbers, and support your own cause.

Printed and Published by G. HILL, 15, Stapleton Road.

Municipal Electoral Poster, 1893.

1893 Manifesto of the Bristol Labor (sic) Candidates, John Sharland, Frank Sheppard, Harold Brabham, William Baster.

in the Starnthwaite affair had more or less resolved their differences eased the way for Bristol socialists to put their full weight into a new initiative. Defeats on the industrial front may have led to a decisive redirection in their strategy, and a focus on securing greater labour representation on the local Council. In the autumn of 1893 the Bristol Socialist Society affiliated to, and worked in unison with, the Bristol and District Trades Council Labour Electoral Association, feeling confident enough that they would be able to put up a good show, in the forthcoming November Municipal elections.

Following the expulsion of the renegades at Starnthwaite, and the subsequent litigation, Gore handed much of his court work over to his brother Arthur, who had recently qualified as a solicitor,[445] providing him with paid employment following his ejection from the Home Colony. Along with Paul Stacy, Arthur also assumed a leading role for the Bristol branch of the Guild of St Matthew in supporting Bristol miners at demonstrations and benefit concerts during the fifteen-week miners' national lockout, which had begun in the last

---

445 The *Bristol Mercury* 29 April 1893 carried a report that Arthur Holmes Gore, articled to Mr H. R. Wansbrough, had passed his final solicitor's exam.

week of July.[446] This gave Gore more time to attend to his public duties on the Town Council, the School Board, his philanthropic work and, in particular, campaigning for the November Council elections.

The unified efforts of the Bristol Socialist Society and the Bristol and District Trades Council Labour Electoral Association in promoting their candidates during the build up to the Council election was starting at last to have an impact. John Sharland, founder member of the Bristol Socialist Society, won the Bristol St. Philip's and St. Jacob's North seat for labour.[447] During his election campaign Sharland spoke at over 90 public meetings, almost losing his voice in the process. He joined Gore (who had, among others, campaigned on his behalf) on the Town Council.[448] By winning the St. Paul's Ward unopposed Frank Sheppard, another member of the Bristol Socialist Society, completed the socialist triumvirate that took their place on the Council benches.

446 For instance see the *Bristol Mercury*, 15 and 18 September 1893.
447 Bryher, *An Account of the Labour and Socialist Movement in Bristol,* Part 2, p. 52.
448 *Bristol Mercury*, 26 and 31 October 1893; Bryher, *An Account of the Labour and Socialist Movement in Bristol,* Part 2, p. 52.

Chapter 13

Prejudice, Religious Discrimination and School Discipline

The relaxation in Gore's workload allowed him to find the time to train as a Bristol rugby football referee,[449] but it was short-lived. In 1894 his brother renounced the legal profession and resigned from his post as a matter of conscience. In a letter to the editor of the *Bristol Mercury* that April he explained that he could not

> approach the ideal of the Catholic Kingdom of Christ so long as I earn my living by maintaining anger and litigation among men whose professed Divine Law is – "Forgive," "Judge not," "Be not angry," "If any men will sue thee at law let him"…[450]

He took to the stage to pursue a theatrical career, which later brought him some success, featuring in popular plays such as *A Sprained Ankle* (1911) and *England's Menace* (1914). His brother Hugh lost invaluable assistance with his court work as well as the company of a like-minded fellow Christian socialist, who had worked tirelessly in support of Bristol miners.

Without the presence of his closest ally and confidant, Gore demonstrated an inability to control the religious fervour which was ever present in his life. This fervour surfaced in a public controversy that was to set Gore apart from the views and principles of the vast majority of his comrades in the Bristol Socialist Society. The rift was deep and bitter. On 29 October 1894, at a meeting of the Bristol School Board, Gore opposed the acceptance of a sixteen-year-old Jewish girl, Rebecca Wolfson, a monitress at Hotwells Girls' School, as a pupil teacher. He feared that the teaching of Christianity at the school would be undermined because he felt that 'the Jewish faith was antagonistic to the Christian faith.'[451]

In the late nineteenth and early twentieth centuries anti-Semitism was pervasive in English society amongst all classes. Some socialists, like Edward Carpenter, were inclined to equate Jews with rapacious financiers and speculators.[452] Racial type-casting was frequently assumed. Gronlund, whose work had also influenced Gore, went further declaring in 1884 that "'Jewism,"

449 He refereed a match between Brighton House Old Boys versus Carlton as a 'probationer' on 10 February 1894, *Bristol Mercury*, 9 and 12 February 1894.
450 *Bristol Mercury*, 6 April 1894.
451 *Western Daily Press*, 30 October 1894.
452 See V. Geoghegen, 'Edward Carpenter's England Revisited', *History Of Political Thought*, Vol. 24 (3), (2003) pp. 509-527 and S. Rowbotham, *Edward Carpenter: A Life of Liberty and Love*, p. 304.

to our mind, best expresses that special curse of our age'.[453] Gore's socialist friend, Charles Ashbee, although half Jewish, wrote in 1918 that

> the Jew is distinguishable, lean, mean, griping, hard-featured, inquisitive, brainy, and every now and then, especially in the faces of young men, with that look of curious dreamy intelligence discerning God, singly, far away through everything.[454]

No evidence of Gore's prejudices towards Jews in terms of physiological sterotypes exists. However, strands of anti-Semitism historically had been an element in Christianity and Gore's rationalisation for his discriminatory behaviour against Wolfson was rooted in his Christian religious beliefs. Adopting the view, expressed by his friend Edward Watson and some traditional Catholics that 'Jewry' had damned Christ,[455] Gore called on other Board members if 'they called themselves Christians' to 'consider very carefully, indeed, whether they were justified in assisting actively in the maintenance of a faith which was opposed to…their own.' His opposition was formally put to the meeting on the grounds of the girl's Jewish faith, which he, in a fiery speech, declared would have prevented her from conforming 'to the rules their pupil teachers had to follow,' as she would have been unavailable to work on the Sabbath and on other Jewish festival days.[456] In the past 'she had been absent for several days on account of religious festivals.'[457]

The discussion that followed became heated, as Gore's anti-Jewish rhetoric fired up emotions. He zealously defended his beliefs admitting that his attitude was indeed one of religious intolerance. Gore openly stated his prejudice against the Jewish faith; 'he could not offer any inducement to anyone who would teach something which was distinctly contrary to the tenets of the faith he had been brought up in.' His objection, having been put to the vote, was defeated by eleven votes to three.[458] The stance he took on this matter enraged his Bristol Socialist Society comrades. On 6 November 1894, a resolution was passed at a meeting of the Bristol Socialist Society, repudiating 'the action and views

453 Gronlund, *The Cooperative Commonwealth in its outlines: An Exposition of Modern Socialism*, p. 50.

454 Crawford, *C. R. Ashbee: Architect, Designer & Romantic Socialist*, p. 175.

455 Letter from James Ramsay MacDonald to Enid Stacy, 1 December 1894, Angela Tuckett Papers, Working Class Movement Library, Salford, Manchester.

456 *Western Daily Press*, 30 October 1894.

457 *Jewish Chronicle*, 2 November 1894, cited in J. Samuel, *Jews in Bristol: The History of the Jewish Community in Bristol from the Middle Ages to the Present Day* (Bristol: Samson & Co., 1997), p. 157.

458 *Western Daily Press*, 30 October 1894.

expressed by Hugh Holmes Gore' at the School Board meeting. They agreed that his opposition to the appointment of a Jewish monitress as a pupil teacher was 'utterly opposed to the spirit and principles of Socialism.'[459]

The reaction of the Bristol Socialist Society to Gore's anti-Semitic outburst led him, just four days later, to give notice that he was quitting the Bristol Socialist Society. In this parting epistle, Gore claimed that the Bristol Socialist Society by repudiating his action in opposing the Jewish girl's appointment, as a pupil teacher, was also repudiating its own, as he was merely carrying out the policy he had been mandated to uphold by the Society. The day after receiving his resignation letter, the Bristol Socialist Society called a meeting at which it made Gore's decision to leave the Society public. This letter was then circulated to the local press for publication. On the face of it, the split was decisive and traumatic. Not only did Gore make an immediate exit from the Society, he also announced in his letter of resignation that he intended to vacate his seat on the Bristol School Board, just before the election, which was scheduled to take place in January 1895, he declared that he was going to stand as an Independent candidate.[460]

Gore's letter revealed an underlying bitterness which he had long suppressed. He felt that his work for the socialist cause over ten years had never been recognised or appreciated by Society members, many of whom, he now alleged, 'preached ideas which were alien and hostile to what we Socialists had been fighting for all along.'[461] He accused them of ignoring Marx and Ferdinand Lassalle's philosophies and of having no clear idea of the meaning of socialism. Although wounded, he said that his resignation from the Bristol Socialist Society did, however, give him the opportunity to speak freely without having to look over his shoulder to check for signs of 'suspicion and trust'. He showed no visible indication of remorse or intimation of despair. He concluded in an upbeat note by vowing to continue to fight for socialism 'as a free-lance in guerrilla warfare.'[462]

This letter was published in full in the local press, as requested by the Bristol Socialist Society. However, at least one of its members, Tom Phillips, was uneasy that in the public mind Gore might be seen as the one wronged and that the Bristol socialists could be viewed as a thoroughly 'disagreeable and intolerant lot.'[463] He retold the whole saga, which differed little from that

459 *Bristol Mercury*, 8 November 1894.
460 Gore to the members of the Bristol Socialist Society, 10 November 1894, *Western Daily Press*, 15 November 1894.
461 Gore to the members of the Bristol Socialist Society, 10 November 1894.
462 Gore to the members of the Bristol Socialist Society, 10 November 1894.
463 Tom Phillips to the editor of the *Western Daily Press*, 15 November 1894, *Western Daily Press*, 17 November 1894.

reported in the Press at the end of October, but took the opportunity to make clear to the public the Bristol Socialist Society's position on religious tolerance and why they had to publically denounce Gore.

> We desire unity, and knowing that religious dogma is, and has been, responsible for much strife, we avoid it, and embrace all men [sic] – Jews or Gentile, Protestant or Catholic, according to equal liberty to each, consistent with the liberty of the whole ... [This is] why we considered the conduct of Mr Gore incompatible with his position.[464]

Phillips' statement reveals a view of a socialism alert to the liberty of individual conscience which differs from Gore's over-arching ideological convictions.

A couple of days later, Gore's friend, the Miners' agent, William Whitefield, wrote to the press expressing his unease with the Bristol Socialist Society's action in condemning Gore. He said that although he disagreed with the position that Gore took, given the sacrifices he had made over the years, and the good work he had done, he wished that Gore 'had been approached in a spirit more befitting the sum total of his life.'[465] More publicity on the matter followed, including a letter to the School Board from Rebecca Wolfson's father. He was a picture frame maker and had a shop in Hotwell Road, Bristol.[466] An immigrant from Russia, Pase Wolfson had come to Britain fleeing the persecution and anti-Semitism Jews faced in his home country. He thanked the Board for not using his daughter's Jewish faith as a reason to exclude her from becoming a pupil teacher and hoped 'that in the near future every vestige of intolerance and bigotry may be effaced entirely, and be a thing of the past.'[467]

The publicity surrounding this incident was seen as potentially damaging for the labour and socialist movement in Bristol. Ramsay MacDonald told Enid Stacy that he felt it serious enough to intervene to give 'both sides some fatherly advice'. On the one side 'there was Bob [Robert] Sharland with his eyes half shut and his legs too emotional to support his body' and on the other Gore's 'silly' reason for excluding the Jewish girl, which MacDonald regarded as really nothing short of Christian bigotry. By knocking heads together MacDonald, with support from Enid Stacy, hoped to bring about reconciliation, 'the Society rescinding the resolution and Gore explaining his position'.[468]

464 Tom Phillips to the editor of the *Western Daily Press*, 15 November 1894.
465 Gore to the editor of the *Bristol Mercury*, 17 November 1894, *Bristol Mercury*, 19 November 1894.
466 *Census Returns of England and Wales 1891*, Ancestry.com, courtesy of the National Archives of the UK, accessed 23 September 2013..
467 Pase Wolfson to the Bristol School Board, *Bristol Mercury*, 27 November 1894.
468 James Ramsay MacDonald to Enid Stacy, 1 December 1894, Angela Tuckett Papers, Working Class Movement Library, Salford, Manchester.

MacDonald's intervention did produce a negotiated compromise. Gore withdrew his notice of resignation from the Bristol Socialist Society 'having undertaken the responsibility of his attitude in the matter of a Jewish pupil teacher'. He recalled his letter of 10 November to the local press which had lambasted the Society and its members. In return the Society rescinded its resolution condemning Gore, and accepted him back into the fold.[469] However, the acrimony proved too great and the truce proved to be only temporary. Another divisive conflict, which had been brewing for some time, erupted. This time Gore was in combat with John Sharland, Frank Sheppard, Reverend Henry John Wilkins (Church of England vicar of St. Jude's, and tireless campaigner for the improvement of housing and sanitary provision in his parish), Bristol Trades Council, and the Bristol Socialist Society.

The origins of their clash can be traced back to 1892, when School Board committee members elected Gore to chair the Industrial Schools Committee. It was the duty of the local authority to ensure that the education department or School Board regulations were not broken in administering corporal punishment. Casual beatings were forbidden and authority to cane or flog pupils was vested in the head teacher. A record of physical punishments had to be kept.[470] However, the local board had some influence in reining back the reliance on corporal punishment, with many radical liberal and socialist board members viewing it 'as an outdated and barbaric instrument of class control.'[471] Gore did not accept this perspective. The colder and harder side of his character emerged in regard to dealing with discipline in Truant schools.

Given Gore's concern about the ill treatment of children and the philanthropic work he carried out in the working class district of St. Philip's, illiberality towards child miscreants seems anomalous. However, Gore maintained a clear-cut separation between harsh discipline towards truants and his boys' club voluntary work. In the case of boys placed in Truant schools, unlike some of the liberally inclined Board members, he believed that discipline could only be kept 'by the application of the rod.'[472] His approach harks back to his own harsh school days, but was at variance with socialist educational ideas. Moreover, his traditional conservative attitude went against the progressive approach of reducing or dispensing with corporal punishment that was beginning to emerge.[473]

469 *Western Daily Press*, 4 December 1894.
470 J. Walwin, *A Child's World: A Social History of English Childhood 1800-1914* (London: Penguin: 1982), p. 54.
471 Walwin, *A Child's World: A Social History of English Childhood 1800-1914*, p. 55.
472 *Bristol Mercury*, 31 January 1891.
473 Walwin, *A Child's World: A Social History of English Childhood 1800-1914*, p. 54.

Seeing that a significant part of Gore's work entailed prosecuting persons accused of ill-treating children, this appears to be at best hypocritical. But he would no doubt have defended his perspective on both religious and social grounds. Strands within Christianity maintained that not all children could be regarded as innocent and the National Society for the Prevention of Cruelty to Children accepted that some children demonstrated delinquent behaviour. Thus, he felt that Truant schools being responsible for putting children on the strait and narrow moral path were right to administer harsh discipline. In Gore's view authoritarian treatment was justified for the long-term interests of the children and society as a whole. Gore's attitude was consistent with his belief that the individual was less significant than a collective organic totality.

In Gore's mind institutional violence, within strictly defined boundaries, was wholly different from the wilful abuse carried out against children behind the closed doors of the domestic home, for which he pushed for prosecution. Those charged with child neglect or inflicting harm on children tended to be the least educated men and women, and the most deprived from the hidden underbelly of the working class. Frequently excessive alcohol consumption on the part of the parent, or parents, was a contributory factor. For those found guilty a short period of imprisonment was usually the punishment. In practice this often meant the children ended up either in industrial schools or in the workhouse, where conditions could be equally grim.[474]

Ironically, Gore's desire to protect children in practice, through the philanthropic Society for the Prevention of Cruelty to Children, could, in practice, result in their being shuffled into authoritarian forms of care. In the words of Steve Humphries, the only alternatives to abuse in the home consisted in

> their enforced confinement in institutions which had little to offer apart from rote learning, rigid discipline[,] manners and morals which were often alien and meaningless, led to a constantly antagonistic atmosphere.[475]

Gore's acquiescence in the harsh alternatives to abuse in the home contrasts sharply with the fun loving rebel defying an indignant farmer and

---

474 For details of workhouse conditions in Bristol see R. Ball, D. Parkin, S. Mills, *100 Fishponds Rd: Life and Death in a Victorian Workhouse* (Bristol: Bristol Radical Pamphleteer, 2nd edition, 2016).

475 S. Humphries, 'Radical Childhood in Bristol 1889-1939', in I. Bild (ed.) *Bristol's Other History*, p. 8. On the severity of punishments in Board schools in London, see A. Davin, *Growing Up Poor: Home, School and Street in London. 1870-1914* (London: Rivers Oram Press, 1996), pp. 127-9.

clambering, with the boys he was leading, over a hedge. Authoritarianism and anti-authoritarianism were interwoven aspects of his character. Again he found himself at odds with his fellow socialists.

In August 1894 the socialist Town Councillor, Frank Sheppard, had written to the Industrial Schools Committee stating that after hearing reports of charges of alleged cruelty against staff at Bristol's Truant School a committee had been formed, comprising the Reverend Wilkins, as its unofficial head, alongside the socialist trade unionist John Sharland, and himself. It had met on 10 August to consider the matter. At this meeting several boys had given testimony supporting these allegations. Due to the seriousness of the charges the committee called upon the School Board to receive a delegation lobbying for a Government inquiry. Gore, who had been Chair of the Industrial Schools Committee with responsibility for overseeing Truant Schools since 1892, read out Sheppard's letter to members of the School Board at their meeting on 24 September, 1894. Following a short discussion, the Board decided that insufficient information accompanied the letter to support the claims made, and the decision was made to write to Wilkins, who already had had a meeting with Gore concerning these allegations, 'to furnish in writing particulars of the case' and supply the names and addresses of the boys concerned.[476]

The following day Wilkins, in a letter to the editor of *Western Daily Press*, challenged the Bristol School Board either to ask for a Government inquiry or to nominate the Industrial Schools Committee's Chair, Hugh Holmes Gore and the School Board's Vice-Chair, Reverend Urijah R. Thomas, to meet with him and other members of his committee to hear evidence which he insisted would prove 'that the conduct of the Bristol Truant School is degrading and against the very first principles of education.' His mistrust of the School Board was evident. He refused to give either the names of the witnesses, or, indeed, provide evidence in writing for fear that in his absence he would get an unfair hearing.[477]

Gore had acquired experience during his tenure as a Town Councillor and School Board member on how to employ the procedures designed, ostensibly to ensure fairness and consistency, to block external scrutiny. He emphasised the fact that the committee set up by Wilkins, Sheppard and Sharland, unlike the Industrial Schools Committee, was an unelected body, and that it had continued to refuse to supply written evidence, despite constant requests to do so. Hence a bureaucratically punctilious Gore maintained that without the specific charges before them, the Industrial Schools Committee could not progress the matter.

476 *Bristol Mercury*, 25 September 1894; *Western Daily Press*, 25 September 1894.
477 H. J. Wilkins to the Editor of the *Western Daily Press*, 25 September 1894, *Western Daily Press*, 26 September 1894.

The complaint consequently proceeded to drag on into December, whereupon it became conveniently impossible to have an inquiry before the elections of a new School Board in January.

John Sharland, however, refused to let the matter drop. On 13 December, just over a week after Gore had been accepted back into the Bristol Socialist Society, Sharland initiated a counter attack on the Bristol School Board by raising the claim of the alleged cruelty by the staff at Bristol's Truant School with the Bristol Trades Council. Sharland informed the Trades Council that a committee, led by Wilkins, had been set up to investigate these allegations. This committee, he said, had good reason to believe that for many years the Truant School, as part of its punishment regime, had inflicted 'systematic and excessive cruelties' on its pupils. These included: birching, caning the soles of the feet, excessive dumb-bell exercise, and insufficient regular food. The Wilkins' Committee also complained of

1. detention of boys over the proper time to cloak cruelty used towards them
2. boys being removed to the hospital and no communication being made with parents, also of boys being ill on the school premises without notification to parents
3. flogging by assistant masters and not in the presence of the head-master
4. degradation of boys by the continual flogging in an exposed condition in the presence of the school, tending to brutalise the lads
5. want of due care of the boys and so permanently injuring their constitution.[478]

Sharland told the Council that on finding evidence to support these allegations his committee had registered its concerns with Gore, the Chair of the Industrial Schools Committee responsible for monitoring the Truant School. Moreover, they had spoken to the Conservative Chair of the School Board, John Henry Woodward, who promised he would support a motion requesting a Government inquiry. This had not materialised; hence he could only conclude that Gore did not want it to happen because if the Industrial Schools Committee had consulted with 'the boys it could have had the charges corroborated.' He concluded that the School Board had side-stepped this option and simply 'passed a resolution that they would facilitate an inquiry but that they would not ask for one,' Sharland asserted it was thus a duty to 'heckle' every candidate in the forthcoming School Board election in order to ensure that the complaints were addressed.[479]

Before the matter was thrown open to discussion, Albert Vincent, the presiding Trades Council officer, reminded delegates that following the attack

478 *Western Daily Press*, 14 December 1894; *Bristol Mercury* 14 December 1894.
479 *Bristol Mercury*, 14 December 1894; *Western Daily Press*, 14 December 1894.

by the Dragoon Guards and Hussars on strikers and their supporters on 'Black Friday' Gore had, 'urged that no public body ought to be able to refuse a deputation.'[480] Then, after due consideration, the Trades Council passed a resolution calling for a Government inquiry over the running of the Truant School in Bristol concerning child cruelty allegations, and beckoned Bristol citizens to pressurise 'future [School Board] candidates to secure more humane treatment for the children.'[481]

At Christmas Enid Stacy returned home to Bristol, and in an attempt to 'reduce the tension' she held council with Gore and his friend, fellow socialist, and advisor, Edward Watson, and others.[482] While on the face of it the Jewish question had been settled, the animosity it had generated continued to fuel the differences between Gore and the Bristol Socialist Society. The conflict over the Truant School thus intensified an already turbulent situation; nothing that Stacy could say or do could alter that. The breach between Gore and his former comrades was irrevocable. It could not be covered over. Bryher described the split between Gore and the Bristol Socialist Society as so wide over the Jewish question and other matters that the Society 'withheld its support of his candidature' in the January 1895 School Board election.[483]

Gore's authoritarian views on maintaining a strong disciplinary regime within the Truant schools had been consistent and well known since he had been elected as Chair in 1892, and had been repeatedly reiterated. This suggests, as Bryher indicates, that as a result of an accumulation of differences Gore's relationship with the Bristol Socialist Society had already broken down. Gore's rash and excitable propensity to erupt quickly over issues without thinking through the consequences had often upset opponents. Now this aspect of his character, which contrasted with his logical legalistic brain, had alienated his former friends and allies.

The School Board election campaign brought matters to a head. Gore, who had recently moved out of his home at the Dings' Club to take up residence at 29 Barton Hill Road, St. Philip's, launched his candidature at a public meeting on 7 January. The Bristol Socialist Society members, John Sharland and William Petherick attended, putting awkward questions to Gore concerning his conduct in respect to dealing with allegations of cruelty at the Truant School. Also present was the secretary of the Bristol Trades Council, John Curle, who asked Gore to explain his justification for opposing the appointment of Rebecca

480 *Western Daily Press*, 14 December 1894.
481 *Bristol Mercury*, 14 December 1894.
482 Tuckett, 'Enid Stacy, The Nineteenth Century Political Radical and Activist for Peace, Social Justice and Women's Rights' (unpublished, edited edition: June 2012), p. 65, Working Class Library, Salford.
483 Bryher, *An Account of the Labour and Socialist Movement in Bristol,* Part 2, p. 55.

Wolfson as a pupil teacher. Gore simply restated the arguments he had already made. He knew he had supporters present.

After Gore had taken questions from the floor of the meeting, the twenty-eight year old Reverend Arthur H. Easton, formerly a curate at St. Francis, Ashton Gate, who was now in charge of the Mission Church, Bedminster Down, proposed unequivocal backing for Gore's candidature.[484] Easton, a Christian socialist, who earlier in the year had been adopted as vice-president of the Bristol branch of the Guild of St. Matthew,[485] and had spoken from a platform at the 1894 May Day demonstration in Victoria Park, had long been a friend of Gore and his brother Arthur. James Watts seconded Easton's resolution. Most notably, Ramsay MacDonald, who had maintained close links with Bristol through Enid Stacy, and was becoming a nationally known figure in the Independent Labour Party, spoke in support.[486] From Gore's perspective a difficult meeting had ended successfully in the passing of the resolution to back his candidature, albeit by a small majority.[487]

The next day the *Bristol Mercury* published a lengthy letter from John Sharland, expressing his belief that Gore, Woodward and Thomas had kept the particulars of the complaints made by his committee from the rest of the School Board members. Once again he provided the details of the allegations of cruelty and concluded with the following remark:

[I]t is an absolute duty on the part of the electorate to see they vote for no candidate who would preserve the present state of things or who have opposed or will oppose a Government inquiry.[488]

The same day, Tuesday 8 January, the Bristol Socialist Society, at its weekly meeting, pledged that as it was not standing a candidate in the School Board election it would not support any contender who was not committed either to the abolition of the Truant School or 'in favour of the board asking for a Government inquiry.'[489]

Gore responded to Sharland's letter to the *Bristol Mercury* with an equally lengthy one, tackling, in detail, the list of complaints and accusations it

484 *Bristol Mercury*, 8 January 1895.
485 Jones, *The Christian Socialist Revival 1877-1914: Religion, Class, and Social Conscience in Late-Victorian England*, p. 135, ftn. 82.
486 James Ramsay MacDonald to Enid Stacy, 1 December 1894, Angela Tuckett Papers, Working Class Movement Library, Salford, Manchester.
487 *Bristol Mercury*, 8 January 1895; *Western Daily Press*, 8 January 1895.
488 John Sharland to the Editor of the *Bristol Mercury*, 7 January 1895, *Bristol Mercury*, 8 January 1895.
489 *Western Daily Press*, 11 January 1895.

contained. Gore maintained that from the day in August 1894, when these complaints had been raised, he had challenged the Wilkins' committee to ask for a Government inquiry. But this it had failed to do. Gore restated the Board's position that they would facilitate any inquiry but would not initiate one. If the Wilkins' committee was confident in the veracity of their claims, he said, it could have approached the Home Office directly.[490]

Rather than go down this road, Wilkins decided to stand as an anti-truant school candidate in the School Board election. John Sharland threw his weight behind Wilkins, whose candidature had been accepted. On 14 January Wilkins outlined his position at a public meeting in St. Jude's. He hoped that after the elections a new School Board would see fit to abolish Bristol's Truant School.[491] On the following day the Bristol Trades Council and Labour Electoral Association introduced its nominee, Henry Jolliffe, the Amalgamated Carpenters and Joiners' Union delegate, who declared he would also support its closure. Frank Sheppard spoke in support of Jollife's candidature, as did another Bristol Socialist Society member, Jason O'Grady.[492] Petherick, who had challenged Gore's position on the Truant School at the candidature meeting, upped the anti-Gore rhetoric. In a letter to the *Western Daily Press* he said

> It would be interesting to me to know what body of citizens "asked" Mr Gore to stand, seeing that the Bristol Socialists…refused to again adopt him as a candidate, believing him to be entirely out of touch with them, inasmuch as he has misrepresented their principles on several occasions in the past'.[493]

Gore, in response, said that Petherick misinterpreted his position. He had not stated that a 'body of citizens' had asked him to stand. What he did say was that three long-standing socialists had nominated or seconded his candidature.[494]

Gore was not without allies. On 14 January a meeting of the Bedminster group of Bristol socialists, many of whom would have been miners, promised to do everything in their power to secure Gore's 'return at the head of the poll.'[495]

490 Hugh Holmes Gore to the Editor of the *Bristol Mercury*, 9 January 1895, *Bristol Mercury*, 11 January 1895.

491 *Bristol Mercury*, 15 January 1895.

492 *Western Daily Press*, 16 January 1895.

493 W. J. Petherick to the editor of the *Western Daily Press*, *Western Daily Press*, 15 January 1895.

494 Gore to the editor of the *Western Daily Press*, 16 January 1895, *Western Daily Press*, 17 January 1895.

495 *Western Daily Press*, 16 January 1895.

And, most significantly, Gore attracted qualified support from the Liberal *Western Daily Press*. In an editorial on 18 January, it backed Gore's actions in keeping the Truant School open believing that many Bristol citizens felt that he deserved some credit for his efforts.

> With regard to the Truant School, which has been the most debated point during this election, it should be possible – and according to Mr Gore's letter it has been possible – to effect improvements without closing a valuable institution…

> Many persons who do not agree with the Socialistic views of Mr Gore, and who regret a particular vote he gave at the Board recently, will yet be of the opinion that he deserves some sympathy in respect of the dead set made against him concerning the Truant School.[496]

The *Western Daily Press* seemed to be in touch with the mood of the voters who were not moved by claims of harsh treatment of truants. Gore topped the poll as an independent socialist with 15,442 votes. The labour candidate, Jolliffe, also did well however, capturing fourth place, out of a field of twenty-one contenders, with 13,868 votes. Wilkins trailed in nineteenth position with 5,651 votes, and, as a result, was one of the unsuccessful candidates.[497]

496 Editorial, *Western Daily Press*, 18 January 1895.
497 *Western Daily Press*, 21 January 1895.

Chapter 14

1895 Parliamentary By-Election in Bristol East

Within a couple of months Gore would be on the campaign trail again. The death on 5 March 1895 of the Liberal Member of Parliament (MP) for Bristol East, and Chairman of the Great Western Cotton Works, Sir Joseph Dodge Weston, who had represented constituents since 1890, triggered a by-election.[498] A heavily industrialised area, the Bristol East constituency had been a safe Liberal seat since it was created in 1885; and in 1890 Havelock Wilson, the Labour candidate, had failed to defeat Weston, trailing in third, after the Conservative James Inskip, with just 602 votes. In 1892 Weston had triumphed again, unopposed, as none of his political opponents, conservative, labour or socialist had even put forward a candidate to contest the seat.[499]

Against this backdrop, four days after Weston's death, a joint meeting was held between the executive committees of the Bristol Socialist Society and Bristol and District Trades Council Labour Electoral Association to consider the selection of a parliamentary candidate who could attract the support of both organisations. At this meeting several names were put forward as possible candidates. These included Gore who, surprisingly, was still an executive member of the Bristol Socialist Society and Tom Mann,[500] secretary of the Independent Labour Party, the new political party formed following the success of Keir Hardie, John Burns and Joseph Havelock Wilson in winning parliamentary seats in the 1892 General Election.

During the discussion that followed, it came to light that the 'hardheaded' E. H. (Harry) Jarvis,[501] assistant secretary of the Bristol branch of the Carpenters and Joiners' Union, had wired Keir Hardie, then Chair and leader of the Independent Labour Party, to see if Mann would be willing to contest the Bristol East seat. Hardie dismissed this possibility and inquired as to whether Gore 'was a likely candidate' and whether he would get the backing of the local labour movement.[502] Unbeknown to the Bristol Socialist Society and Bristol

498 Lyes, 'The 1895 By-Election in Bristol East', *Transactions*, Volume 130, pp. 279-293, is the only published account of this by-election.
499 Jordan, Ramsay and Woollard, *Abstract of Bristol Historical Statistics, Part 3: Political Representation and Bristol's Elections 1700-1997*, p. 201.
500 Minutes of the Joint Meeting of the Executive Committees of the Bristol Socialist Society and the Bristol and District Trades Council Labour Electoral Association, 9 March 1895.
501 Bryher's description in Bryher, *An Account of the Labour and Socialist Movement in Bristol*, Part 2, p. 51.
502 Letter from Hardie to Jarvis reported in Minutes of the Joint Meeting of the Executive Committees of the Bristol Socialist Society and Bristol and District Trades Council Labour Electoral Association, 9 March 1895.

and District Trades Council Labour Electoral Association, Gore had written to Hardie on 7 March saying he was confident of picking up some of the Liberal vote if he were to stand, and disclosed how he had already been assured support from the Liberal Unionist Party for his guarded antagonism to Irish Home Rule.[503]

This reversal of his previous position established for the first time that Gore now opposed Home Rule. It was a truly surprising turn-around; Gore was the secretary of the Guild of St. Matthew Bristol branch under Charles Marson's presidency, and the Guild advocated Home Rule.[504] Previously too, he had backed the demand for Irish Home Rule, protesting against Dillion's imprisonment under the Coercion Act in 1888. It had also featured in Whitefield's 1890, and Edwards' 1892, election manifestos, which Gore had helped to write. Intriguingly, a fictionalised reference to Gore's policy shift over Home Rule appears in the novel, *The Image Breakers*, written by his erstwhile Clifton and Bristol Christian Socialist comrade, Gertrude Dix. In her storyline she depicts how support for Home Rule among socialists was assumed and reflects on the incongruity of the sole socialist (a thinly disguised Gore) who opposed Home Rule 'and *he* was a Christian Socialist. It was just as though Christianity were bound to water things down somewhere.'[505]

Gore's political manoeuvring smacked of opportunism. However, it is doubtful that at the time the executive committees of the joint bodies, the Bristol Socialist Society and Bristol and District Trades Council Labour Electoral Association, would have been aware of the support he had secured from Liberal Unionists. Nevertheless, they still had little hesitation in saying to Hardie that 'they could not officially support' Gore, as he could not be trusted.[506] This suggests that the antagonism of past disputes went deeper than even the specific issues and constituted a visceral suspicion of Gore's whole mind-set. With the candidature question unresolved, the meeting between the executive committees of the joint bodies adjourned.

On Monday night, 11 March 1895, the two executive bodies resumed their talks and after considerable discussion they decided to invite Will Thorne,

503 Howell , *British Workers and the Independent Labour Party 1888-1906*, p. 387.
504 Sutcliffe, *The Keys of Heaven: The Life of Revd Charles Marson, Christian Socialist & Folksong Collector*, Kindle file, location, 3077.
505 Gertrude Dix, *The Image Breakers* (New York: Frederick A. Stokes, 1900), p. 351.
506 Minutes of the Joint Meeting of the Executive Committees of the Bristol Socialist Society and Bristol and District Trades Council Labour Electoral Association, 9 March 1895, Bristol Central Reference Library. Lyes, in 'The 1895 By-Election in Bristol East' reported that the joint meeting 'resolved that they would not run anyone for the seat except a *bona fide* Labour candidate and this would exclude Gore.' This was submitted as an amendment to the resolution to 'not officially support Gore.' but this amendment was lost.

General Secretary of the National Union of Gasworkers and General Labourers, to stand as their parliamentary candidate for Bristol East.[507] The next day, when the local secretary of the Gasworkers' union, Harold Brabham, relayed this invitation to Thorne, it yielded a swift but firm refusal. Brabham suspected 'there had been wire pulling going on, by someone amongst them.'[508] Gore clearly had powerful connections in the national leadership of the Independent Labour Party. A deputation was sent to London to see Thorne to try and persuade him to change his mind. While Thorne agreed to meet them and hear what they had to say, he was still resolute in withholding his consent, despite getting the nod from his Union Executive Committee that they would not stand in his way.[509]

The feeling at the Thursday 14 March joint meeting of the Bristol Socialist Society and the Bristol and District Trades Council Labour Electoral Association was a growing sense that some behind-the-scenes shenanigans were going on concerning the selection process of a suitable labour candidate. However, Thorne and the National Organiser of the Gasworkers' Union, Pete Curran, who had also been invited to stand, denied that their decision to decline was 'influenced by interested parties outside.'[510] Curran, an Independent Labour Party member, had been based in Bristol in the early 1890s and had gained the respect of Bristol trade unionists before he left to become a National Organiser.[511]

When Gore, as a member of the Executive Committee of the Bristol Socialist Society, presented himself at the conjoined Thursday meeting he was asked to leave because of a conflict of interest. At first he resisted, but he reluctantly agreed to withdraw following the intervention of the guest speaker, Fred Brocklehurst, secretary of the Labour Church in Manchester, and a leading member of the Independent Labour Party.[512]

Once Gore had left the meeting the London deputation reported that having met with some Independent Labour Party members, including Hardie, and asking them if they had approached Gore on the candidacy, any such approach was firmly denied. This disclaimer did little to stop the growing suspicion that

507 Minutes of the Adjourned (9 March) Meeting of the Executive Committees of the Bristol Socialist Society and Bristol and District Trades Council Labour Electoral Association, 11 March 1895.

508 Minutes of the Joint Meeting of the Executive Committees of the Bristol Socialist Society and Bristol and District Trades Council Labour Electoral Association, 12 March 1895.

509 Minutes of the Joint Meeting of the Executive Committees of the Bristol Socialist Society and Bristol and District Trades Council Labour Electoral Association, 14 March 1895.

510 Minutes of the Joint Meeting of the Executive Committees of the Bristol Socialist Society and Bristol and District Trades Council Labour Electoral Association, 14 March 1895.

511 *Western Daily Press*, 14 July 1891.

512 Minutes of the Joint Meeting of the Executive Committees of the Bristol Socialist Society and Bristol and District Trades Council Labour Electoral Association, 14 March 1895.

outsiders were secretly backing Gore to stand. Pressure to nominate Gore, however, began to mount. A deputation from the Bristol East Ratepayers' Association arrived at the meeting expressing its desire to co-operate 'in seeking the return of a Labour Candidate' naming Gore as its favoured nominee.[513]

After this deputation had left, Brocklehurst admitted that while there had been no communication between Gore and the Independent Labour Party as a Party, Hardie had corresponded personally with Gore over the Bristol East by-election. Having cleared the air, Brocklehurst relayed a message he had brought from Hardie. It said that in order to gain support from the Bristol Socialist Society and Bristol and District Trades Council Labour Electoral Association for Gore's candidature, Hardie would be willing to

> sign an agreement to the effect that he [Gore] would abide by the decision of the Local Labour Party [an alternative name given to the joint bodies of the Bristol Socialist Society and Bristol and District Trades Council Labour Electoral Association] and give way to their nominee whosoever he be, at the next General Election.[514]

Unsurprisingly, given that at best Hardie had been disingenuous over his contact with Gore in regard to the forthcoming Bristol East by-election, the meeting rejected the offer and expressed a united and categorical opposition to 'any recognition of H. H. Gore as a Labour candidate for Bristol East.'[515]

Despite the outright rejection of Gore's candidature, Brocklehurst left the meeting on friendly terms conveying that 'as far as the Independent Labour Party were concerned the matter was ended, as they would not run any candidate who had not got the support of the Local Labour Party'.[516] The meeting closed with the decision that under no circumstances would they support Gore, and regretted that they could find no candidate to run for Labour. By Saturday 16 March, however, relations between the local Labour Party in Bristol, and the Independent Labour Party, and its President, Keir Hardie, were coming under severe strain. Unconfirmed reports emerged that Hardie was in fact intending to run Gore as an Independent Labour Party candidate in the Bristol by-election.

513 Minutes of the Joint Meeting of the Executive Committees of the Bristol Socialist Society and Bristol and District Trades Council Labour Electoral Association, 14 March 1895.
514 Minutes of the Joint Meeting of the Executive Committees of the Bristol Socialist Society and Bristol and District Trades Council Labour Electoral Association, 14 March 1895.
515 Minutes of the Joint Meeting of the Executive Committees of the Bristol Socialist Society and Bristol and District Trades Council Labour Electoral Association, 14 March 1895.
516 Minutes of the Joint Meeting of the Executive Committees of the Bristol Socialist Society and Bristol and District Trades Council Labour Electoral Association, 14 March 1895.

In response the Bristol Socialist Society and Bristol and District Trades Council Labour Electoral Association met on Saturday 16 March to discuss the matter. They decided to adopt the Chairman of the Trades Union Congress Parliamentary committee and President of the Amalgamated Weavers' Association, David Holmes, as their candidate provided he could find the money to run his campaign. This was a clear sign of desperation, as Holmes was well known for his anti-socialistic views.[517] The Bristol Socialist Society Executive had severe reservations about this choice, but they went along with it for the sake of unity. At this crucial juncture, and timed to perfection, Gore, supported by Independent Labour Party member, Samuel (known as Sam) Hobson, arrived at the meeting to try, once again, to secure a compromise that would enable him to run for the Bristol East seat as the local Labour candidate.[518]

The decision taken by the meeting to invite Holmes to contest this seat was immediately relayed to Gore, who, somewhat irritated, explained that he had been given to understand that a suitable candidate could not be found and, therefore, following an approach 'by certain persons' he had agreed to stand. Since he had incurred considerable expense in preparation for fighting the election, if the conjoined committees wanted him to withdraw he gave notice that he would want compensation for the money spent or losses incurred. He insisted that they let him know their decision by six o'clock the following evening. Before retiring from the meeting Hobson appealed to those present to think again on the basis 'that they [Independent Labour Party] would take no part [in the election] whatever against the expressed wish of the conjoined committees.'[519]

To complicate matters further, it materialised the next day that the Bristol Trades Council and Labour Electoral Association executive member, William G. Renwick, an insurance agent, had directed the request for money to support Holmes' candidature to Sir William Henry Houldsworth, Conservative MP for Manchester North West, and Chairman of the Bimetallic League.[520] Renwick was a supporter of Bimetallism as a remedy for industrial depression.[521] This

517 See, for instance the *Hull Daily Mail*, 18 September 1890; *Burnley Express*, 12 September and 3 November 1894.

518 Minutes of the Joint Meeting of the Executive Committees of the Bristol Socialist Society and Bristol and District Trades Council Labour Electoral Association, 16 March 1895.

519 Minutes of the Joint Meeting of the Executive Committees of the Bristol Socialist Society and Bristol and District Trades Council Labour Electoral Association, 16 March 1895.

520 The League's aim was to establish international bimetallism that was to adopt the same mint ratio between gold and silver internationally, each country to convert its currency into specified amounts of gold and silver. See *Manchester Courier and Lancashire General Advertiser*, 4 May 1895 for Sir W. H. Houldsworth argument for adopting bimetallism standards.

521 *Western Daily Press*, 23 April 1895 and 19 September 1895.

development compelled the conjoined committee to write to Holmes explaining that they were withdrawing their invitation to him to contest the Bristol East seat and why they had done so. It seemed that Hobson knew of this development, and considerable concern was expressed that someone from the conjoined committees had leaked this information to him. The situation was left on the tacit understanding that all parties, including the Independent Labour Party, would remain neutral in respect to Gore standing as an independent socialist.[522]

On 19 March Gore, with the Unionist vote in mind, submitted his nomination as an independent Unionist-socialist candidate for Bristol East. Notably, Harold Brabham, who had just a day or so before supported Gore's exclusion as a candidate, jumped ship. He had been one of Gore's proposers, and it came to light that Brabham was the insider who had informed Gore of the Bristol Socialist Society and Bristol and District Trades Council Labour Electoral Association deliberations on the selection of a candidate over the previous week.[523] He, along with Gore's other proposer, the miners' agent, William Whitefield, was to be an invaluable ally in the election campaign.

Gore had issued his manifesto to the Bristol East electorate on the previous day. His programme included shorter working hours; higher wages; a local public works programme to help alleviate unemployment; provision for old age by pensions or other means; more adequate inspection of mines, factories, and work shops; nationalisation of the railways; full suffrage for everyone, subject to qualification by age; the disestablishment of the Welsh Church and an inquiry established to look into its revenues and endowments;[524] the abolition of the hereditary principle in the House of Lords; a generous measure of local government for Ireland, but not Home Rule; opposition to compulsory vaccination; municipalisation of the drink traffic; and opposition to the Local Veto Bill, which earned him the label of being a friend of the drink trade.[525] This was the Bill he had supported previously, when acting as Edwards' election agent in the 1892 Dover parliamentary election. Its object was to allow the majority of the local ratepayers in a locality to control the drink trade in their area. The Bill proposed to allow ten per cent of local inhabitants to demand a ballot on whether there would be a total prohibition or a reduction of the

522 Minutes of the Joint Meeting of the Executive Committees of the Bristol Socialist Society and Bristol and District Trades Council Labour Electoral Association, 17 March 1895.

523 Minutes of the Joint Meeting of the Executive Committees of the Bristol Socialist Society and Bristol and District Trades Council Labour Electoral Association, 23 March 1895.

524 Disestablishment of the Welsh Church would have required the Church in Wales be reconstituted as a separate ecclesiastical province.

525 Western Daily Press, 18 and 19 March 1895; Bristol Mercury, 18 March 1895; Lyes, 'The 1895 By-Election in Bristol East', Transactions, Volume 130 (The Bristol & Gloucestershire Archaeological Society: 2012), p. 286.

number of alcohol-sellers by the suppression of licences.[526] The idea behind the Bill was to reduce through legislative means the amount of alcohol consumed by the working class.

Eighteen months later, Gore explained the rationale underpinning his contentious position on the licensed drink trade, in the 1895 by-election, at the Church Congress held in Shrewsbury in October 1896. Gore had little sympathy with the temperance cause. He argued that

> [t]he public-house is today the centre of social intercourse for the great body of Englishmen; it is there that we find such fellowship as exists among the great working classes. We want to illuminate that fellowship with the Holy Ghost. Centuries back our forefathers in the Church controlled the public-house, the house to which we all had access; but gradually the modern public-house has usurped the place formerly occupied by the hospice or clergy-house. We have got to recover our possession of the public-house, make it a centre of our work, and not ignoring or being actively hostile towards it, but meeting it in a friendly spirit, find that through it we may enable some to realise their duties as Churchmen.[527]

However, as Gore well knew, in 1895 there was a less lofty, if convenient element in his stance on the drink trade and Home Rule. The two issues were attractive to both Tory and Liberal Unionist voters. The Conservatives were not contesting the seat, whilst his opponent, the Liberal candidate, Sir William Henry Wills, was not a Unionist and supported Irish Home Rule.[528] Gore prioritised social reforms in his propaganda asking east Bristol workers 'to sink their politics and vote for the candidate who looked upon the unemployed and other social problems as of greater importance than Home Rule or Welsh disestablishment.'[529]

Wills' campaigning strength was his past experience as an MP in Coventry from 1880-85, the reputation of his family business, the tobacco company W.D. & H. O. Wills, as a good employer (it operated an eight-hour day, the first firm in Bristol to do so, and paid an annual bonus to its employees), and his

---

526 *The Spectator*, 13 April 1895; J. Greenaway, 'United Kingdom Alliance (UKA)' in J. S. Blocker, D. M. Fahey and R. Tyrrell (eds.) *Alcohol and temperance in Modern History: An International Encyclopedia* (Santa Barbara, California: ABC-CLIO eBook: 2003), pp. 627-8.
527 Text from a speech made by Hugh Holmes Gore in *The Official Report of the Church Congress, held at Shrewsbury, October 1896* (London: Bemrose and Sons: 1896), p. 115.
528 Lyes, 'The 1895 By-Election in Bristol East', *Transactions*, Volume 130, p. 289.
529 *Western Daily Press*, 21 March 1895.

unerring support for Home Rule.[530] He also supported votes for women based on property qualifications and unlike Gore he backed the Local Veto Bill.

The election campaign took place just a week or so after the imposition of a national lockout of boot and shoe workers, which in the Bristol area affected around 1,600 union hands and thousands of non-unionists employed by forty manufacturers belonging to the Kingswood Association of Boot Manufacturers, as well as manufacturers located in east and central Bristol.[531] The lockout quickly became one of the key issues in the by-election. The employers took this action in order to break the National Union of Boot and Shoe Operatives' opposition to the abolition of piecework and the introduction of time rates and team working. Employers demanded changes to traditional payment methods, along with organisational changes such as team working, in order to extract greater productive effort from their investment in new machinery.[532] It was an industrial war in which the employers were seeking greater control over the labour process. Victory for the employers would have also inflicted a defeat on the socialists, who had established a significant foothold in the Union. Hobson, who, along with Brocklehurst and Enid Stacy, had put his energy into propagating the Independent Labour Party's socialist position to boot and shoe workers across the country, argued that the employers, many of whom were Liberals, looked on 'the Socialist-Labour movement with a bitter hatred. They are fighting because the National Union of Boot and Shoe Operatives is a Socialist society.'[533]

In Bristol the union certainly had leaders sympathetic to socialism. William Knew, the President of the Bristol Branch of National Union of Boot and Shoe Operatives, was a member of the Bristol Socialist Society; and among the proposers and seconders of Gore's nomination were John Hallaran, the local secretary of the Kingswood Branch of the Union, and John Caines its president. On 18 March around 6,000 to 7,000 of their members and supporters, as well as Bristol operatives, gave a warm reception to Gore when he spoke at their demonstration in Kingswood, during which he took the opportunity to promote his candidature for Bristol East.[534]

The boot and shoe lockout allowed Gore to annul the opinion expounded by his opponents that the interests of capital and labour were as one, and call

530 Lyes, 'The 1895 By-Election in Bristol East', *Transactions*, Volume 130, p. 283-4.
531 *Western Daily Press*, 11 March 1895; *Bristol Mercury*, 18 March 1895.
532 For a full account of this dispute see E. Brunner, 'The Origins of Industrial Peace: The Case of the British Boot and Shoe Industry', Oxford Economic Papers, New Series, Vol. 1, No. 2 (June, 1949), pp. 247-259.
533 "The Boot War', *The Labour Leader*, 13 April 1895, cited in Howell, *British Workers and the Independent Labour Party 1888-1906*, p. 103.
534 *Western Daily Press*, 19 March 1895; *Bristol Mercury*, 19 March 1895.

upon workers to think 'whether or not they would for ever send to Parliament from east Bristol representatives who represented capital instead of workers?'[535] Enid Stacy spoke with passion and fervour at public campaign meetings, moving workers to support Gore 'in a straight fight between one capitalist and one representative of labour, with no other issues thrown in, and no straight three-cornered fight.'[536]

Other key speakers that came to Bristol to electioneer on Gore's behalf included Tom Mann, Keir Hardie, Ramsay MacDonald and Sam Hobson. Local speakers included the Reverend Easton, Brabham, Whitefield and Dr Cunningham, a representative of the Bristol East Ratepayers' Association, who presided at a meeting in an east Bristol School in support of Gore's candidature. The gathering was so large that an 'overflow' meeting was quickly arranged and held outside afterwards.[537] Many of Gore's supporters provided assistance during the campaign including J. J. Hamilton, a Fabian activist and secretary of the Wiltshire Agricultural Labourers' Association.[538]

Gore, the ever-astute politician, as well as securing solid support from boot and shoe workers, attracted the backing of the electoral committee of licensed victuallers. The committee welcomed Gore's pledge to vote against the Local Veto Bill and his opposition to Sunday closing, and placed advertisements in the local press calling for all those in the licensed trade 'to vote and work for Mr Hugh Holmes Gore'.[539] Fearing closures of local public houses the licensed victuallers' district agent, A. J. Harris, distributed notices that were displayed in most public houses appealing to working men 'Vote for Gore, who will oppose all teetotal tyranny and injustice.'[540]

On 19 March, at an open-air meeting outside the Lysaghts' Galvanising works in St. Philip's, Gore dismissed the rumour circulating that his campaign was funded by Church money as a disgrace and the charge that he was a Tory in disguise as nonsense. And responding to a question concerning his position on adult suffrage he 'declared himself in favour of manhood suffrage and the payment of members' and 'in favour of women who were rated having votes but he did not believe in any property qualification for man or woman.'[541]

Ostensibly standing as an independent socialist candidate, Gore received a rapturous welcome when Tom Mann introduced him at a packed gathering at Barton Hill on the evening of 19 March. Later, Tom Mann told the meeting

535 *Western Daily Press*, 19 March 1895.
536 *Western Daily Press*, 19 March 1895.
537 *Western Daily Press*, 19 March 1895.
538 *The Times*, 22 March 1895.
539 *Bristol Mercury*, 19 March 1895; *Western Daily Press*, 19 March 1895.
540 *Western Daily Press*, 22 March 1895
541 *Western Daily Press*, 20 March 1895.

that he 'rejoiced' at being connected to the Independent Labour Party and announced that an Independent Labour Party branch had been formed in Bristol East that very night, implying that a vote for Gore was also a vote for the Independent Labour Party.[542] The following day Gore's campaign team was greeted enthusiastically at eleven well-attended meetings held in the constituency. And on the night of the election Enid Stacy reported that hundreds of children displaying a portrait of Gore in their caps paraded the streets chanting '"Vote for Gore," "Good old Gore,"' ... 'with a terribly intimidating effect!'[543]

Following the closing of voting stations, the count proceeded and it soon became evident that Gore and Wills were running neck and neck. Gore was with family 'quietly supping with his mother' when he was called in.[544] 'Excitement was intense, Sir William Henry Wills looking as red as a turkey cock. Everyone was on the tip-toe of expectancy!'[545] In fact at one point the Liberals thought they had lost. Enid Stacy witnessed this moment:

> Just before the declaration of the poll I was sitting in the room next to the counting room, among the friends of Sir W. H. Wills. They thought Gore was in and ascribed it "to the present most unfortunate dispute in the boot trade, which had temporarily demoralised the men": whereat I smole [stole] a smile.[546]

However, Gore failed by a whisker to get elected: His opponent William Henry Wills won with 3,740 votes to Hugh Holmes Gore's 3,558, a Liberal majority of 182. When the result was first announced Gore was thought to have received 3,608 votes but 50 spoilt papers had inadvertently been included. Gore, nonetheless, claimed a moral victory for socialism. Measured by any standards for a political outsider to come so close to winning was an amazing achievement, and the 'enthusiasm that followed was intense.'[547]

There were between fifteen and twenty thousand people waiting at the polling station, Gore's supporters being in the majority. After his opponent, Wills, had driven away in a horse and carriage and the singing of the *Marseillaise* had died down, Gore addressed his supporters. He exclaimed that 'never before

---

542 *Western Daily Press*, 20 March 1895.

543 Enid Stacy, 'The Bristol East Election', *The* Clarion, 30 March, 1895; Paul Stacy, in the *Labour Prophet*, May 1895, IV, 41.

544 This is the one piece of evidence found that despite the fact that his mother was not a socialist, and moreover a member of the Bristol and Clifton Total Abstinence Society, she was at hand to support her son at such an important time.

545 *The Labour Leader*, 6 April 1895, p. 2.

546 Enid Stacy, 'The Bristol East Election', *The Clarion*, 30 March 1895.

547 Enid Stacy, 'The Bristol East Election', *The Clarion*, 30 March 1895.

in parliamentary annals would they find that workers themselves had managed to find no fewer than 3,600 votes'. He concluded his speech with the words 'East Bristol properly belonged to labour, and labour's it should be', which was greeted by loud cheers.[548] He was then carried shoulder high by his supporters, including his friend William Whitefield, to Lawrence Hill, several hundred yards away, where further speeches were made.[549] The tour through the Bristol East ward continued to St. George, Hanham and Kingswood. After such a long day Gore's devotees insisted on escorting him home. He was put in a carriage, along with Enid Stacy. The horses were unhitched

> and for over two miles, without stop or stay, the carriage was pulled through St. George's down to St. Philip's. If ever the practice was excusable it was then. Here were no factory hands pulling their master to his West End residence, but electors dragging their fellow elector and co-worker down to his own home among them.[550]

Gore was cheered all the way with cries of '"Next Time Mr Gore!" "No more capitalists for East Bristol!"[551]

The closeness of the vote came as a shock to the Liberals and the local press. They were quick to claim, however, that the Tories and Liberal Unionist electors had turned out to vote for Gore, which almost swung the election his way. Commentators in the press argued that Gore's popularity, earned through his commitment to philanthropic undertakings, educational work, running the Dings' Boys' club, and support for workers in struggle, rather than his socialism, accounted for his extraordinary good showing in only missing victory by a marginal amount.[552]

Immediately after the election Gore sent a resignation letter to the Bristol Socialist Society notifying them that he wanted his name removed from the Society's membership list. They gladly approved.[553] On Sunday 24 March he travelled to London to fulfil a commitment he had made to the Christian Social Union to deliver a lecture entitled 'The Unskilled Labourer' at the Parish Hall, Sloane Square. He used the occasion to raise concerns over poor working conditions and their social impact on the unskilled working class. He stressed the fact that in contrast to the skilled artisan their pay was poor and their work precarious. Yet, he added, their labour 'requires, if not technical skill, a power

548 *Western Daily Press*, 22 March 1895.
549 *The Labour Leader*, 6 April 1895.
550 Enid Stacy, 'The Bristol East Election', *The Clarion*, 30 March 1895.
551 Enid Stacy, 'The Bristol East Election', *The Clarion*, 30 March 1895.
552 *Bristol Mercury*, 23 March 1895.
553 Minutes of the Executive Committee of the Bristol Socialist Society, 26 March 1895.

of physical endurance.' They do necessary work and form the largest class in the community. For those in employment after a long tiring day

> he(*sic*) returns home to a tenement of two or three rooms with no quiet, no privacy: a wife probably irritated by the constant worry of household cares, and the continuous necessity of looking after the children.[554]

Gore went on to tell his audience that for recreation the unskilled had three choices, a workman's club, the public house and hanging about the streets, and of these choices the public house offered the most agreeable atmosphere for this class of workers, but their hard-earned money is soon transferred from their pockets to the tills of the brewers.

Although Gore's remarks resonated with his audience, his remedy was unclear. On the one hand he intimated that people of a higher social status must take responsibility to encourage the non-craft worker 'to improve his conditions' and 'teach him self-respect', and on the other warned that they must go among the unskilled 'with the desire to learn, not to teach. The rich have much to learn from the workers.' Given the socialist orientation of his audience, in all probability the call for people to take responsibility and encourage and teach workers to stand on their own feet was, in part, an indirect appeal to trade unions to organise the unskilled, enabling them to act collectively and increase their chances of securing better working conditions through their own efforts, which in turn would raise their self-esteem.[555]

Just over a week later, back in Bristol, the fallout between Gore's supporters and the rest of the local labour movement over him running as a candidate in the by-election continued. A large contingent of the Bristol Socialist Society in Bedminster, strong backers of Gore, left to form a branch of the Independent Labour Party.[556] More resignations followed. Paul Stacy gave notice of withdrawal. His sister, Enid, wrote to the Bristol Socialist Society, threatening to quit the Society if it did not disassociate itself from Robert Weare's characterisation of the selection contest, which had led to Gore standing as a candidate, as 'a dirty job'.

Subsequently she did resign from the Socialist Society, not because of Weare's comments, which she was to learn had not been endorsed by the Society, but for its strong condemnation of Hardie, Mann, Hobson, and other members of the Independent Labour Party in

554 *The Labour Leader*, 30 March 1895, p. 5.
555 *The Labour Leader*, 30 March 1895, p. 5.
556 Minutes of the Executive Committee of the Bristol Socialist Society, 2 April 1895.

that their action [in supporting Gore's candidature in opposition to the decision of the joint bodies of the Bristol Socialist Society and the Bristol Trades Council and Labour Electoral Association] was both mean and despicable, and calculated to injure, and bring the Socialist Movement into contempt.'[557]

This she thought was a bit rich coming from an organisation colluding with others in 'negotiating with such an antagonist to Socialism as David Holmes' with a view to him standing as a candidate in the Bristol East by-election.[558]

This was not the end of the matter. At the Bristol Trades Council meeting, held on 4 April 1895, Herbert Spencer, a Trades Council delegate, publicly accused Gore of receiving financial support for his election campaign from the Bristol North Liberal Unionist, Arthur Lee.[559] This Lee denied unequivocally,[560] leading Spencer to withdraw his allegation, only to add that if the money did not come from this source, the Independent Labour Party or any local organisation, then it must have been 'furnished by the enemy', a veiled reference to the Conservative Party.[561]

Spencer continued to attack Gore. At a previous meeting the Trades Council had decided to accept an invitation from the Guild of St. Matthew to join in a Labour Day service at St. Thomas' Church in central Bristol. Spencer proposed that the Council rescind this decision. He argued that the action of the leading Guild members, Gore and Paul Stacy, 'had been unworthy of men claiming to be in sympathy with the Labour movement.'[562] He condemned Gore's connection with the formation of a branch of the Independent Labour Party in Bristol.[563] Due to the shortage of time to fully discuss the issue, the matter was adjourned until the next meeting. On 18 April the deferred debate was reopened. After some harsh words, Spencer's motion to rescind the invitation from the Guild of St. Matthew was put the meeting and adopted by 25 votes to 17.[564]

Quick to exploit Gore's by-election 'success', the Independent Labour Party established an east Bristol Branch (No. 1). At a general meeting of the branch,

557 Minutes of the Special Monthly Meeting of the Bristol Socialist Society, 2 April 1895; Minutes of the Executive Committee of the Bristol Socialist Society, 23 April 1895.
558 Minutes of the Special Monthly Meeting of the Bristol Socialist Society, 2 April 1895.
559 *Bristol Mercury*, 5 April 1895. Mistakenly, the report names Herbert Spencer as Herbert Stacy. A later report, *Bristol Mercury* 19 April, refers correctly to Herbert Spencer.
560 *Bristol Mercury*, 5 April 1895.
561 *Bristol Mercury*, 19 April 1895.
562 *Bristol Mercury*, 5 April 1895.
563 *Western Daily Press*, 5 April 1895.
564 *Bristol Mercury,* 19 April 1895.

held at the Dings' Club on 23 April, Gore was elected as president; Richard Thomas Daniel, vice-president; John Walker, treasurer; Paul Stacy, secretary; Ted Childs, assistant secretary; and Frank Mills, financial secretary. Tapping into the Gore's near success at the by-election, the east Bristol Independent Labour Party branch decided to take a contraposition to the Trades Council and accept the invitation from the Guild of St. Matthew to attend a Labour Day service at St. Thomas' Church. From Gore's perspective, this provided some welcome publicity for the Guild of St. Matthew and Christian socialism.[565]

As the excitement of the closely fought election died down, however, Gore began to question the degree of progress socialists had made. Socialists, he thought, placed too much store in expounding 'what the Socialist state will be, and how it differs from the present commercial anarchy', never stopping to consider whether the people were ready and prepared to consciously accept 'the wisdom, even the necessity of its accomplishment.'[566] While socialists were prepared to embark on the journey towards the ideal state, little attention had been paid to whether the masses were ready to follow; it was just assumed that they would.

One of the lessons that Gore drew from his narrow defeat in the parliamentary by-election was that the socialist consciousness of individuals needed to be developed in order 'to prepare and equip the army of Labour for its journey' to the Promised Land. Socialists, he contended, had a tendency to detach themselves from the realities of everyday human experiences. 'We have kept ourselves aloof from the anti-social sinner in our own economic bethel.'[567] Gore advocated that rather than standing aloof and preaching to the masses, socialists should engage with them in all their activities, recreational, work, and even with those in the army, navy and reserve forces to win them over to socialism. He concluded that it would be a long slow mission, but his time spent looking after a boys' club had shown him that while

> it is as hard to help ten boys to become good Socialist citizens as to give five years to street preaching … I am firmly convinced it is greater to have infused into even five boys the spirit of Human Brotherhood than to win a seat in the name of Socialism in the Imperial Legislature.[568]

However, the short but demanding election campaign, the recriminations that followed, his estrangement from former comrades, and the establishment

565 *Bristol Mercury*, 25 April and 2 May 1895.
566 *The Labour Prophet*, Vol. IV. No.41, May 1895.
567 *The Labour Prophet*, Vol. IV. No.41, May 1895.
568 *The Labour Prophet*, Vol. IV. No.41, May 1895.

of Independent Labour Party branches in Bristol, took its toll on Gore's health, despite the exhilaration he must have felt in almost gaining a surprise victory. Within a couple of months of resuming his 'normal duties' his doctor ordered him to take an immediate rest from work. His brother Arthur took a break from his stage career and kindly stepped in to cover his commitments in court.

Chapter 15

Retreat and Ill-Health

The deterioration in Gore's health coincided with the infamous trials of Oscar Wilde. Incensed by his son's love affair with the playwright, the Marquis of Queensbury, John Douglas, denounced Wilde as a 'Sodomite'. Wilde sued him for libel, lost, and, having spurned chances to escape to the continent, was arrested and charged with gross indecency. After two trials, he was convicted and sentenced to two years hard labour. Following the first trial, the Christian socialist, and affirmed ritualist, Stewart Headlam, posted bail for Wilde. Not only did this action provide Headlam's enemies with ammunition against him personally, it also cast a slur upon the Anglo-Catholic Guild of St. Matthew which he had founded.[569] Innuendo persistently linked radical Anglo-Catholicism with an effete masculinity, which was equated with homosexuality.

The publicity around the Wilde case fed into an anxiety about masculine vigour within mainstream middle class culture. It also made the homosexual the scapegoat for a visceral loathing of the effeminate idleness and immorality of the leisure-class.[570] Both of these crude assumptions held the potential to threaten Gore who was already vulnerable. His views, combined with his scornful irascibility, laid him open to exposure from his political and professional enemies. Up to this time Gore had successfully camouflaged his homosexuality. Now, even though he did not fit the stereotypical image of the homosexual as fop, associated with the decadent aestheticism, which was part of Wilde's pose, he would have found himself in a situation of heightened danger. The shock of Wilde's conviction, combined with the moral panic surrounding the sentence, must have caused Gore apprehension and anxiety. Gore drew great satisfaction from his ability to protect his high standard of honour, an image which was key to his popularity with the voters. Moreover, he cherished the respect he had gained from the boys in the Dings' Club. Fear of exposure must have jolted him out of his customary confident complacency and checked that outward expression of optimism, which had been sustained by his popularity. The fallout from the Wilde trial fatally undermined the psychological buoyancy that had characterised his public commitment.

According to Enid Stacy's niece, the Communist solicitor, Angela Tuckett, the threats that Gore confronted were explicit, as well as implicit. She writes

569 Orens, *Stewart Headlam's Radical Anglicanism: The Mass, The Masses and the Music Hall*, p. 118.

570 A. Sinfield, *The Wilde Century, Effeminacy, Oscar Wilde and the Queer Moment* (New York: Columbia University Press, 1994), pp. 43-45, 68.

that in the weeks following Gore's near success in the by-election at the end of March 1895, some of his enemies started to exploit the public paranoia about 'deviant' sexual behaviour and 'point a finger at a popular socialist activist in a sensitive professional position.'[571] While such allegations never surfaced in the local or national press, there is no doubt that such accusations would have seriously troubled Gore.

In June, Gore pulled out of some important engagements, presumably because of poor health. Towards the end of the month the local press confirmed that Gore had been 'laid aside by illness'.[572] In early July he was scheduled to be one of the volunteer captains on the children's summer camp at Barton,[573] but his malaise forced him to withdraw, though his sister, Caroline, attended the girl's camp as deputy superintendent.[574] It had become clear that because of his weak disposition he would not be able to contest the July parliamentary election for the Independent Labour Party, which was a serious setback for them. In the July edition of *The Labour Leader*, the Party expressed its concern over Gore's well being, placing the blame on the conduct of some Bristol socialists:

> We are all grieved to hear that Hugh Holmes Gore, the candidate for East Bristol, has completely broken down in health. Nervous prostration followed his gallant contest of a few months past, and he is now on the continent looking for his lost health. A man of sensitive temperament, he was deeply hurt by the cruel and insensate calumnies heaped upon him by the Bristol Socialists, whilst they were charging him with obtaining Tory money (they having agreed to support a man who would run on Liberal and Bimetallism money) he was meeting his election charges mainly out of his own pocket. He was too delicate to blazon it abroad. I [Anon.] can personally testify that Hugh Holmes was deeply hurt at the way his whilom comrades turned upon him and tried to rend him.[575]

Gore had travelled to Bern in Switzerland to convalesce. Sam Hobson stepped in to fill the void, but could not muster the local support that Gore had received in the March by-election and was easily beaten by Wills who received 4,129 votes to Hobson's 1,874. Elsewhere no Independent Labour

571 Tuckett, 'Enid Stacy, The Nineteenth Century Political Radical and Activist for Peace, Social Justice and Women's Rights' (unpublished, edited edition: June 2012), p. 65, footnote 9, Working Class Library, Salford.
572 *Bristol Mercury*, 26 June 1895.
573 *Bristol Mercury*, 14 May 1895.
574 *Bristol Mercury*, 8 July 1895.
575 'Our London Letter', East Bristol, *The Labour Leader*, 6 July 1895, p. 3.

Party candidates were returned in this General Election. However, given Gore's local popularity and his showing a few months before, if he were to have run the result in Bristol East might have been a much closer affair.

Gore's poor health continued to be of concern, although he resumed his public and private work at the end of July. His doctor, however, advised him to curtail his public work. His diagnosis was that prolonged mental stress had left Gore physically and mentally exhausted. A decade of constant activism, running a solicitors' practice, and a demanding work schedule had taken its toll. Reluctant to give up his educational and philanthropic activities, he decided not to seek re-election to the Town Council in November, a position he had held since winning the South St Philip's seat in 1889.[576]

Gore's response to the impact of severe stress was to go into retreat both physically and psychologically. Moving out of his home in the heavily populated and deprived working class area of Barton Hill, he took up residence at Avon House, near Shirehampton, then a small village overlooking the banks of the river Avon, five miles from the centre of Bristol. Unlike the overcrowded back-to-back dwellings of Barton Hill, his new home had a coachhouse, a stable and a garden and was conveniently close to a railway station. Gore sought solitude in this quiet settlement in an attempt to get away from the sources of his depression.

By September signs of improvement in Gore's health were evident. Feeling fit enough to carry on in what he loved to do, he took on the position of honorary secretary of the Bristol Rugby Union, and resumed refereeing rugby matches on a regular basis.[577] Nevertheless, he stuck to his decision not to contest the South St. Philip's seat again, despite being pressed to do so. In his place the Independent Labour Party East Bristol Branch selected its vice-president, Richard Daniel, as its candidate to stand in the November municipal election. Once again lack of unity between the Socialist and labour organisations left the Independent Labour Party to run its candidate alone.[578] Daniel, an insurance agent, trailed in third place with 270 votes behind James Smith Naish, the Independent Conservative candidate, who won the seat with 612 votes and the Liberal, Albert Essey with 479 votes.[579] Labour did not regain this seat until 1911, and then it only held on to it for just one year. It was not until after World War One that Labour would prove capable of retaining it for a sustained period of time.

576 *Western Daily Press*, 23 August 1895.
577 This information was gleaned from sports' reports in the local press, for instance see the *Bristol Mercury*, 16 November 1895 and the *Western Daily Press*, 30 December 1895.
578 Bryher, *An Account of the Labour and Socialist Movement in Bristol*, Part 2, p. 63.
579 *Western Daily Press*, 2 November 1895.

While Gore cut back on his political commitments signs of stress and depression were still present. He seemed unable to stay away from controversy. During November, he became involved in a minor spat over the commercialisation of rugby, venting his contempt for the 'theatrical exhibition' and 'acrobatic performances' of the Bristol Rugby Club players in order to attract bigger gates. His adversary, William Henry Cowlin, had argued that attracting more spectators and charging for admission were essential not just to meet expenses, such as rents, but also for the general health of the game.[580] Gore and Cowlin had a political history — Gore had defeated his opponent in two local elections. Moreover, Gore, as the honorary secretary of the Bristol (Rugby) Football Club, carried some weight, when he publicly aired his views on the subject.

In early December 1895 Gore travelled to Scotland to deliver a lecture on 'Sport' for the Independent Labour Party.[581] While he was there he took the opportunity to visit Edinburgh and call on Patrick Geddes, a Scottish biologist, pioneering town planner, and co-author of *The Evolution of Sex*,[582] a book that Gore had read. Despite having mutual friends, Gore and Geddes' paths had never crossed before. Geddes, besides knowing Carpenter, was friendly with the former Clifton College master, Cecil Reddie. During his student days at Edinburgh University in the early 1880s, Reddie had studied under Geddes and retained strong connections with him after he left. In 1889 Reddie put some of Geddes' educational ideas into practice when he established Abbotsholme, a progressive public school.[583] Notwithstanding these connections, Gore soon discovered he had little in common with Geddes, 'our sympathies are not in the same direction'. He thought Geddes 'a most uncongenial man'. Disappointed he had returned to his home in Shirehampton in such a bleak frame of mind that he neglected to send Carpenter New Year greetings, for which he was 'infinitely ashamed'.[584]

In his letter to Edward Carpenter on 3 January 1896, thanking him for his New Year Greetings and apologising for his 'long silence and neglect', he said that although Bristol was 'more or less a nightmare' to him, it was easier to earn a living there 'than it would be in new fields.' The letter indicates his troubled state of mind. Gore told Carpenter he knew no one in the village and he did not 'desire acquaintances'. He questioned 'whether time for thought' was desirable and only read books that did not demand much mental exercise, which 'for the

580 *Western Daily Press*, 26 November 1895.
581 *Dundee Courier*, 7 December 1895.
582 P. Geddes and J. A. Thompson, *The Evolution of Sex* (London: Walter Scott: 1889).
583 H. Meller, *Patrick Geddes: Social Evolutionist and City Planner* (London: Routledge, 1990), p. 40, ftn 57.
584 Gore to Edward Carpenter, 3 January 1896, Carpenter Collection, Sheffield Archives.

time being' he liked.[585] He was trying to clear his mind in readiness to begin the search for a new direction in life. He said that he was 'growing much older in some senses', yet he felt that he was possibly at the beginning of some sort of rejuvenation, 'a chrysalis state' not that he thought he would transform into a 'butterfly'. He went on to say but 'I may sow some sort of seed. Only What?' In January 1896 he was thirty-one years old.

The emotional reaction to the stress that Gore experienced in 1895 had led him to social and political withdrawal, although he was still able to carry on with his professional duties. He told Carpenter that 'he did not write much' but he had had some contact with their close friend, Charles Ashbee who had sent him 'a short note or two'. Their other mutual acquaintance, Cecil Reddie, who was busy running Abbotsholme, had, however, 'fallen out of' his 'list of correspondents'. He had 'few or no Oxford friends left now' and had been 'entirely severed from Clifton College.'[586] It is possible that this severing was linked to the Chinese whispers circulating after the General election questioning Gore's sexual orientation. Gore had worked closely with the College on the boys' summer camps in Somerset, however, the College headmaster, the Reverend Michael Glazebrook, was a member of the National Vigilance Association, and would have wanted to remove any hint of scandal. On the other hand, Gore maintained his work with the Children's Help Society, an organisation that was also supported by Clifton College, and where his father officiated as President.

Despite the hostility existing between Gore and John Sharland, Gore avoided any direct mention of this to Carpenter, communicating that the Sharlands were 'well', although Harold Sharland, Robert's son, was still not fit enough to do 'hard work of any sort.' He also reported that Robert's work was 'slack' and that he had 'offered them all a home in the country' but seemingly Robert was 'loathe to leave the town.'[587] It appears from the way in which Gore evinced thoughtfulness about Robert and Harold's well being, that Gore's rift with John had not seriously damaged his personal relations with the rest of the Sharland family. However, he ruled out the likelihood of political cooperation with the Bristol socialists again. He told Carpenter that '[t]he labour movement has little cheer for me now. I find dissension about everywhere, and here [Bristol] the split is complete.'[588]

Gore's isolation accentuated the feelings of fear and vulnerability which had arisen as a result of his political conflicts. His anxiety focused on the forthcoming visit of a man called James Marchant, informing Carpenter that

585 Gore to Edward Carpenter, 3 January 1896.
586 Gore to Edward Carpenter, 3 January 1896.
587 Gore to Edward Carpenter, 3 January 1896.
588 Gore to Edward Carpenter, 3 January 1896.

Marchant was coming to Bristol 'for a day or two'. He does not explain why this was significant to him, presumably assuming that Carpenter would have known the reason. The twenty-nine year old Marchant was touring the country as a public speaker for the Christian Evidence Society. Concerned about the problem of non-belief this organisation took on the mission of presenting the case for Christianity to a wide audience base,[589] challenging the views of atheists, agnostics, and secularists, and counteracting 'the propaganda of infidelity'.[590]

Established in 1870 by Anglicans and Nonconformists in an unusual spasm of unity, the Christian Evidence Society was 'a selfconsciously ecumenical venture', attracting moderate and evangelical churchmen, rather than High Anglicans, like Gore.[591] Christian apologists, like Marchant, defended their faith – especially against Free Thinkers, such as the secularist Charles Bradlaugh – 'with new affirmations of the certainty of Christianity.'[592] Moreover, Marchant had been active in the National Vigilance Association, since it was formed in 1885 'for the enforcement and improvement of the laws for the repression of criminal vice and public immorality', a reference to the Criminal Law Amendment Act passed on 14 August 1885,[593] an Act that would be used to send Oscar Wilde to prison in 1895 for committing an acts of gross indecency with other male persons.

Initially, the social reformer, Josephine Butler, and the Ladies National Association were affiliated to the National Vigilance Association which had assisted in the Repeal of the Contagious Diseases Acts. However, the National Vigilance Association's subsequent policy of supporting the enforcement of the Criminal Law Amendment Act against brothels made women responsible for prostitution, not men. This led Butler, and many of her associates, who strenuously defended women's individual rights, to break ties with the Association and oppose its activity as repressive.[594] Marchant, as a moral crusader, remained a vocal supporter of the National Vigilance Association's repressive line, which had extended beyond condemning prostitution and homosexuality to attack music halls and denounce works by Honoré de Balzac,

589 D. A. Johnson, 'Popular Apologetics in Late Victorian England: The Work of the Christian Evidence Society', *Journal of Religious History*, Vol.11: 4, p. 558.
590 *John Bull*, 31 May 1884, p. 347.
591 Johnson, 'Popular Apologetics in Late Victorian England: The Work of the Christian Evidence Society', p. 558.
592 Johnson, 'Popular Apologetics in Late Victorian England: The Work of the Christian Evidence Society', p. 558.
593 *The Times*, 22 August 1885. See L. Bland, *Banishing the Beast: English Feminism & Sexual Morality 1885-1914* (London: Penguin: 1995), for a full account of the Criminal Law Amendment Act and the National Vigilance Association, pp. 97-101.
594 L. Bland, *Banishing the Beast: English Feminism & Sexual Morality 1885-1914*, p. 99.

Oscar Wilde at Bow Street, 1895.

Émile Zola and François Rabelais.[595] In Bristol, for instance, the National Vigilance Association instructed the solicitor and fellow Vigilance Association member H. R. Wansbrough, to prosecute a shop owner and his son for unlawfully publishing and selling 'obscene' literature, including translations of Zola's novels, from their shop in the Lower Arcade, Bristol. The defendants were found guilty and fined; and, by Court order, all the offending books were destroyed.[596]

Between 1889-1893 Marchant had held the position of lecturer on Christian apologetics to the Bishop of St. Albans. Two years later he was made minister of an independent Congregational church in Plymouth.[597] This appointment gave him the freedom to lecture across the country for the Christian Evidence Society, which brought him to Bristol in January 1896.[598] He was evidently a controversial figure, for just two weeks after Gore had penned his letter to Carpenter, Marchant arrived at St. James' Hall to deliver the first of two

595 J. R Walkowitz, 'Male Vice and Female Virtue: Feminism and the Politics of Prostitution in Nineteenth Century Britain' in A. Snitow, C. Stansell and S. Thompson(eds.), *Powers of Desire: The Politics of Sexuality* (New York: Monthly Review Press, 1983), p. 428.
596 *Western Daily Press*, 15 March 1889.
597 Sir J. Marchant's Obituary, *The Times*, 22 May 1956.
598 *Bristol Mercury*, 22 January 1896.

Christian Evidence Society's lectures on an anti-Roman Catholic theme, 'The Confession Box' and 'An Unholy Trinity – Saints Benedict, Dominec (*sic*) and Francis De Assissi (*sic*)', these attracted a band of 'disturbers' who managed to get hold of tickets.[599] As Marchant mounted the speakers' platform this excitable body of protesters took possession of the area beneath the podium, hurled abuse at him and then stormed the stage chasing off the chairman, Marchant, and his supporters.

> [O]ne elderly yet nimble woman mounted the platform table, and, amid the exciting cries of those about her, whirled an umbrella wildly over her head, at the same time giving utterances to expletives as to what she would do, if the opportunity afforded , to the lecturer.[600]

The meeting had to be abandoned and a prearranged lecture due to be delivered two days later, Sunday, 19 January, at the Victoria Rooms in Clifton, was cancelled. Fearing more trouble the agents of the Rooms revoked the booking.

Despite the attack on free speech by the protesters who, it seems, were Irish Roman Catholics, there was some sympathy voiced for them in the local press, because of Marchant's hostility to Catholicism. One anonymous observer (Laicus) remarked that he or she was 'not surprised at Catholics, Irish or otherwise' disrupting what they deemed would be an attack on Catholicism given that 'they have held on to their faith through the bitterest persecution', expressing the belief that 'prejudice and suspicion is taking the place of mutual respect and toleration.'[601]

Gore and Marchant were in opposing camps on religion, though they shared an hostility to the impact of the industrial system. Moreover, in 1895 Gore had been able to work amicably with local Vigilance Association activists in Bristol. These activists included the Reverend Urijah Thomas, with whom Gore had cooperated in the Bristol Children's Help Society, along with several other Bristol clergymen and Justices of the Peace. Gore also cooperated with Mary Ralph and Margaret Tanner, members of the Vigilance Association as well as the Bristol Women's Liberal Association.[602]

An explanation for these apparent discrepancies probably lies in the nuances of the social purity agenda. Initially, social purity campaigns had called for a single moral standard for both sexes. But by the mid 1890s the discourse within

599 *Bristol Mercury*, 22 January 1896.
600 *Bristol Mercury*, 22 January 1896.
601 *Bristol Mercury*, 25 January 1896.
602 The Annual Meeting of the Bristol and South Western branch of the National Vigilance Association 5 February 1895, notice of in the *Bristol Mercury*, 2 February 1895, report of in the *Western Daily Press*, 6 February 1895.

the National Vigilance Association was shifting under the impact of ideas of degenerative contagion in which decadence, homosexuality, and a supposedly innate masculine vice were conceived as threating 'the integrity of both family and State.'[603] Marchant's interpretation of the social purity agenda, with its obsession with 'societal degeneration', would have been likely to trouble Gore. The rhetoric of the social purity zealots, like Marchant, must have borne down on him in isolated retreat in Shirehampton. Moreover, it was being voiced in a wider oppressive context.

Following the trial of Oscar Wilde, fear of the danger of blackmail intensified among men with same-sex passions. The weight of prurience must have been crushing. Gore's idealism withered as moral pressures closed in on him, markedly affecting his emotional state and his ability to think clearly. Psychological factors were compounded by and contributed to his failing health and loss of self-esteem.

In contrast, Marchant's fulminations against *fin-de-siècle* decadence gained him a public platform. Becoming a leading voice in the morality business in the early twentieth century led to his advancement.[604] He went on to hold the posts of Director of the National Council for the Promotion of Race Regeneration and Organising Secretary of the National Social Purity Crusade eventually being awarded the Commander of the Order of the British Empire and Knight Commander of the Order of the British Empire.[605]

603 A. Smith, *The Victorian Nude: Sexuality, Morality, and Art* (Manchester University Press: 1996), p. 217.
604 G. R. Searle, *A New England? Peace and War 1886-1918* (Oxford: Oxford University Press, 2004), p. 74.
605 *Dundee Courier*, 8 August 1921, D. C. Thompson & Co. Ltd., courtesy of The British Library Board.

Chapter 16

Thornbury and *The Red Flag*

Although Gore's road to recovery seems to have been disturbed by Marchant's visit to Bristol, his physical removal and political detachment from the Bristol labour movement had released him from coping with the political battles, previously such a significant part of his everyday life. Gradually he was regaining some of his old strength.

In June 1896 his political ally, friend and work colleague, Edward Watson, passed the Incorporated Law Society's final examination,[606] and thus could provide greater professional assistance. Consequently, Gore felt able to continue with his work on the School Board. Throughout 1896 and 1897 he regularly attended meetings, discussing issues such as night schools, children's attendances, and temperance teaching in schools. With Gore's support the School Board introduced 'Citizenship' lectures, some of which Gore delivered, suggesting that he was slowly regaining some of his verve and pride.[607]

However, Gore acquired adversaries on the Board, in particular the evangelical Reverend Frederic J. Horsefield, vicar of St. Silias' Church, St. Philip's Marsh, and the teaching of 'Citizenship' proved a point of some contention. Horsefield was an amateur historian and author of *Life in a Cornish Village*, which he wrote on convalescence leave from the Albert Memorial Church, Collyhurst, northeast Manchester.[608] On recovery he returned to his Collyhurst church in 1894 and delivered a series of sermons 'in defence of Evangelical Protestant truth', attacking Catholicism and the ritualists of the Church of England.[609] From the Evangelical viewpoint High Anglican ritualists were akin to their great opponent, 'Popery'.

Since arriving in Bristol with his wife and baby daughter in 1895 to take up his appointment as vicar of St. Silas, Horsefield had become a leading member of the Bristol and Clifton Protestant League, an active member of the local branch of National Vigilance Association, and the Christian Endeavour Union. Elected to the Bristol School Board in January 1897, he quickly made his mark. At the July Board meeting Horsefield opposed Gore's resolution to appoint the solicitor, George Duncan Grey, a contemporary of Gore at Bristol Grammar School,[610] to deliver 'lectures on the life and duties of citizens at

606 *Bristol Mercury*, 7 July 1896.
607 *Bristol Mercury*, 21 October 1896.
608 F. J. Horsefield, *Life in a Cornish Village* (Turo: Lake and Lake, 1893).
609 *Manchester Courier and Lancashire General Advertiser*, 30 October 1894.
610 *Western Daily Press*, 4 January 1898.

the Castle and Merrywood schools'. His concern was that such lectures 'must include political questions, and politics were precluded by rule of the board.'[611] Despite his objection the resolution was passed and, buoyed by this victory, Gore further proposed that the prominent evolutionary psychologist, Professor Conwy (Conway) Lloyd Morgan, Principal of University College, Bristol, should also be adopted as a lecturer. The Board accepted Gore's proposals leaving Horsefield and his supporters aggrieved.[612]

Lloyd Morgan was a particularly enlightened choice. A former student of the Darwinist, Thomas Huxley, he was well respected, both locally and nationally. Gore knew Lloyd Morgan through the Footpath Preservation Society (see Chapter Four).[613] Lloyd Morgan had built his reputation in the 1890s in the new field of mental evolution.[614] His pioneering writings on psychology drew on his scientific knowledge of geology, as well as upon philosophy. In the opening pages of his book, *An Introduction to Comparative Psychology*, he explained his 'monistic' theory to knowledge, which rejected subject and object as independent existences. Basing his thinking on actual experience, unlike some monists, he believed that hypotheses or assumptions were vital to philosophy, as there are many unknowable elements. The interpretation of these 'possibilities of experience' was a necessary supplement to 'actual experience.'[615] As a regular attender at Church, Lloyd Morgan's interest in geology, evolution, psychology or philosophical monism did not lead him down the path of agnosticism, instead, according to Peter Bowler, he engaged in 'the kind of scientific writing which appealed to liberal religious thinkers.'[616]

Lloyd Morgan was by no means a dangerously heterodox figure but Horsefield was indifferent to the virtues of liberal religious thinkers. Moreover, in the process of establishing himself in the local community, Horsefield had embarked on a vehement crusade against High Church Anglican clergymen, whose beliefs and practices, he professed, could 'hardly be distinguished from the Roman Catholic doctrine'.[617] Horsefield's hostility to the High Church wing of the Church of England necessarily put him at odds with Gore. After

611 Bristol School Board Report, *Bristol Times and Mirror*, 27 July 1897.

612 Bristol School Board Report, *Bristol Times and Mirror*, 27 July 1897.

613 *Bristol Mercury*, 6 June, 1888, listed Lloyd Morgan as a member of the Footpath Preservation Society and recorded that he moved a proposal, at a meeting of the Society on 5 June, 1888, calling for the Bristol society to support their colleagues in a legal case being fought in the Lake district.

614 G. C. Field and Rev. J. F. M. Clark, 'Morgan, Conway Lloyd (1852-1936), Oxford Dictionary of National Biography (Oxford University Press, 2004-14).

615 C. Lloyd Morgan, *An Introduction to Comparative Psychology* (London: The Walter Scott Publishing Company: 2nd revised edition, 1903, first published 1892), pp. 1-10.

616 See P. J. Bowler, *Evolution: The History of an Idea* (California: University of California Press: 2003, first published 1983), p. 323.

617 *Bristol Mercury*, 2 May 1896.

clashing over their choice of lecturers, their disdain for one another was evident in a series of clashes at School Board meetings over issues such as Gore's support for the reduction of scripture instruction time,[618] and Horsefield's repeated attempts to push through a resolution to close public houses on a Sunday.[619] Gore's position on scripture lessons followed that of the Guild of St. Matthew, which believed the Church, rather than secular schools, should administer religious instruction.[620] On the question of temperance Gore was at one with the Guild in opposing the imposition of Sunday closing upon public houses, as it would remove places of relaxation, social interaction and public discourse from the working poor. These differences were not just political. Without realising it Gore had acquired an opponent whose animosity was visceral. Horsefield abhorred every aspect of Gore's values and outlook.

Gore's withdrawal from party political activity to focus on his School Board work did not preclude him from continuing to defend socialists in the courts. His track record in upholding the right of free speech and right to protest brought him to Thornbury Police-court in August 1897. He had been called upon to represent Gilbert Williams, a carpenter from Alveston, and Samuel Britton, a basket maker from Oldbury-upon-Severn who, under the 72nd Section of the 1835 Highway Act, were charged with obstructing the highway called the 'Plain' in the main street running through Thornbury.[621] They appeared in court with their socialist associate London-based Jim Connell, an Irish born, socialist lecturer and poet who in 1889 had written the socialist anthem *The Red Flag* which was partly inspired by the London dock strike. Connell had been in the Marxist Social Democratic Federation but by 1897 he had left and joined the Independent Labour Party.

Jim Connell conducted his own defence and Gore appeared for Williams and Britton. H. P. Thurston outlined the prosecution case to a packed courtroom. He said that on the evening of Friday 20 August a large crowd had gathered to hear the defendants speak at a meeting organised by them 'in accordance with public notice' which resulted in the blockage of the public highway. At this juncture, the police asked Connell and by implication his associates, Williams and Britton, to terminate the meeting. They refused. The police then proceeded to command members of the crowd to move on. They resisted the order and the crowd became denser, extending to around 300, which the prosecutor contended presented 'an element of danger to the public.'[622]

618 Bristol School Board Report, September 1897, Bristol Record Office.
619 Bristol School Board Reports, *Western Daily Press*, 30 November 1897 and *Bristol Mercury*, 29 March 1898.
620 A. V. Woodworth, *Christian Socialism in England* (London: Sonnenschein & Co., 1903), p. 119.
621 *Bristol Times and Mirror*, 28 August 1897.
622 *Bristol Times and Mirror*, 28 August 1897; *Gloucester Journal*, 28 August 1897.

In defending Williams and Britton, Gore presented a case based on the argument that the law should treat individuals in similar situations equally:

> [I]f all meetings on the Plain were henceforth prohibited he should save the time of the court by asking his clients to at once plead guilty but he did object to favouritism being shown to one section of the community and being denied to another…religious meetings had been held there at which a number of people assembled and had not been objected to and no prosecution had occurred. But if the Socialists who held a meeting there were to be singled out because they were Socialists, and their opinions were not shared by the inhabitants then they must go on with the case.[623]

It was a long-standing disagreement around the right to speak in public. Socialists and anarchists had clashed with the police around the country on the issue on many occasions. It was often the case that religious speakers were allowed greater leeway. Unsurprisingly, therefore, the magistrates eschewed Gore's cogent argument and, after the defendants refused to plead guilty, proceeded with the case.

Connell put up a stout defence. He brought to the court's attention that the meeting in question was peaceful until a local shopkeeper tried to break it up by driving his pony and trap through the crowd several times, once 'at a furious pace'. From the witness stand the police constable's version of events differed only on one aspect, the speed of the trap, which he said was 'a gentle trot'. Connell then put to the constable a hypothetical scenario: What if someone had been knocked and killed as a result of the shopkeeper's actions. Would he have been charged with manslaughter?[624]

The chairman of the court intervened to tell the witness not to answer this question. Picking up on Gore's opening remarks, Connell proceeded to ask the witness another question:

> If this had been a religious meeting, a meeting called to celebrate the Jubilee of the Queen, or a Tory meeting, and there had been many people thereat, would you have thought it your duty to prosecute the promoters of it and allow the brawlers to escape?[625]

---

623 *Bristol Times and Mirror*, 28 August 1897.
624 *Gloucester Journal*, 28 August 1897.
625 *Gloucester Journal*, 28 August 1897.

Again the chairman instructed the witness not to answer the question. At this point Gore rose to his feet exclaiming that the defendant had 'a right to ask that question.' He was told to sit down, as he was not defending Connell. Gore ignored this request and restated his point of order, only to receive a further rebuke. From this point on there was little doubt what the verdict would be. All three defendants were found guilty and fined subject to fourteen days' imprisonment in default of distress.[626]

Both Connell and Williams had insufficient money or goods to disburse the penalty and costs imposed on them, and despite offers of help from their friends they refused to allow them to pay the fines. Therefore, they were taken to Horfield Prison on the outskirts of Bristol to serve their sentences, oakum picking.[627]

Again, Gore had displayed an unprofessional volatility in court. For Gore the issues raised in this case, such as the right to hold public meetings, fairness, and equality before the law, stirred his core beliefs. They were a reminder of principles he had fought for, first as an active member of the Clifton and Bristol Christian Socialists, and then the Bristol Socialist Society, before relations with the latter organisation had been irreparably broken. The emotions that this evoked were evident in his conduct of the defence. He intervened not only on behalf of the rights of his own *clients'* but also for Connell, who was defending himself, despite being rebuked by the Magistrates' chairman.

The day after the jailing of Williams and Britton, some of Gore's old comrades from the Bristol Socialist Society joined socialist delegations from Gloucester, Worcester, Cheltenham, Berkeley, Sharpness, Stroud and Cardiff in Thornbury at the 'Plain', to hold a protest meeting against the action of the presiding magistrate at Thornbury police court. On arriving at the 'Plain' they were met by the Superintendent of the police, who assured them 'that no other body, political or otherwise, should meet at the disputed spot in future' and offered an alternative meeting place for the gathering of hundreds of people, which was accepted.[628] Whether Gore was present at this protest is unknown but his contribution to the whole affair was of some significance, and it is not unreasonable to conclude that, intellectually at least, he continued to hold fast to socialist ideals. The unprofessional anger he displayed in court suggests that he was still not completely able to handle the formal distancing which was part of his professional role.

Two days later, on Monday 30 August, he attended the regular monthly meeting of the School Board as an elected representative. His profound

626 *Gloucester Journal*, 28 August 1897.
627 *Gloucester Journal*, 28 August 1897.
628 *Gloucester Journal*, 4 September 1897.

commitment to extending education meant he was resolved to prioritise participation on the Board despite the breakdown in his health. At this meeting Gore was one of five named to form a sub-committee to confer with the Boards of Horfield, Stapleton, St. George and Bedminster, which were to be merged into one Greater Bristol School Board. He objected to the co-option of Tom Butler, (son of the staunch Methodist William Butler the owner of a chemical firm in Crew's Hole, St George), onto the Board in advance of this merger, suggesting that they should wait until the general school election, which was due to be held in January 1898.[629] He was overruled, however, by his fellow Board members who were keen to 'have a gentleman who was associated with a firm employing a good deal of labour and contributing largely to the rates.'[630] It must have been frustrating for Gore to see the appointment of a new Board member most likely to support what Raymond Williams was later to describe as 'the continued relegation of trade and industry to lower social classes and the desire of successful industrialists that their sons should move into the now largely irrelevant class of gentry'.[631] However, Gore need not have worried for in January 1898 Butler decided not to seek re-election.[632]

Over the years, the stresses and strains of public life upon Gore had been eased somewhat by his enthusiasm for sporting activities. As well as rugby football, he loved swimming, walking, athletics, boxing, sailing and cycling.[633] Physical activity had played an important part in balancing his emotions, lifting his motivation and decreasing his anxiety levels. Gore held the view that rugby football, in particular, along with boxing, played an important part in character building, as it made 'the player courageous, and require[d] control of temper.'[634] Unsurprisingly, however, as he approached his mid-thirties he became less physically active on the playing fields, though sport continued to play an essential part in his life. Gore's involvement in sport was transferred to administration. Early in 1897 the Bristol Bicycle and Tricycle Club announced that it was pleased to have secured 'the popular Hugh Holmes Gore',[635] 'a scholar and a gentleman',[636] as its President following the resignation of the Liberal, C.

629 *Bristol Times and Mirror*, 31 August 1897.
630 *Bristol Times and Mirror*, 31 August 1897.
631 R. Williams, *The Long Revolution* (London: Chatto and Windus, 1961), p. 143.
632 *Bristol Mercury*, 3 January 1898.
633 *The Bristol Bicycle and Tricycle Club Gazette, Monthly Gazette*, 1 November 1897 (Bristol; Printed and Published by W. S. Bishop, Artistic Printer, 12 John Street), Bristol Central Reference Library, p. 108.
634 *The Bristol Bicycle and Tricycle Club Gazette, Monthly Gazette*, 1 July 1897, p. 67.
635 *The Bristol Bicycle and Tricycle Club Gazette: A Retrospect, 1876-1897* (Bristol; Printed and Published by W. S. Bishop, Artistic Printer, 12 John Street), Bristol Central Reference Library.
636 *The Bristol Bicycle and Tricycle Club Gazette, Monthly Gazette*, 1 November 1897, p. 108.

FORMED · 1876   EDITED BY H. J. PARKES

No. 8.   AUGUST 1st, 1897.   VOL. 1.

Header from the Bristol Bicycle & Tricycle Gazette, 1897.

E. A. George. In November Gore presided over the Club's 21st annual dinner at which his father appeared as one of the guest vocalists, suggesting that they were on good terms despite holding opposing political positions. The month before he had been re-elected as vice-president of the Gloucester County Rugby Football Union.[637] Despite being so clubbable and popular in his social, as well as his professional and political activities, Gore nevertheless had to contend with the watchfulness of the public eye.

637 *Gloucester Journal*, 2 October 1897.

Chapter 17

Religious Sectarianism and Gore's Disappearance

Whether willing or not, at election time candidates had to do as much as they could to catch the attention of prospective supporters. Gore was not immune; in the School Board election of January 1898 he went on the stump on an independent ticket, holding meetings in the Dings, his home territory, attracting welcoming bands of supporters. During the dinner hour of Tuesday 4 January he was to be found addressing a large gathering outside the Stapleton Gas Works, where he received a warm reception. He had the backing of the local President of the Gas Workers' Union and Independent Labour Party member, John Walker. Gore could still rely, too, on some old socialist friends to speak on his behalf. The following Saturday evening at another election rally held outside the Bush Hotel in Totterdown, Edward Watson and the long-serving Republican member of the Bristol Socialist Society, William Baster, stood side by side with Gore stressing his past record and asserting his desire to see children in Bristol Board Schools well educated.[638] As in previous elections, Gore knew he could rely on the Bristol Licensed Victuallers' Association, who openly opposed the Sunday closing of public houses, to rally behind him, and indeed attract the votes of many working men.[639]

Hours after the polling stations had closed and the count had begun, the early signs indicated that Horsefield would top the poll. It looked as if Gore's position would not be as high as he had previously experienced.[640] Since arriving in Bristol in 1895 Horsefield had acquired a celebrity status through his denunciation of the ritualistic practices of the High Anglican Church. With his Church situated in the heart of St. Philip's, he was Gore's local rival. Unexpectedly, despite Horsefield doing relatively well in the election, he was pushed into third place by Gore, who showed he still had popular support. Neither man gained enough to defeat the radical Liberal candidate, Reverend James Trebilco, who topped the poll beating Gore by 357 votes, a margin of 1.7 per cent.[641]

Following the School Board elections in 1898 Gore was at last able to enjoy several months of relative calm. Blithely unaware that a life-changing crisis lay ahead, he continued to carry out his representative role on the School Board. At the March meeting he helped block a renewed attempt by some Board members,

638 *Bristol Mercury*, 10 January 1898.
639 *Bristol Mercury*, 10 January 1898.
640 *Bristol Mercury*, 14 January 1898.
641 *Bristol Mercury*, 15 January 1898.

including his adversary Horsefield, to adopt a memorial to Parliament in favour of the Sunday closing of premises licensed to sell alcohol.[642]

However, Horsefield was moving away from the Temperance cause to become utterly engaged in the militant wing of the anti-ritualist movement. This was, of course, anathema to Gore, breeding enmity between them. Both men became more prone to act injudiciously. Their arrogance and animosity were evident at the School Board meetings. Constructive communication broke down, turning into personal attacks and angry accusations. Controversy resonated in the Anglican Church itself, which, from the mid-1890s, was experiencing virulent conflicts over ritualism.

Horsefield had come to revere John Kensit, a forty-two year old founder member of the Protestant Truth Society. Kensit had adopted a new strategy of Evangelical direct action, systematically interrupting services conducted by Church of England ministers he considered to be introducing Romanist ritualist teachings and practices. Kensit had gained notoriety on Good Friday, 8 April 1898, in a dramatic protest against an unauthorised service called the Veneration of the Cross, at St. Cuthbert's, South Kensington. Kensit had grabbed the cross, raised it above his head and exclaimed, 'In the name of God I denounce this idolatry in the Church of England; God help me.'[643] An undignified scuffle ensued.

A few weeks later, Kensit, described the 'idolatrous' practices at the ritualist church of St. Cuthbert's as having been 'conducted by a "priest in petticoats." The congregation were poor specimens of men. ... They seemed a peculiar sort of people, very peculiar indeed.'[644] This was an allusion to accusations of effeminate priests prevalent during the 1860s, when antagonism towards High Anglicans had been particularly fierce. It also played on Oscar Wilde's sympathy with ritualism and Catholicism. Not only had Wilde's association with rent boys conflated homosexuality with the growing paranoia over social degeneration, Kensit stirs up prejudices against High Anglicans and Roman Catholics.

In this homophobic environment Kensit's suggestive language, and his persistence in sabotaging Church of England services he deemed ritualistic, heightened his popularity within the Protestant Alliance, though not, it seems, with voters in the London School Board elections, of November 1897, where

---

642 *Bristol Mercury*, 29 March 1898.
643 Martin Wellings, 'Kensit, John (1853–1902)', *Oxford Dictionary of National Biography*, Oxford University Press, 2004 [http://www.oxforddnb.com/view/article/34289, accessed 17 May 2014]; G. I. T. Machin, 'The Last Victorian Anti-Ritualist Campaign, 1895-1906, *Victorian Studies*, Vol. 25, No. 3 (Spring, 1982), p. 287.
644 Hilliard, 'Unenglish and Unmanly: Anglo-Catholicism and Homosexuality', p. 9.

he only secured 973 votes out of 38,663.[645] However, similar incidents to the one that occurred at St. Cuthbert's were to follow; one of them led to Kensit appearing in court. On 8 May 1898, after disrupting a church service at St. Michael's, Shoreditch, Kensit was charged with 'brawling' when he pushed aside a churchwarden in order to take a seat near the pulpit, thus bringing the ceremony to temporary halt.[646] In the court case that followed his followers turned up in support, waving their hats and umbrellas in the air, cheering and chanting 'No Popery!'[647] Following this incident Kensit agreed to a temporary respite with the Bishop of London, Mandell Creighton, who in return promised 'to present a petition to the Upper (that is, episcopal) House of the Convocation of Canterbury.'[648] Not satisfied with the outcome however, after a two-month truce Kensit resumed and indeed intensified his anti-ritualist activity.

The new Bishop of Bristol, Dr. George Forrest Browne, had experienced Kensit's disruptive dissenting activities while serving as the Bishop of Stepney between 1895 and 1897. Aware that the problem needed addressing, upon his arrival in Bristol he initiated a consultation process on how to deal with Kensit's tactics. This was at an advanced stage when the Reverend Horsefield and his curate, Humphrey Hurst, stepped up their anti-ritualist campaign in the Bishop's Bristol and Gloucester diocese. Increasingly concerned, the Bishop wrote to Horsefield begging him 'to abstain from identifying [himself] with men the natural outcome of whose proceedings has so shocked the religious conscience.'[649] On the following morning Horsefield received a further letter from the Bishop calling on him to attend a one-to-one meeting between them at 10.30am on 8 September 1898.[650]

During the interview that followed Horsefield, seemingly unperturbed by the situation, revealed his intent to take the chair at a meeting to be addressed by Kensit within the Bishop's diocese, and asked the Bishop for permission to do so. Shocked at receiving such a brazen request the Bishop responded with a categorical 'No'! That afternoon he wrote an open letter to Horsefield, which was published in the *Bristol Mercury* on 9 September, outlining the substance of what he had said along with the confirmation of his ruling.

---

645 James Britten, *A Prominent (Mr John Kensit) and the Protestant Truth Society* (London: Catholic Truth Society, 1911), p. 14.
646 *London Standard*, 10 May 1898.
647 *Reynolds' Newspaper*, 22 May 1898; Machin, 'The Last Victorian Anti-Ritualist Campaign', 1895-1906, p. 287.
648 Machin, 'The Last Victorian Anti-Ritualist Campaign, 1895-1906', p. 287.
649 The Bishop of Bristol to the Reverend Horsefield, 5 September 1898, published in *Bristol Mercury*, 9 September 1898.
650 *Bristol Mercury*, 9 September 1898.

The agitation led by Mr Kensit has produced results so shocking…that their continuance is a disgrace to the forces of law in this kingdom …
I forbid you to take the chair or appear on the platform at any public meeting on this kind of question in my diocese at which Mr Kensit is to speak.[651]

In effect the Bishop delivered an Episcopal prohibition of Horsefield appearing with Kensit on any occasion in his diocese.

Shrewdly, Horsefield managed to orchestrate a propaganda campaign against the Bishop by sending all the relevant correspondence between them to the local press, which they published with little hesitation. He attached a copy of his reply to the Bishop's letter which made plain that it was 'the terrible lawlessness on the part of a certain section of the clergy of our church' that made it necessary for him 'to withhold any absolute pledge to permanently abstain from such meetings as referred to.'[652]

The story spread quickly to the national press attracting much attention.[653] Displeased, the Bishop sent another letter on 10 September to Horsefield rebuking him for publishing his letters without asking permission.[654] Events were moving swiftly, however. Kensit had already sent a letter of complaint concerning the Bishop's action against Horsefield to the editor of *The Times*, which was published on 10 September.[655] That evening a protest meeting was held in a tent at Frampton Cotterell, (a rural Gloucestershire village, northeast of Bristol), against the Bishop of Bristol's decision barring Horsefield from attending what they viewed as lawful meetings. Arriving an hour late and with a contingent of police present John Kensit delivered a lively speech condemning both the Bishop who 'the sooner they told him to get another berth the better', and the ritualistic practices of Frampton Cotterell's local rector, Reverend Dr. Belcher.[656]

Despite pleas for peace the conflict dragged on. Horsefield continued to receive plaudits for his spiritual leadership,[657] being hailed by his supporters as 'Luther the Second'.[658] His ego was thus in the ascendant when, at the School

651 *Bristol Mercury*, 9 September 1898; see also and also *The Times*, 9 September 1898.
652 Reverend F. J. Horsefield to the Bishop of Bristol, 9 September 1898, published in the *Bristol Mercury*, 10 September 1898.
653 For instance see *The Times*, 9 and 10 September 1898.
654 Reverend F. J. Horsefield to the Bishop of Bristol, 10 September 1898, published in the *Bristol Mercury*, 12 September 1898.
655 John Kensit to the Editor of *The Times*, 9 September 1898, published in *The Times* on 10 September 1898.
656 *Bristol Mercury*, 12 September 1898.
657 See 'The Kensit Meetings', *Bristol Mercury*, 13 and 17 September 1898.
658 *Bristol Mercury*, 12 October 1898.

Board meeting held on 26 September 1898, he and Gore became involved in an argument. It appeared to be a minor quibble at first. Gore had supported the resolution passed the previous July, authorising the curtailment of time given to scripture lessons at Merrywood School by a quarter of an hour. Horsefield wanted it rescinded stating that the teachers supported him. Gore demanded that he give the names of these teachers. Horsefield declined, saying he could not release their names without consent. Whereupon Gore could not resist making the sardonic comment 'What about the Bishop?'[659] The chairman intervened on this direct reference to the Bishop of Bristol's displeasure at Horsefield releasing his private letters to the press without his permission. He told Gore that his remark was 'most unwarrantable'. Gore responded with a strong riposte:

> Unwarrantable remark! If it is discourteous to mention a teacher's name without consent, surely it is more so to publish letters from the Bishop without authority.[660]

This dispute between Gore and Horsefield erupted in a public arena, and was reported in the press as 'a lively incident'.[661] It took place just four days after the sacking of St. Stephen's church in central Bristol. In an attack on the church's ritualistic practices, the cross in the centre of the communion table was ripped from its moorings and thrust under the organ along with one of the candlesticks. A silk bookmarker emblazoned with a cross was removed, a picture of the Crucifixion destroyed, and a notice board in the chancel spoiled.[662] Such an extreme onslaught appears to have been a rare occurrence; nevertheless, concern was being voiced among both Nonconformists and Anglicans over Romanist ritualism.

Several days after the outrage at St. Stephen's, E. G. Sargent, a Baptist, banker and member of the Anchor Society, a charity politically influenced by radical Liberals, raised alarm over the increase of ritualist practices, stating at the anniversary of the City Road, Baptist Chapel in Bristol that the spread of ritualism was 'a national calamity.'[663] Moreover, alleged ritualistic excesses in the Church of England were the subject of the Bishop of Gloucester (Dr. Ellicott's) address to the Gloucester Diocesan Conference held on 19 October 1898, in which he referred to the controversial exchange of letters between Horsefield and the Bishop of Bristol published in the local and national press. In a long speech, he acknowledged that

659 *Bristol Mercury*, 27 September 1898.
660 *Bristol Mercury*, 27 September 1898.
661 *Bristol Mercury*, 27 September 1898.
662 *Bristol Mercury*, 28 September 1898; *Reynolds' Newspaper*, 2 October 1898.
663 *Bristol Mercury*, 6 October 1898.

'the bounds of Anglican ritualism [had] been reached' but was confident that 'loyalty to the Church of England would prevent further departure from … the directions and teachings of the Book of Common Prayer' and, with a concerted effort, illegal practices in unauthorised services could be stopped.[664]

The Gore-Horsefield confrontation at the end of September 1898 brought to the surface the hostile relations that had long existed between them and which reflected their deeply felt ideological and theological differences. This was not just a case of political jousting. It had gone beyond that, though whether it had reached a stage sufficient to point to any specific manifestation of ill will toward Gore by Horsefield in respect to what happened next is open to conjecture.

The timing is, however, suggestive. The 26 September School Board meeting, at which Gore had clashed with Horsefield, turned out to be his concluding one.[665] A wall of silence descended. In the second week of October E. T. Morgan was elected to replace Gore as the chair of the Physical Exercises Committee of the School Board.[666] Gore's last chronicled court appearance was on 27 September 1898. Gore withdrew from his practice – leaving his loyal partner, friend and comrade, Watson, as sole proprietor. The precise timing of this secession from his solicitor's practice cannot be determined. But after December 1898 Gore's name does not appear in *Matthew's Bristol and Clifton Street Directory*. In 1899 E. J. Watson is recorded as the sole person running what had been their joint legal practice in St John's Arch.[667] So all that can be inferred is that at some point between early October and the end of December 1898 Gore broke completely from his former profession. Henceforth Gore vanishes entirely from view. He did not practise in the legal profession again.

He would not have taken such a decision lightly, especially as he had so painstakingly established a practice that reflected his social and ethical values. What could have induced him to disappear of his own volition? Gore did not appear to be in financial difficulty. There is no record of him being struck off the solicitors' rolls, or of him filing for bankruptcy. Neither is there any record that he had fallen out with Watson or any of his clients.

The mystery is that the sudden eclipse of a man who was both a significant local public figure and known nationally evoked no comment in the press. Gore's withdrawal from public visibility strongly suggests a crisis in his personal life, and one that was hidden from view. The absence of information leaves us with speculation.

---

664 *Bristol Mercury*, 20 October 1898.
665 His position on the School Board was automatically terminated in April 1899, due to his absence for six consecutive months.
666 *Bristol Mercury*, 18 October 1898.
667 *Matthew's Bristol and Clifton Street Directory* (Bristol: John Wright: 1899, compiled late 1898).

Chapter 18

Searching for a Reason

Clues about Gore's plight and disappearance can be drawn out of the response from a few of his closest friends and associates. When Edith Ellis wrote that concerned letter to Carpenter on 15 November 1898, asking what had become of him (see Introduction), she herself knew very well what it was to experience the fear of public humiliation. Earlier that year, the scholarly and pioneering book on homosexuality and lesbianism, *Studies in the Psychology of Sex: Sexual Inversion*, written by her husband, Havelock Ellis, had been seized from the bookshop of the free thinker George Bedborough. On 31 May 1898 Bedborough was arrested for selling copies of the Ellis' book, on the grounds that it contained lewd and wicked material. In June, at the preliminary hearing, the book was described as 'bawdy and obscene'.

Bedborough's free thought network linked him to advocates of free love and anarchists who the police were watching. Moreover, Ellis' publisher, Roland de Villiers, turned out to be guilty of fraud and fled the country to avoid arrest. By that October, when the trial took place, Bedborough proceeded to strike a deal with the prosecution in order to reduce his charges.[668] Both Havelock and Edith Ellis were intimidated and shaken by the publicity and the trial.[669] The Police investigation reflected a wider social climate in which police subversion and sexual deviation were conflated. The late 1890s saw a reawakening of fears of violent anarchist subversion and this became associated with the issues of homosexuality and obscenity.

In August 1898 the passing of an extension to the 1824 Vagrancy Act, the Vagrancy Amendment Bill, had increased the danger of homosexual men being unmasked as it allowed those men or women who 'in any public place persistently solicits or importunes for immoral purposes', or was found 'masquerading in female attire', to be dealt with in the same way as vagabonds.[670] Gore was a man who did not lack enemies and this Act laid him open to exposure, false allegations, even blackmail. However, in the second edition of *Studies in the Psychology of Sex: Sexual Inversion, Volume II*, published in 1901, after Gore went missing, Havelock Ellis explains

668 This brief account is based on *The Bedborough Case* (London: Free Press Defence Committee, 1898), LSE pamphlets and Phyllis Grosskurth, *Havelock Ellis: A Biography* (New York: New York University Press, 1985), pp. 191-201. Roland de Villiers was eventually arrested in 1902, and died in police custody.
669 Grosskurth, *Havelock Ellis:* A Biography, p. 201.
670 A. Mclaren, *The Trials of Masculinity: Policing Sexual Boundaries, 1870-1930*, (Chicago: Chicago Press, 1997), p. 16.

graphically why homosexual men like Gore might disappear and in some instances even take their own lives.

> Whenever a man is openly detected in a homosexual act, however exemplary his life may previously have been, however admirable it may still be in all other relations, every ordinary normal citizen, however licentious and pleasure-loving his own life may be, feels it a moral duty to regard the offender as hopelessly damned and to help in hounding him out of society. At very brief intervals cases occur, and without reaching the newspapers are more or less widely known, in which distinguished men in various fields, not seldom clergymen, suddenly disappear from the country or commit suicide in consequence of some such exposure or the threat of it.[671]

In this post-Wilde hostile environment, Gore's disappearance must have been very distressing for his family. Yet, throughout this period Gore's father continued to carry out his court duties as normal, and Gore's brother, Arthur, seems to have fulfilled all his theatrical commitments. Did Gore's disappearance relate to some threat of exposure about his homosexuality? Could his father's connections have effected a suppression of press coverage? There are more questions than answers in this mystifying and intriguing episode. The scant traces that remain come only from collections of personal letters.

As well as Edith Ellis' letter, one direct reference to Gore's personal crisis came from his friend, the architect and designer, Charles Ashbee. On the 17 January 1899 he wrote to Gore offering his love and support.

> I have heard of your misfortune & I write to send you my love as of old & to tell you that there are friends of yours here, & I am one of them, who still believe in you & do not allow the opinion of the world to shake their confidence in you…

> I think that in these matters that affect our own personal conduct & where no injury to others is concerned there is only one rule – the rule that Socrates laid down & confirmed – the rule of temperance, & the definition of this lies in each man's own heart – if he transgresses he is his own severest judge.[672]

671 Havelock Ellis, *Studies in the Psychology of Sex: Sexual Inversion, Volume II (Philadelphia: F. A. Davis, 1901, 2nd revised and expanded edition)*, p. 203. On the directive of J. A. Symonds' widow, this edition and subsequent editions were published solely in the name of Havelock Ellis.
672 Charles Robert Ashbee's copy of his letter to Hugh Holmes Gore, 17 January 1899, the Papers of Charles Ashbee, CRA/1/5 held at King's College, Cambridge.

The Bristol labour movement maintained a loyal silence about Gore's predicament. Bryher was to make no mention of Gore's troubles when he wrote *An Account of the Labour and Socialist Movement in Bristol* in 1929, yet it is difficult to believe that he and others in the local labour movement were not aware of them. Just one voice broke the silence in the autumn of 1902. The anarchist, David Nicoll had restarted *Commonweal* in April 1902.[673] In the September 1902 edition of *Commonweal* he published a tirade, penned by himself, against 'abnormal sexuality' that he said was 'a vice of the upper classes', which 'leads to nerve disease and ultimately insanity. Its proper treatment is not a term of brutal imprisonment, but kindly restraint where needful, and medical care.'[674] In an article published in the October issue, he asserted that, like some before him, Gore had fled the country to escape from the charge of homosexuality.[675] Moreover, he denounced Gore and H. H. Champion as Jesuits and homosexuals and accused Edward Carpenter 'as one of the chief agents of these scoundrels, who not only corrupt the young' but who by their association with Jesuits 'have caused the wholesale murder of men, women and children in South Africa', a reference to the Boer War.[676]

The historian of British anarchism, John Quail, author of *The Slow Burning Fuse*, believed that by this point in his life Nicoll was seriously paranoid, as did most of Nicoll's contemporaries.[677] Nicoll had developed an hostility to Gore from the role he played in the defence of the Walsall Anarchists, financed by the fund raised by Carpenter and others. Nicoll never forgave them for concentrating on a narrow legalism rather than an *exposé* of the corrupt action of the police and their use of *agents provocateurs*.[678] Several years later, and in response to another rant by Nicoll against Jesuits, including Nannie Florence Dryhurst, who was active in the Anarchist Freedom Group,[679] the German anarchist and historian, Max Nettlau, conceded that Nicoll 'despite his incipient insanity,' was 'not far wrong in his denunciation of the Jesuitical and reactionary forces that were at work to deflect the attack of militant socialism into other channels.'[680]

673 David Nicoll's *Commonweal* was published from April 1898 under his editorship and control at 6 Windmill Street, London, *Reynolds' Newspaper*, 22 May 1898.
674 D. Nicoll, 'The Crisis of Despotism' *Commonweal*, Vol. 11, No. XIX, September 1902.
675 D. Nicoll, 'The Crimes of the Priests' *Commonweal*, Vol. 11, No. XX, October 1902.
676 D. Nicoll, 'The Crimes of the Priests' *Commonweal*, Vol. 11, No. XX, October 1902.
677 Quail, *The Slow Burning Fuse*, p. 210.
678 I am grateful to John Quail for this explanatory comment (email 23 May 2014). Also see Quail, *The Slow Burning Fuse*, p.117, and chapter 10 in this book.
679 David Nicoll's scribblings on a post card to Mrs Dryhurst, Freedom Offices, Nettlau Papers, International Institute of Social History, Amsterdam, Archive 1001, 28.
680 Nettlau Papers, International Institute of Social History, Amsterdam, Archive 1001, 28, p.211.

Whatever 'Jesuitical reactionaries' or actual Jesuits were up to, Nicoll's claim that Gore and Champion were associated with the Jesuit order itself has no foundation. His disclosure that Gore was a homosexual and his assertion that Gore fled the country to avoid prosecution are the only explicit contemporary references to Gore's sudden disappearance, though they are corroborated implicitly by Ellis and Ashbee's references to Gore's 'misfortune', which point to a connection between Gore absconding and the exposure of his homosexuality.

Confirmation that this indeed was the case came from a surprising source the Bristol Training Ship Association Minutes (4 October 1898). The training ship was an industrial reform venture aimed at boys deemed to be delinquent. Just as this book was going to press Alyson Green contacted me to say that she had found references to Gore in these minutes. On checking I found that on 22 September 1898 an accusation of attempted indecent assault was brought against Gore by a boy who had been placed under his supervision. The police were informed and a warrant for his arrest was issued on the 27 September (BRO 38087/NS/A2) the day after his argument with Horsefield. No further evidence has come to light.

Chapter 19

The Philippines

The exact circumstances of Gore's disappearance, and precisely *when* he left the country, are not known. What we can be certain of, however, is that he entered the Philippines before the end of the Filipino-American War, which did not officially conclude until 8 September 1902. The contents of a letter sent by Gore to Edward Carpenter on 20 September 1902 suggests that he had been living in the Philippines in July 1902 and indeed may have arrived there as early as 1901:

> My Dear Ted, your cheery letter of July 22 reached me in due course about a week ago, and gave me 'unspeakable pleasure.'

Towards the end of the letter he spoke of a man who had 'lived in my house here for nine months', which indicates that Gore had been in the Philippines at least since 1901. [681] However, this revelation raises yet more mysteries.

The Filipino-American War began on 4 February 1899, just two days before the U.S. Senate ratified the Treaty of Paris ending the Spanish-American War, which provided the United States with its first overseas empire. The subsequent fighting between American forces and their former allies, the Filipino nationalists, lasted three years and resulted in the death of more than 4,200 American troops, 20,000 Filipino fighters, and 200,000 Filipino civilians. [682]

Britain had adopted a neutral position during the Spanish-American War, but following Spain's defeat, Britain suggested that the United States acquire the Philippines, fearing that Germany would take advantage of the situation and step in. Britain, already overstretched in defending its existing empire, was unwilling to take on the extra costs associated with the defence and administration of the islands. [683] A complicating factor for the imperial powers was the change in the attitude of the leader of the Filipino Revolutionaries, Emilio Aguinaldo, towards the United States. Aquinaldo had fought with the Americans against the Spanish but during 1898, as America's imperialist intentions became clear, Aquinaldo became their opponent, On 12 June 1898

681 Gore to Edward Carpenter, 20 September 1902.
682 F. S. Weaver, *The United States and the Global Economy: From Bretton Woods to the Current Crisis* (Lanham, Md.: Rowman & Littlefield, 2011), p. 9.
683 Ruel V. Pagunsan, 'British Consular Reports on Filipino Anti-Colonial Struggles and Philippine-British Relations, 1896-1902', *Philippine Social Science Review*, Vol. 62, No.1, (2010) p. 141-2.

Aguinaldo declared Philippine independence and established a Revolutionary Government. In January 1899 he was sworn in as the first president of the new, self-governed Philippine Republic. The United States refused to recognise the Aguinaldo regime and proceeded with its mission of 'benevolent assimilation'.[684] This precipitated the start of the Filipino-American War.

Though Britain had adopted a neutral position to the war, it 'allied itself with the U.S., and eventually supported ... the latter's occupation of the Archipelago.'[685] Britain's business interests in the Philippine Archipelago heavily influenced its policy towards American intervention. Between 75 and 80 per cent of foreign enterprises located there belonged to British-owned companies, including the Manila Railway Company and two of the three leading banks. Britain also dominated the import and export trade through its merchant houses dotted around the islands.[686] Nevertheless, some British residents, and indeed certain British merchants, actually offered help to the Filipino revolutionaries. Two companies, Smith, Bell & Co. and Warner, Barnes & Co. were accused by the Americans of 'aiding and abetting' the insurgents.[687] In its desire to protect their interests, the British in the Philippines were walking a diplomatic tightrope. Not knowing the outcome of the war they did not want to provoke undue hostility from the main actors.

All in all the Philippines could not have offered Gore an exactly peaceful retreat. As well as the horrifying bloodshed sustained in what had turned into a Guerilla War, fought in thirty-four of the seventy-seven provinces in the Philippines,[688] appalling conditions prevailed on the islands. Gore arrived amidst drought, famine, plague, poverty and disease. When a cholera epidemic swept through the islands from March to November 1902, leaving many dead, Gore lost two young friends, one of whom was the man who had lived with him for nine months. Both were what Gore termed 'enthusiasts', and 'one was a frequent companion' on his travels.[689]

Nevertheless several factors may have attracted Gore to settle in the Philippines, particularly after the war was concluded. First, there was no

684 Munro Smith, 'Record of Political Events', *Political Science Quarterly*, Vol. 14, No. 2 (June 1899), p.358.

685 Pagunsan, 'British Consular Reports on Filipino Anti-Colonial Struggles and Philippine-British Relations, 1896-1902', p. 142.

686 Pagunsan, 'British Consular Reports on Filipino Anti-Colonial Struggles and Philippine-British Relations, 1896-1902', p. 131.

687 Pagunsan, 'British Consular Reports on Filipino Anti-Colonial Struggles and Philippine-British Relations, 1896-1902', p. 149.

688 B. M. Linn, *The Philippine War, 1899-1902* (Lawrence, KS: University of Kansas Press, 2000), p. 185.

689 Gore to Carpenter, 29 April 1903.

extradition treaty between American occupied Philippines and Britain. Second, under American military control the capital city, Manila, had begun 'to resemble a boom town. With the lifting of the siege and the opening of the port, business men, criminals, prostitutes, adventurers, and other assorted camp followers flocked into the city'.[690] It was not difficult to hide oneself amidst the confusion. Third, by the end of 1901, in the areas that were largely pacified, the Americans began to establish a colonial administration, which included the formation of municipal governments and recruitment of civilians to support the reconstruction of a war-torn country with a stress on health, education and legal reform.[691]

Gore's correspondence to Carpenter in September 1902 strongly suggests that he was one of those recruited to assist the colonial administration. Not only did he refer to his travels, he wrote 'my position as a person who inspects and advises, with an income more than sufficient for my daily needs is an easy one.' The Americans had introduced the Municipal Code Act in January 1901, which recognised the *pueblos* (town, township or community of indigenous people) of the Philippine Islands as municipal corporations with the same administrative boundaries as before.[692] Each municipality required inspectors to provide support that would enable the corporation to discharge their duties. Gore was well qualified to work for one of these municipal corporations, given his experience as a councillor on Bristol's local authority, and it seems more than likely that one of these corporations would have hired him as an inspector. This would explain why, since his arrival in the Philippines, he had taken such a keen interest in the technical workings of municipal government. In fact, as Gore told Carpenter, he had begun to write a critique of the municipal system, which he said he was thinking about publishing.[693]

Gore's position as a government employee, therefore, did not mean he wholly approved of American policy. He would have been aware of Carpenter's attitude to the Raj in India, commenting, 'my government means well, but it has the impertinence to think that oriental people want their western civilisation. They want nothing of the kind.' Exasperated at what he saw as the people's docility, Gore told Carpenter 'They want to be left alone, willing slaves of the Chino half-caste, who cunningly runs the show.'[694]

690 J. Gates, *Schoolbooks and Krags: The United States Army in the Philippines, 1898-1902* (Westport, Conn.: Greenwood Press, 1973), p. 63.
691 Gates, *Schoolbooks and Krags: The United States Army in the Philippines, 1898-1902*, pp. 216-7, and 278-282.
692 Chan Robles, Virtual Law Library, http://www.chanrobles.com/scdecisions/jurisprudence1916/dec1916/gr_l-9819_1916.php, accessed 21 July 2014.
693 Gore to Edward Carpenter, 29 April 1903.
694 Gore to Edward Carpenter, 20 September 1902.

This animosity towards people of Chinese or mixed Chinese and Filipino descent was common. Economic depression in the 1880s fuelled anti-Chinese prejudice leading to calls for the suspension of Chinese immigration in the mid 1890s. Despite efforts to discourage targeting people of Chinese or mixed Chinese and Filipino descent, Filipino nationalists acted violently against them. The Americans, however, recognised qualities in the Chinese community that would assist them in conducting a war in an unfamiliar and hostile environment and enlisted their support: 'As contractor and entrepreneur, as laborer and carter, the Chinese made it possible for the Americans to fight a type of war to which they were not well-adapted, in a strange and debilitating climate.'[695]

Yet divisions did exist among Americans over the war. The American President, Theodore Roosevelt, in a Memorial Day speech at Arlington Cemetery, on 30 May 1902, ignored criticisms from anti-imperialists such as Storey Moorfield, an American lawyer and civil rights leader, who had remonstrated with his government for having 'visited upon this weaker people every horror of war'.[696]

> In his 'indignant' speech, Roosevelt defended the U. S. Army against charges of 'cruelty' in the ongoing Philippine-American War by racializing the conflict as one being fought between the forces of "civilization" and 'savagery'. He dismissed the Filipinos as 'Chinese half-breeds', and insisted 'this is the most glorious war in our nation's history'.[697]

Moorfield's accusation that American 'Imperialism has thrown aside its mask of benevolence'[698] does not appear to have been shared by Gore, who viewed the Filipinos as 'too childlike and docile' and in need of guidance from a colonial power.[699] Despite his criticism of Western hegemonic assumptions, Gore's actions serve as evidence of his tacit support for the American policy

695 P. Ginsberg, 'The Chinese in the Philippine Revolution', *Asian Studies, Journal of Critical Perspectives on Asia*, (8.1: April 1970), p 152.
696 Storey Moorfield, 'Statement against Acquiring the Philippine Islands' (c. January-February, 1900), The Historical Society of Pennsylvania, Philadelphia, PA, Historical Society of Pennsylvania Autograph Collection (Collection 22A), Philippine Islands, http://digitalhistory. hsp.org/pafrm/doc/statement-against-acquiring-philippine-islands-c-january-february-1900 accessed 28 July 2014.
697 Arnaldo Dumindin, "Philippine-American War, 1899-1902." *Philippine-American War, 1899-1902*. (Web publication: 2006), http://philippineamericanwar.webs.com accessed 23 July 2014.
698 Moorfield, 'Statement against Acquiring the Philippine Islands'.
699 Gore to Edward Carpenter, 20 September 1902.

that believed 'only through American occupation' was 'the idea of a free, self-governing and united Filipino commonwealth at all conceivable.'[700]

He was confronted with some formidable dilemmas of governance. The system the Americans inherited, of governing through the *pueblos*, required the headmen of *barrios* in rural villages, comprising between ten and thirty farmers, to furnish their local municipality with labour for a certain number of days per year and sell their produce at fixed prices.[701] Apart from these commitments rural *barrios* had been left to run their affairs without outside interference, holding weekly meetings under the direction of a headman. Gore noted in his letter to Carpenter in 1902 that this 'subjection to the community' was soon to go and would be replaced by 'individual liberty'. He felt divided. While unconvinced 'that the virtual slavery of the communal life' was 'satisfactory', he recognised that 'no one starved' and 'the interest of each was the interest of all and vice versa.' Charmed rather than convinced by the practice of some basic aspects of primitive communism, Gore struggled to see a way forward, believing that 'our [American] methods are ridiculous and preposterous.'[702]

In January 1899, President William McKinley had resolved that the 'paramount aim of the military administration [was] to win the confidence, respect, and admiration of the inhabitants of the Philippines by assuring them in every possible way that full measure of individual rights and liberties which is the heritage of free peoples'.[703] However, such ideas were repressed by the realities of war, and the administrative emphasis of the regime was geared towards non-military pacification. The apparent endorsement of the model of local autonomy as democratically liberating was illusionary, as the powers of provincial governments were limited. Under the umbrella of the War Department's Bureau of Insular Affairs insular bureaus took control of key service sectors, particularly the constabulary, education, forests, mines and lands.[704]

By 1903, Gore felt increasingly alienated from 'official acquaintances' in the Colonial administration, who he viewed as being 'on the make' and not really caring 'one jot for the people who' were 'taxed to maintain them.' Gore's sense of obligation to the Filipino people, driven by his commitment to duty, the socialistic principles of the Guild of St. Matthew, and the inspiration

---

700 Dumindin, "Philippine-American War, 1899-1902." *Philippine-American War, 1899-1902*.
701 Gore to Edward Carpenter, 20 September 1902.
702 Gore to Edward Carpenter, 20 September 1902.
703 President McKinley's Proclamation of Benevolent Assimilation issued on 4 January 1899 cited in B. M. Linn, *The U.S. Army and Counterinsurgency in the Philippine War, 1899-1902* (Chapel Hill, North Carolina: The University of North Carolina Press, 1989), p. 20.
704 D. P. Barrows, *A Decade of American Government in the Philippines 1903-1913* (New York: World Book Company, 1914), p. 16.

he drew from his High Anglican religious faith, set him apart from his fellow administrators. The Americans' success in securing participation of the Filipino elite in the colonial administration, as part of its strategy of benevolent assimilation, occasioned Gore to remark in his correspondence to Carpenter how 'servile to authority' the Filipinos were. 'They would not dare to breathe a syllable of criticism of their own administration for fear of losing their job.'[705]

Gore's participation in the colonial administration was a temporary expedient. With an eye to the future he bought a valley and had a house built as his residence. He purchased two horses, one for himself and the other for his servant, allowing them 'to run wild in the rich grasses of the valley'. He also maintained a town house. He had made the Philippines his home. He still cared to hear about old friends and wished that Carpenter would visit him.[706] However, he had come to doubt his belief in democracy and the possibility of unifying all humankind. In his letter to Carpenter he wrote:

> Does it ever occur to you that the idol "democracy" is all false too; and that only the Spirit of Christ is what animates the world to a fuller & more eternal life? The comradeship of Whitman is a selfish platitude which never will unify humanity.[707]

Moreover, in the same letter Gore broke a seemingly surprising piece of news:

> This is my home, and someday I hope to share it with my brave sweetheart in England, who cannot join me [in the Philippines] while *her* [my emphasis] parents live.[708]

It seems likely that the reference to 'her' in Gore's letter is a cover for a male lover, who perhaps had been the occasion for Gore's disgrace and exile.[709] This 1903 letter comprises the last testimony to Gore's enigmatic personality, while the details of and reason for his flight elude us. Gore was not present at the funerals of his mother in June 1915 or his father on 1 October 1919; neither did he send any public messages expressing grief or sorrow. Even the date of his death is unclear. Apart from one hazy reference to his death long ago in the

705 Gore to Edward Carpenter, 29 April 1903.
706 Gore to Edward Carpenter, 29 April 1903.
707 Gore to Edward Carpenter, 29 April 1903.
708 Gore to Edward Carpenter, 29 April 1903.
709 For a reference to the possibility of substituting 'her' for 'him' as an example of early coded homosexual talk see J. N., Katz, *Love Stories: Sex between Men before Homosexuality* (London: The University of Chicago Press, 2001), p. 175.

Philippines, which appeared in an edition of the *Western Daily Press* on 17 April 1948, no further record of Gore has been found:

> The death of Miss Caroline Edith Holmes Gore will remind elderly Bristolians of a time when members of her family were very well known... Hugh Holmes Gore [her brother] took a leading part in the early history of the Socialist movement in Bristol, but died the writer understands, some time ago in the Philippines.

The strange disappearance of Hugh Holmes Gore retains its mystery.

Appendix 1

The Guild of St. George Objects

1. To determine, and institute in practice, the wholesome laws of laborious (especially agricultural) life and economy, and to instruct first the agricultural, and, as opportunity may serve, other labourers or craftsmen, in such science, art, and literature as are conducive to good husbandry and craftsmanship.
2. The acquisition by gift, purchase, or otherwise, of plots or tracts of land in different parts of Great Britain and Ireland.
3. The acquisition by gift, purchase, or otherwise, and the erection of Schools, Museums, and other educational establishments, in different parts of Great Britain and Ireland.
4. The acquisition by gift, purchase, or otherwise, of such pictures, sculptures, books, and objects of art and natural history, as may be properly adapted for the cultivation of taste and intelligence among rural labourers and craftsmen.
5. The erection of dwelling-houses for agricultural labourers, and of farm buildings, and the repair thereof.
6. The selling, aliening, and disposing for such consideration, in money or otherwise, and upon such terms and conditions, and in such manner in all respects, as may in each case be thought best, of all or any part of the property and effects of the Association, and the acquisition of other property and effects of a like character in place thereof, or the application towards such other of the objects of the Society as may in each case be thought best of the money to arise from any such sale, alienation, or disposal.
7. The holding, tilling, cultivating, leaving uncultivated, turning into waste or common land, or otherwise applying to such purposes as, having regard to the nature of the soil and other surrounding circumstances, may in each case be thought most generally useful, of all or any of the said plots or tracts of land.
8. The leasing for any term or terms of years at such rent, and under and subject to such covenants and conditions, and upon such terms and in such manner in all respects, as may in each case be thought best, of all or any of the said plots or tracts of land, schools, museums, dwelling-houses, and farm buildings.
9. To make grants of money out of the funds of the Association to or in aid of Associations having similar objects, either by way of gift or loan with or without interest.
10. The doing all such other lawful things as are incidental or conducive to the attainment of the above objects.[710]

710 Memorandum of Association of the Guild of St. George, E. T. Cook and Alexander Wedderburn (eds.), *The Works of John Ruskin*. London: George Allen, 1909, Volume XXX, 'The Guild and Museum of St. George', p. 5.

Appendix 2

The Guild of St. George Codes

The Guild's codes had to be written, and signed, in the applicant's own hand:

1. I trust in the Living God, Father Almighty, Maker of heaven and earth, and of all things and creatures visible and invisible. I trust in the kindness of His law, and the goodness of His work. And I will strive to love Him, and keep His law, and see His work, while I live.

2. I trust in the nobleness of human nature, in the majesty of its faculties, the fulness of its mercy, and the joy of its love.

3. And I will strive to love my neighbour as myself, and, even when I cannot, will act as if I did.

4. I will labour, with such strength and opportunity as God gives me, for my own daily bread; and all that my hand finds to do, I will do with my might.

5. I will not deceive, or cause to be deceived, any human being for my gain or pleasure; nor hurt, or cause to be hurt, any human being for my gain or pleasure; nor rob, or cause to be robbed, any human being for my gain or pleasure.

6. I will not kill nor hurt any living creature needlessly, nor destroy any beautiful thing, but will strive to save and comfort all gentle life, and guard and perfect all natural beauty, upon the earth.

7. I will strive to raise my own body and soul daily into higher powers of duty and happiness; not in rivalship or contention with others, but for the help, delight, and honour of others, and for the joy and peace of my own life.

8. I will obey all the laws of my country faithfully; and the orders of its monarch, and of all persons appointed to be in authority under its monarch, so far as such laws or commands are consistent with what I suppose to be the law of God; and when they are not, or seem in anywise to need change, I will oppose them loyally and deliberately, not with malicious, concealed, or disorderly violence.

9. And with the same faithfulness, and under the limits of the same obedience, which I render to the laws of my country, and the commands of its rulers, I will obey the laws of the Society called of St. George, into which I am this day received; and the orders of its masters, and of all persons appointed to be in authority under its masters, so long as I remain a Companion, called of St. George.[711]

---

711 The Code of the Guild of St. George, E. T. Cook and Alexander Wedderburn (eds.), The Works of John Ruskin. London: George Allen, 1909, Volume XXVIII, Fors Clavigera, Letter 58, p. 419.

Name Index

Adams, Richard, 41

Aguinaldo, Emilio, 162, 163

Ashbee, Charles Robert, 38, 57, 58, 61, 110, 140, 159, 161

Ashman, Herbert, 71

Aveling, Edward, 17

Bailey, Harriet, 60

Bailey, James, 60

Baker, William, 99

Bale, Samuel, 40

Balzac, Honoré de, 141

Barnett, Francis Gilmore, 15, 69

Baster, William, 18, 19, 71, 107, 152

Battola, Jean, 82-85

Bax, Belfort, 17

Bedborough, George, 158

Belcher, Reverend Dr., 155

Bell, George Charles, 7

Benson, Edward White, Archbishop of Canterbury, 40

Besant, Annie, 26

Binfield, Richard, 104

Black, Clementina, 73

Blatchford, Robert, 104

Bow, Harry, 95, 98

Bowen, Edward Earnest, 61

Bowler, Peter, 146

Brabham, Harold, 94, 107, 123, 126, 129

Bradlaugh, Charles, 19, 141

Bradley, Katherine, 14,

Bramble, Lieutenant Colonel James Roger, 9, 10, 11, 13, 18

Britton, Samuel, 147, 148, 149

Brocklehurst, Fred, 123, 124, 128

Brown, James, 86

Browne, Dr. George Forrest (Bishop of Bristol), 154

Bryher, Samson, 117, 168

Burns, John, 33, 34, 121

Butler, Dr A. J., 5

Butler, Josephine, 141

Butler, Tom, 150

Butler, William, 150

Cailes, Victor, 82-85

Cann, Superintendent, 93

Carpenter, Edward, VI, 1, 14-16, 18, 23-24, 29, 36-38, 43, 55, 57, 82, 83, 100, 109, 121, 139-142, 147, 158, 160, 162, 164, 166-167

Cave, Justice, 33

Champion, Henry Hyde, 14, 33-34, 82, 160-161

Charles, Fred, 82-86, 100

Childs, Edward, 104

Childs, Ted, 134

Coathupe, Edwin W., 90-91

Connell, Jim, 147-149

Cooper, Edith, 14

Copeland, Herbert, 5-6

Cossham, Handel, 34, 64-65

Cotterell, J. N., 82

Coulon, Auguste, 84-85

Cowlin, William, 51, 91, 93, 139

Creighton, Mandell (Bishop of London), 154

Croix, Gaspard de la, 93

Cunningham, Dr., 129

Cunninghame Graham, Robert Bontine, 64

Curle, John, 117

Curran, Pete, 123

Dakyns, Henry Graham, 37

Daniel, Richard Thomas, 134, 138

Daniell, Miriam, 47-48, 51, 69

Darwin, Charles, 15

Davitt, Michael, 65, 67

de Villiers, Roland, 158

Place Index

General Index